Post-colonial Syria and Lebanon

In memory of my beloved mother, Nadia Youssef Bek El-Zein

POST-COLONIAL SYRIA
AND LEBANON

THE DECLINE OF ARAB NATIONALISM

AND THE TRIUMPH OF THE STATE

Youssef Chaitani

I.B.TAURIS

LONDON · NEW YORK

Published in 2007 by I.B.Tauris & Co Ltd
6 Salem Road, London W2 4BU
175 Fifth Avenue, New York NY 10010
www.ibtauris.com

In the United States and Canada distributed by Palgrave Macmillan,
a division of St. Martin's Press, 175 Fifth Avenue, New York NY 10010

ISBN: 978 1 84511 294 3
Library of Middle East History 11

A full CIP record for this book is available from the British Library
A full CIP record for this book is available from the Library of Congress
Library of Congress catalog card: available

Typeset in Minion by Dexter Haven Associates Ltd, London
Printed and bound in India by Replika Press Pvt. Ltd

CONTENTS

ACKNOWLEDGEMENTS

Special thanks go to Dr Raghid el-Solh for his constant encouragement, understanding and valuable advice. Dr Solh took a personal interest in seeing the completion of the study in a manner that corresponds to his high research standards and dedication to Arab regional integration. The study could not have been concluded without him.

I would also like to specially thank Prof. Sami Zubeida. Prof. Zubeida's support goes far beyond the intricacies that went into the preparation of the manuscript.

My special thanks go to Dr Patrick Seale, Prof. Roger Owen, Prof. Kamal Salibi, Prof. Eugine Rogan, Prof. Charles Tripp, Prof Atif Kubursi and Prof. Paul Kingston for their suggestions and constructive criticisms. They took the time to read the manuscript and proposed improvements.

In addition, I extend my sincere thanks to Mr Nadim Shehadi, who provided the crucial support in tackling the numerous difficulties I faced related to the archival material utilised in the study.

My profound gratitude goes to my former professors at the History Department at the American University of Beirut, in particular Professors Samir Seikaly, Abdel Rahim Abu Hussein and John Meloy, as well as to the dedicated staff of the Jaffet Library at the American University of Beirut for facilitating my access to the research material I needed.

I thank Mr Fadi Shaker, whose research skills and dedication contributed to the enrichment of the study. My gratitude also goes to Mr Sarmad Salibi, Daniel Neuwirth, Abigail Fielding-Smith and Gretchen Ladish for their unfailing support.

My eternal gratitude goes to ESCWA Executive Secretary and Under-Secretary General Mervat Tallawy for her boundless support.

Most importantly, I shall be eternally indebted to my parents, Nizar and Nadia, as well as my brother Hussein and sisters Randa, Riem and Hana, for their enormous sacrifices. Without them I would have never been able to have got as far as I did. Sacrifices and unlimited support were also made by my in-laws, Mahmoud and Haifa Nasreddine, my sister-in-law, Ruwan and my uncle Abdel Latif el-Zein.

Last but not least, my heart goes out to my wife Lara and our two children, Karim and Yasmine. Their love makes all the hardships and hard work easily endurable.

ACKNOWLEDGEMENTS

FOREWORD

O f all the Arab world's political relationships, none displays such a tormented combination of attraction and repulsion, of love and hate, as that between Syria and Lebanon. Although indispensable to each other, they have often found coexistence onerous and troublesome. They cannot live together, yet they cannot live apart. They seem forever trapped in a repetitive cycle of conflict and reconciliation. The most recent falling out – and a spectacular one – occurred in 2005, when outrage over the assassination of Rafiq Hariri, the billionaire former Premier and architect of Lebanon's post-civil war revival, aroused a groundswell of anti-Syrian feeling – a veritable political *tsunami* – which forced Syrian troops to leave the country after a stay of nearly three decades. Lebanon seemed determined to break free from what had become a suffocating Syrian tutelage. The protagonists seemed irreconcilable and the breach final. Yet, peering into the uncharted future, one can be certain of only one thing – that Syria and Lebanon will eventually make it up.

A permanent estrangement is indeed unthinkable. For one thing, ties across the common border of family and friendship, of commerce and strategic interest, are so dense as to rule out the possibility of divorce. What Syrian family does not have a relative that has married in Lebanon, or has a Lebanese business partner, or an account in a Lebanese bank, or has been treated at a Beirut hospital, or has perhaps settled there to escape one or other of Syria's authoritarian or socialist regimes, or has humbly worked in Lebanon on a building site or laboured in the fields at harvest time? And what Lebanese has not bargained and shopped and eaten and traded in the souks of Damascus, always so much cheaper and more 'authentic' than those of cosmopolitan Beirut, and has not then carried home a precious box of Syrian sweetmeats, without dispute the best in the world?

Whatever their quarrels, the one issue that has united Syria and Lebanon is their hostility to Israel, the common enemy to their immediate south. Israel seized Syria's Golan plateau in the 1967 war and shows no inclination to return it. Israel also invaded Lebanon, not once but twice – in 1978 and then again on a larger scale in 1982, when it killed some 17,000 Lebanese and Palestinians and besieged and bombarded Beirut with the aim of driving out the Syrians, destroying the PLO (which had set up house there after being expelled from Jordan in 1970) and bringing Lebanon into its orbit.

These aggressive aims might well have succeeded had Syria and its local allies not managed to wrest Lebanon out of Israel's grip and abort an agreement – in effect a separate peace – which the United States brokered between Israel and Lebanon in 1983. Nevertheless, Israel remained in military occupation of a substantial slice of southern Lebanon for 22 years until finally driven out by Hizballah guerrillas in 2000.

With Damascus less than 20 kilometres from the Lebanese border and the heart of Syria vulnerable to a thrust up the Beqa' valley, a fundamental principle of Syrian policy has been to prevent any hostile power, and Israel in particular, from establishing itself in Lebanon, or mounting hostile operations against it from Lebanese soil. Syria has thus striven to keep Lebanon within its own sphere of influence and away from any relationship with Zionism (an option that some Lebanese Maronites, seeking allies against their Muslim environment, flirted with from time to time throughout the twentieth century).

Big-brotherly control of Lebanon has in recent decades served Syria well: it has lent it regional and international weight; it has provided a buffer against Israel; and it has been a source of wealth for well-placed Syrians in the army and security services, in the political elite and the business community. These assets and advantages were threatened by the crisis over Hariri's murder, but there is no evidence that Syria is ready or willing to give them up altogether. With its local friends and allies, it will fight, and perhaps even kill, to retain a measure of real influence in Beirut, if no longer of direct control.

There is another imponderable. Deep in the Syrian consciousness, among the public and the leadership alike, is the feeling that Lebanon is not really a foreign country, but rather more like a long-lost province over which Syria has some ancient if indeterminate claim.

For some four hundred years until 1918, the countries we now call Syria, Lebanon, Jordan and Israel, together with what is left of Palestine, were known collectively as 'Syria', or rather as the Syrian provinces of the Ottoman Empire. These countries cannot easily opt out of their common history or their common environment, however much one or two of them may long to do so. Although each has developed a distinct identity, they are doomed to interact with each other because they are all, as it were, carved out of the same flesh – and none more so than Syria and Lebanon. These, then, are some of the factors that bind the two neighbours indissolubly together.

There are others, however, that drive them just as firmly apart. Of these, the first is undoubtedly the role of the Maronite Church in shaping Lebanon's particular identity over the past one thousand years. Links between Franks and local Christians were forged at the end of the eleventh century when the Crusaders built their castles and established Catholic enclaves, such as the Kingdom of Jerusalem and the County of Tripoli. Early in the twelfth century, the Maronite Church made contact with the Papacy and accepted Catholic doctrine, a relationship with Western Christendom that flowered over the centuries, resulting in a formal agreement with the Papacy in 1736 and the benevolent protection of France. The Maronite Patriarch – and the French ambassador – remain to this day inescapable actors on the Lebanese political scene.

There are other, more secular, sources of Lebanese particularism. Two local emirs, Fakhr al-Din in the first half of the seventeenth century and Bashir II of the Shihab dynasty in the early nineteenth century, won a certain temporary independence from the Ottoman Empire and are therefore counted among Lebanon's founding fathers. Both managed in their time to extend their rule over the whole of present-day Lebanon and even somewhat beyond – establishing what Lebanese nationalists like to call their country's 'natural and historic frontiers'. But both came to grief. Their ambitions were stifled and their emirates were defeated when Ottoman rule was restored.

In more recent Lebanese history, an important landmark was the privileged status Mount Lebanon secured from the Porte in 1861, following a bloody civil war the previous year between Druzes and Maronites. The massacre of Christians on the mountain, and also in Damascus, alarmed Europe and triggered a French intervention. Under pressure from the European Powers, it was agreed that Mount Lebanon would be a separate province, a *mutasarrifiya*, ruled by a Christian (non-Lebanese) governor, appointed by the Ottoman government with the consent of the Powers and assisted by an administrative council representing the various sects and communities. Relative peace and prosperity prevailed until the Turks put an end to this privileged regime at the start of the First World War. Kamal Salibi, the prominent historian of Lebanon, argues that Lebanon's identity was, for the first time, given legal definition by the Mount Lebanon *mutasarrifiyya* between 1861 and 1914. To be Lebanese was to enjoy citizenship of this unusual province, as well as the various tax and other privileges, such as freedom from military service, which went with it. Others, however, have suggested that Mount Lebanon's special status was little more than an institutional device by the Porte to reassure newly emancipated non-Muslim subjects of the Empire after the 1860 massacres. On this argument, the real aim was to restore Ottoman control, not to encourage Lebanese separatism. Nevertheless, those years of semi-autonomy under European sponsorship undoubtedly contributed to shaping Lebanon's early identity.

After the First World War, the victorious Allies, Britain and France, chopped up the Arab provinces of the Ottoman Empire to suit their respective interests. France, which had established long-standing commercial and educational ties with the Levant, had to wrestle with the puzzle whether Lebanon should become a separate state or be merged into a wider Syrian entity. After intense lobbying by Lebanese nationalists at the Versailles Peace Conference, the matter was settled on 10 November 1919, when the veteran French Prime Minister, Georges

Clemenceau, gave the Maronite Patriarch, Mgr Pierre-Elias Hayek, an undertaking that an enlarged *mutasarrifiya* would be given independence under French protection.

Accordingly, France proclaimed the state of Greater Lebanon – *Le Grand Liban* – in 1920. It was intended as a haven for the predominant Maronite community, France's main clients, but, in terms of geopolitics, it was also conceived as a French fortress in the eastern Mediterranean, which could be used against European rivals as well as against Arab nationalists of the Syrian interior. These rebellious nationalists heartily disliked the League of Nations' Mandates given to France over Syria and Lebanon, which, in practice, provided little more than a fig leaf for a colonial regime.

To give depth and width to the new French-created and French-protected Lebanese state, France attached four Syrian *cazas*, or districts, to Mount Lebanon, including the Beqa' valley in the east, Tripoli and its hinterland in the north, Tyre, Sidon and the Jabal 'Amil in the south, as well as the thriving merchant port city of Beirut, which became the capital of Greater Lebanon. These areas taken from Syria were inhabited mainly by Muslims, both Shi'i and Sunni, which were soon to pose a demographic, and hence a political, challenge to the dominant Maronite community. The four *cazas* were to be the source of enduring controversy between the wars: Arab nationalists wanted these 'disputed territories' returned to Syria, while Lebanese nationalists defended their expanded state with equal passion. The matter was only resolved when it became clear to Arab nationalists in Lebanon – and to Sunni leaders like Riad el-Solh in particular, who was to become the first Prime Minister of independent Lebanon – that recognising Lebanon's sovereignty within its expanded frontiers was the only way to persuade the Maronites to join the independence struggle against France.

After a great deal of acrimony – and a last spiteful bombardment of Damascus in 1945 – French troops finally withdrew from the Levant states the following year. But by this time, Syria and Lebanon had developed different natures and different ways of life, which greatly complicated their post-independence relations. Having lost Palestine (southern Syria) to the Jews, Alexandretta to the Turks, the Beqa' valley and much of its Mediterranean frontage to Lebanon, Syria was reduced to a mere rump of the country it had aspired to be. It had always been conservative, pious and inward-looking but, as a result of these amputations, it became prickly, defensive, ultra-nationalistic, and intensely anti-French.

Economically, it was still an unreformed agricultural country, with grain production largely in the hands of a score of 'feudal' landowners. Although it was beginning to develop some light industries, these demanded protection, reinforcing a tendency towards isolationism. To add to Syria's problems, Paris had tied its currency to the franc, which, in the turmoil after the Second World War, led to unwelcome devaluations and a wish to break loose from French entanglements altogether.

The contrast with Lebanon could not have been greater. Open to the Mediterranean and the Western world, Lebanon had become a laissez-faire merchant society, thriving on trade, transit and tourism. It was deeply penetrated by the French language and European ways of living. Two great centres of learning, the American University of Beirut and the Jesuit University of St Joseph, educated a sophisticated middle class. In the summer months, visitors from Egypt, Iraq and other hot countries flocked to its cool mountain villages. It was a place of *villégiature*, a place where people came to rest, to talk, to eat, to play with their children and to have fun.

In addition, some of its Christian elites had embraced the myth of 'Phoenicianism', the notion that present-day Lebanese were somehow the descendants of the seafarers and traders, famous for their gold and metal working, their glass-blowing and ivory and woodcarving, who had settled on the eastern Mediterranean coast in about 3000 BC, before extending their influence from Biblos and Beirut south to Jaffa and Acre, and across the sea to Carthage, Cyprus and Andalusia. As a contribution to Lebanon's identity, Phoenicianism won many, mainly Christian, devotees between the wars and continued to do so well into the 1970s.

Such, in broad brushstroke, is the background to Youssef Chaitani's ground-breaking study, which deals in absorbing detail with the crucial period from 1943 to 1950, which saw the final struggle with the French and then the early years of independence. Inexperienced, hard-pressed and virtually bankrupt governments in Damascus and Beirut were faced with the intractable problem of how to reconcile the fundamentally different interests of their respective economies and societies, while at the same time confronting, as best they could, the challenge from Israel, which emerged victorious from the 1947–48 war.

A problem that was to preoccupy them throughout those years, and to which they failed to find a solution, was how to unscramble to their mutual satisfaction the edifice of so-called 'Common Interests' left to them by the French. These included a joint Customs Directorate, which compelled them to seek agreement on tariffs and quotas and other factors governing their foreign trade. It was a vain enterprise. As a producing country, Syria favoured protectionism and did not hesitate to use the weapon of its grain exports, on which Lebanon depended for its daily bread, to blackmail Beirut into falling in line with its economic policies. In contrast, Lebanon, which produced very little of anything except *douceur de vivre*, favoured a free import policy to provide cheap goods for its population as well as the amenities that tourists demanded.

Basing himself on diplomatic archives, but also – and this is a major contribution – on the vituperative, wounding exchanges between Syria's nationalist newspapers and Lebanon's dailies, Youssef Chaitani leads us through the maze of failed negotiations to the inevitable rupture, when Syria and Lebanon went their separate ways.

Fascinating in itself, his account shows that the 1940s provide an illuminating precedent for the problems of friendly coexistence that the two sister states face today, so close and yet so different, so inseparable and interdependent and yet so determined to be free of each other.

Patrick Seale

INTRODUCTION

I n the late nineteenth and early twentieth centuries, it was widely thought in the Arab world that once foreign control came to an end, the Arab territories would be reunified. The writings of veteran Arab nationalists such as Sati' al-Husri, Nabih Amin Fares and George Antonius attest to this line of thinking. Al-Husri in *Ara' wa ahadith fi al-qawmiyya al-'arabiyya* maintained that it was because of colonial greed that Arab land, which consisted of one people who had the same interests and aspirations, was divided into several states after World War I. Al-Husri asserted that colonial powers continued to prevent the unity of Arabs, singling these powers out as the only obstacle to Arab reunification.[1] Antonius, in *The Arab Awakening: A Story of the Arab National Movement*, contended that first and foremost the Sykes–Picot Agreement cut up Arab land in such a manner as to place artificial obstacles in the way to Arab unity. Antonius maintained that this scheme was in conflict with the natural forces at work. He suggested that the 'national movement was now a force with the plank of Arab unity as well as independence in the forefront of its aims'.[2] Arguing along similar lines, Fares in *Haza al'alam al-'arabi* wrote that Western states adopted a policy of dividing Arab land into states and Arab people into rival factions and parties. Fares argued that the challenge facing the Arab cause was the West, which would continue to prevent the union of Arab land in order to safeguard its interests and ensure its domination of the Arabs.[3]

This line of thinking remained well beyond the second half of the twentieth century, as the writings of the Arab unionist Michel 'Aflaq indicate. 'Aflaq in *Fi sabil al-ba'th* wrote that Arab national unity had been the subject of attacks and plots from colonialism. 'Aflaq held that the West was fully aware that Arab unity would mean the end of colonialism in Arab land. He firmly believed that an end of colonialism would bring about the unification of Arab land that in turn would bring the end of underdevelopment and all that which 'was not worthy of life'.[4]

In the case of Syro-Lebanese relations, these beliefs were reinforced by the special relationship envisaged by the Lebanese Arab nationalists, Syrian unionists and – paradoxically enough – radical Lebanese nationalists. The aim of this book is to examine this assumption by focusing on the formative years of Syro-Lebanese relations. A thorough study of the formative years of the relationship of two newly

1

independent states is essential to an understanding of their relations. In the case of Lebanon and Syria these years fall between 1943 and 1950, during which Syro-Lebanese bilateral relations were shaped. This book begins in 1943, when the French order in the Levant collapsed, bringing with it the emancipation of Lebanese and Syrians. Independence brought forth a whole series of new challenges to Lebanese and Syrian policymakers. For most there were no serious differences concerning the future presence of foreign troops that were still on Lebanese and Syrian soil. Rather, it was the nature of future Syro-Lebanese relations that came to be the primary subject of intense debate between the opinion-makers and ruling elites of the two states. Although this debate continues to the present day, March 1950 was a milestone in Syro-Lebanese relations, the point at which formal 'separation' took place between the two states.

The dissolution of the Syro-Lebanese partnership was not an abrupt matter. Rather, it was an evolutionary process into which internal as well as external political and economic factors came into play. This work thus begins by tackling Syro-Lebanese relations from 1943 to 1946 and describing the forging of new alliances between the Lebanese and Syrian nationalist movements. Related to this period is how the new Lebanese and Syrian ruling elites' concern with liberating their respective states outweighed the functional aspects of their bilateral relations. The watershed in bilateral relations came with the withdrawal of foreign troops in 1946.

From 1946 to 1950, the functional aspects of Syro-Lebanese relations became one of the leading concerns of the ruling elites and opinion makers of both states. Subsequent chapters of this book, while following chronologically, are so divided as to focus on the development of the functional relations between Lebanon and Syria. It scrutinises the influence of internal politics upon bilateral relations. In this regard there is an extensive discussion of the manner in which crucial Syro-Lebanese functional relations developed into conflicting interests between the two states. Unable to come to terms, Beirut, and in particular Damascus, utilised numerous means of economic pressures, such as frequent border closures and food blockades, to enforce an agreement. As shall be seen, such methods only led to the deepening of the schism between the Lebanese and Syrian elites that had jointly, and only a few years earlier, successfully ousted France from their homelands.

In order to better trace the manner in which relations developed between the ruling elites of both states, how the perceptions of their respective constituencies were affected, and the role played by the latter, this study makes extensive use of editorials and press reports in addition to memoirs and archival material.

The debate between Syrian and Lebanese Arab national movements as well as the Lebanese nationalists was occurring amidst favourable circumstances. Urbanisation and the expansion and intensification of commercial relations were coupled with the proliferation of newspapers, literary salons, private clubs and coffee houses, through which news and ideas were disseminated and exchanged. The literary salons and political clubs, which 'turned political neophytes into political activists', contributed to a heightened political atmosphere and to the emergence of an ever-widening modern 'public sphere' in Lebanon and Syria.[5]

The influence of newspapers was not limited to the literate. Not only were newspapers exchanged in informal settings like coffee houses, but street-corner vendors shouted out the headlines of the latest editions.[6] By 1943, the Lebanese and Syrian press was relatively advanced and contributed to, rather than merely recorded, the debates between the Lebanese and Syrian elites. Significantly, by that time a number of Lebanese journalists had joined the ranks of the ruling elites. In this capacity, they used their papers to enhance their political status, which in turn gave their papers added significance. One of these papers was *al-Qabass*, which was one of the most important and respected dailies in Syria. *Al-Qabass*, owned by Najib al-Raiyyes, was known as a mouthpiece of the National Bloc. Al-Raiyyes, a member of the Syrian parliament, was very close to the Syrian President, Shukri al-Quwwatly. He was also known to have exercised great influence over the most prominent politicians of Syria.[7]

Another daily that falls within this category was *al-Nahar*, which was at that time one of the most widely read newspapers in the Arab world. *Al-Nahar* was owned by Jubran Tweini, a Lebanese Arab nationalist Orthodox Christian. A member of parliament, he held ministerial posts in various governments and served as Lebanese ambassador to a number of countries. After his death in 1948, the paper was taken over by his son Ghassan, who followed in his father's footsteps as parliamentarian and minister.[8] Two other important Lebanese Arab nationalist dailies were *Beirut al-Masa'* and *Beirut*. *Beirut al-Masa'* was founded by 'Abdallah al-Mashnuq, a Muslim Arab nationalist parliamentarian who served in a number of governments. Mashnuq was known for his charisma and his ability to mobilise the masses.[9] Meheddine Nsouli was the owner of *Beirut*. Nsouli, an Arab nationalist with an Islamist bent, served as a minister during the Mandate period. He was also the founder of the Najadeh party, a Lebanese Arab nationalist party whose primary function was to safeguard the rights of the Sunni community.

Facing the Arab nationalist press were the mouthpieces of the Lebanese nationalists as well as the radical Lebanese nationalists. The most prominent figures representing the two camps were George Naccache, the editor-in-chief of *L'Orient*, and Michel Chiha, his counterpart in *Le Jour*. Both French-language newspapers were the most influential dailies during the Mandate and after. *L'Orient* first appeared in 1924, its motto being 'the protection of Lebanon from Syrian Unity'. During the 1930s it supported Emile Eddé's vision of a smaller Christian Lebanon.

Le Jour was born with the emergence of the Constitutional Bloc in 1934, which was headed by Chiha's brother-in-law, Bshara al-Khuri. Chiha, a close advisor in the corridors of power during the first ten years of independence, was a strong supporter of a Greater, multi-confessional, Lebanon. Chiha is said to have had great influence over the shaping of Lebanon's foreign and economic policies. His followers included members of his own family, who, aside from President Khuri, were Henri

Phar'oun, Salim and Philip Takla, Habib Abi Chahla and Charles Helou – all of whom occupied key positions in the Lebanese state after independence. Chiha was at the heart of this 'Consortium' of families who were competing in the world of business and who supported Bshara al-Khuri, preparing him for and sustaining him in power.[10]

As stated, most of those men mentioned above were key political actors who had considerable influence upon the political milieu of the time.[11] Contemporary press reports of the various political debates within, and between, Syria and Lebanon reflect the reactions of Syrians and Lebanese to the clash of nationalisms – notably pan-Arabism and radical Lebanese nationalism – within the context of Syro-Lebanese relations. This book will reveal how Lebanon's conflicting nationalisms converged to face a Syrian Arab nationalism that, throughout the late 1940s, had in fact developed into Syrian particularism, at least where Syro-Lebanese relations were concerned.

Studies focusing on the history of Syro-Lebanese relations between 1943 and 1950 are rare. Classics such as Albert Hourani's *Syria and Lebanon* and George Haddad's *Fifty Years of Modern Syria and Lebanon* tackled the impact of Westernisation in the two countries. Hourani scrutinised the impact of changes in intellectual and social conditions upon the political life. Haddad presented an overview of the main political and economic developments during the first half of the twentieth century. Nicola Ziadeh's *Syria and Lebanon* is an account of the Syrian and Lebanese political scene, focusing on both states' disposition towards the League of Arab States, the Baghdad Pact and Israel. Robin Fedden's *Syria and Lebanon* and Eugenie Abouchdid's *Thirty Years of Lebanon and Syria* provided an historical overview, starting with the Phoenicians and ending in the first half of the twentieth century. Both works emphasise the importance of grasping Syria's past to understand the causes of the country's instability.

Most of this literature was written in the first half of the twentieth century and consequently did not have access to archival material. Moreover, these studies did not make extensive use of the press. All the scholars designed their works as general introductions to or overviews of the two Levantine states. Consequently, the dynamics of Syro-Lebanese relations were not extensively investigated.

Other basic references on Lebanon and Syria that focus on a more specific period, and made extensive use of archival material, include Philip Khoury's *Syria and the French Mandate*, Stephen Longrigg's *Syria and Lebanon under the French Mandate* and Peter Shambrook's *French Imperialism in Syria*. These works provide detailed analyses of the politics in the Levant under the French Mandate, so restrict themselves to the period up to 1945.

The aforementioned studies contribute greatly to our understanding of the 1943–1950 period. In their writings one can discern several key elements that are pertinent to this period, such as the emergence of the various national movements, their aspirations and sensitivities; the alliances among the Lebanese and Syrian ruling elite; and the contexts and repercussions of the establishment of Lebanon and Syria as well as the administrative apparatuses founded by the French Mandate that resulted in an 'imposed economic union' between Lebanon and Syria. As shall be demonstrated, all these elements played a central role in post-independence Syro-Lebanese relations, and were extensively referenced by politicians and opinion makers during their debates on the bilateral interests of both states.

Scholars have tended to identify the various national movements in their work. Their studies tend to group Syrian Arab nationalists and Lebanese Arab nationalists into one category. However, an investigation of the bilateral relations of the two Levant states reveals divergent and even conflicting interests in the Arab nationalist camp. Consequently, and for the purpose of this study, the major nationalist movements at play are divided into three categories: the Syrian Arab nationalists, the Lebanese Arab nationalists and the Lebanese nationalists.

The Lebanese nationalists, most of whom were drawn from the Lebanese Christian-Maronite community, strove for an independent Lebanese state – *Grand Liban* – within what they perceived to be its historical and natural borders, extending from the Mediterranean in the west to the Anti-Lebanon mountains in the east, and from the Kabir River in the north to Ras al-Naqura in the south. With its capital in Beirut and claimed historic links with ancient Phoenicia, the state was to be a refuge for Christians in an Arab/Muslim-dominated Middle East. The Syrian Arab nationalists as well as their Lebanese counterparts, on the other hand, had their own vision – that of a united, independent Arab nation, stretching from the Mediterranean in the west to the Syrian desert in the east, from Cilicia in the north to the Sinai desert in the south.[12]

Works such as Kamal Salibi's *The Modern History of Lebanon* and John Spagnolo's *France and Ottoman Lebanon, 1861–1914* trace the rise of the national movements to the end of the Ottoman era. In general terms, during their four centuries of rule the Ottomans divided Syria into a variety of administrative districts. After 1864, these consisted of three vilayets, those of Aleppo, Damascus and Beirut, the province of Jerusalem and the *mutasarrifiya* of Mount Lebanon. Except for Mount Lebanon, which enjoyed a certain degree of special cohesion and autonomy, these units had little more than administrative significance. They bore no great political meaning, nor did they interfere with communications or the movement of people and goods across administrative lines.

Philip Khoury's *Urban Notables and Arab Nationalism: The Politics of Damascus 1860–1920* and C. Ernest Dawn's *From Ottomanism to Arabism: Essays on the Origins of Arab Nationalism* argue that, as long as they were part of an empire, the ruling elites of the major Syrian and Lebanese towns saw that there was no urgent need for them to link up in a common political front, even though they had identical social roots and classified their interests in a similar manner. This changed with the Young Turks Revolt of 1908. The Young Turks' emphasis on centralisation and Turkification of the Arab provinces sufficiently threatened the interests of a significant number of the Syrian political elite to provoke a violent reaction. To legitimise their opposition, the Syrian political elite relied on a mixture of traditional Islamic and modern secularist elements. At their core lay an emphasis on the specificity of the Arabs, their great cultural influence upon Islam, and their language, from which an ideological weapon, Arabism, was fashioned. By using Arabism, disaffected members of the urban elite could both justify and advance their opposition movement.[13]

In Mount Lebanon the situation was similar. The Lebanese nationalists – led by Christians, especially Maronites – called for greater political autonomy for the *mutasarrifiya*. Lebanese nationalists' demand for political autonomy was coupled with efforts to ensure Lebanese economic viability.[14] Kamal Salibi's *The Modern History of Lebanon*, Philip S. Khoury's *Syria and the French Mandate*, Kais Firro's *Inventing Lebanon*, Jean Karl Tanenbaum's *France and the Arab Middle East* and William Shorrock's *French Imperialism in the Middle East* maintain that the Young Turk Revolution of 1908, and growing Ottoman efforts to tie the Empire's provinces more tightly to Istanbul, led the Lebanese nationalist movement to adopt ideas of political separatism and territorial expansion under French protection. France's financial, political and religious investments in the region were concentrated in Beirut and Mount Lebanon, thereby encouraging the ambitions of the radical Lebanese nationalists. Thus, whereas the Syrian interior became more economically interdependent, Beirut and Mount Lebanon were more closely tied to France. Their economic relationship with France allowed the Christians of Beirut and the *mutasarrifiya* to reap the lion's share of economic and political benefits created by the overall French involvement in Syria. By 1914, the effects of this unbalanced French expansion were already visible in the divergent political aspirations of Lebanese Maronites and Syria's Muslim majority.[15]

Longrigg's *Syria and Lebanon under the French Mandate* placed the beginning of Syria's modern history at the onset of World War I, when Syria abruptly emerged from 'the shabby obscurity of an Ottoman province'[16] to become the focus of Great Power concern. At the centre of this transformation was the British government's effort to build alliances for its war efforts against Germany. Towards this end, it made vaguely worded promises regarding the Syrian territory to three different parties. In the Husayn–McMahon correspondence, ten letters exchanged between July 1915 and March 1916, London promised parts of Syria to be brought under the control of the Ottoman governor of Mecca, Sharif al-Husayn. In the Sykes–Picot Agreement of May 1916, Britain and France took over Syria.[17] In the Balfour Declaration of November 1917, Great Britain endorsed 'the establishment in Palestine of a national home for the Jewish people'.

British forces took control of the area from the Mediterranean Sea to Iran in a campaign that began with the Arab Revolt of June 1916 and ended with the conquest of Aleppo in October 1918. In Syria, the British forces stopped short of

Damascus, allowing Faysal, the Sharif's son, to take over the city and establish an Arab administration in Syria. With this act, the British indicated their support for an Arab rather than a French administration in Damascus, while enhancing Faysal's stature.

James Gelvin's *Divided Loyalties* holds that the division of the Ottoman Empire destroyed the 'overarching political structure that had loosely linked an emergent stratum of Westernising elites with much of the remainder of the population'. As a result the period during the war, as well as the two-year period that separated the end of the war and the French invasion of inland Syria, was one of rigorous rivalry during which different and sometimes opposing visions of Syria's future competed with one another.[18] Gelvin points out that although the Arab movement became dominant after the outbreak of the Arab revolt, Syrian enthusiasm for it diminished with the end of the war,[19] while local Syrian and Lebanese tendencies became stronger once 'liberation from the Ottomans' became a reality. In his work Eliezer Tauber argues that at the end of World War I, the Arab nation split into two main ideological streams. The Arab movement strove to establish a single greater Arab state in the territories of the former Arab provinces of the Ottoman Empire, while a Lebanese national movement strove for an independent Lebanon with extended boundaries.[20]

Under King Faysal's brief reign the number and activities of parties, popular committees and societies increased profoundly. They assisted in influencing and, to a certain degree, moulding popular perceptions towards the shape of Syria. This was to have a direct bearing on Syria's relations with Lebanon. Syrian independence, if not within the framework of an Arab union, was the main objective of all Syrian parties and popular committees. A Lebanon separated from an Arab union or Greater Syria scheme was completely rejected.[21]

The Lebanese nationalists rejected annexation or unification with a Syrian state. Many of them were also pro-French and gave credit to France for its educational, cultural and relief projects in the region before the war. In contrast to the Syrians, they were more open to the idea of French aegis. During this period – and in the years preceding the war – the partisans of Lebanese independence, with or without foreign patronage, and Lebanese national distinctiveness were much stronger than the factions that wanted to be connected with Syria.[22]

At the San Remo Conference in April 1920, a mandate over Syria and Lebanon was granted to France, and a British Mandate established over Palestine and Iraq. Three months later, the French army, under the command of Henri Gouraud, defeated the Arabs at Maysalun, occupied Damascus and expelled Faysal and his government from Syria, thus bringing their dreams for independence and unity to an abrupt end. For the next quarter-century, France would control Syria and Lebanon.

Throughout the course of its mandate, notes Spagnolo, France preferred to emphasise social and cultural differences between the Syrians and Lebanese, interpreting these as the product of sectarian divide. This rather 'over-simplistic' interpretation of the nature of Syrian (and Lebanese) societies in terms of sectarian conflict also incorporated the French notion of 'progress', which, in terms of Syria and Lebanon, pitted a numerically weak but socially and culturally more advanced Christian minority (Lebanon), with 'an unquenchable thirst' for European knowledge and values, against a large community of fanatical, narrow-minded, and intellectually underdeveloped Muslims (Syria) bent on obstructing progress in all areas of life.[23] With a constant fear of being swamped by the surrounding Arab/Islamic majority, most radical Lebanese nationalists came to identify themselves with France, thereby formalising Syrian and Arab national resentment against anything Lebanese. As shall be seen, in post-independence Syro-Lebanese disputes, Syrian Arab nationalists were always wary of French influence over Lebanon and were convinced that a Lebanese refusal to toe the Syrian line was a prelude to France's return to the Levant. On the other hand, the radical Lebanese nationalists were convinced that the Syrians were plotting to 're-take' Lebanon. Consequently, Syro-Lebanese economic disagreements frequently developed into rows where Lebanese and Syrian intentions were respectively classified as either conspiratorial or expansionist.

Philip Khoury, Meir Zamir and Stephan Longrigg indicate that this resentment reached new levels in the battle of Maysalun,[24] which came to be engraved on Syria's collective memory as a symbol of the nation's heroic defence of its independence. It was the first devastating blow to the Arab nationalists during the long and bitter years of the French Mandate. The Arab nationalists regarded France not as a friendly nation – which was, as defined by the mandate, to help and guide them towards independence and statehood – but as a colonial, Christian, Western, anti-Muslim power, which had denied their national aspirations and was threatening their religion, culture and language. After being stripped of their independence, they received no less severe a blow when France shattered their dreams of unity by dismembering Syria. They helplessly witnessed the partition of their lands and the imposition of artificial borders by two European Powers, and watched as France surrendered Palestine to Britain and eventually to the Zionists, Cilicia and later Alexandretta to Turkey. France then carved up Greater Syria, exploiting its religious, ethnic, sectarian and geographic diversity, into what the nationalists regarded as artificial entities: Greater Lebanon, the Alawite region, Jabal al-Druze and the autonomous province of Alexandretta. The interior was further divided into the statelets of Damascus and Aleppo.[25]

Zamir notes how Syrian Arab nationalist politicians, intellectuals and opinion makers often portrayed Lebanese nationalism both as an artificial idea supported by a small minority that refused to recognise the aspirations of the Arab nation, and as an isolationist movement inspired by religion and sect, led by the clergy and backed by a colonial power. While the radical Lebanese nationalists were undermining Arab independence and unity, Arab nationalism, they declared, upheld equality for all, regardless of religion or sect.[26]

Marwan Buheiry's *Beirut's Role in the Political Economy of the French Mandate, 1919–39* and Khoury's *Syria and the French Mandate* put great importance on the subsequent division of Greater Syria into British and French Mandates as well as the creation of Greater Lebanon, which served to secure French domination over the area and isolate Damascus. The city was now less than 15 miles from the Lebanese border, and the vital road and railway systems in the Beqa' valley linking it to Homs, Hama and Aleppo, and to Tripoli, Beirut and northern Palestine, were under French and Lebanese command. With the Beqa' valley, Beirut and Tripoli within its territory, Lebanon now completely controlled access to Damascus from the sea. Damascus subsequently lost much of its standing to Beirut, which became the main political, administrative, economic and cultural centre of the French mandated territories, enjoying its status as the seat of the High Commission.

The Damascenes envied Beirut's prosperity and believed it had been achieved largely at their expense. Indeed, there was a sharp contrast between the prosperous 'Christian-French Beirut with its elegant quarters, wide avenues, modern universities and large European communities, and grim, conservative Muslim Damascus'.[27] Judging from the numerous editorials written by Syrian Arab nationalists, it was expected that Damascus would regain its pre-eminence over the Lebanese capital – or at least gain an equal footing with Beirut – once the Lebanese Arab nationalists came to power. In contrast with Damascus, Beirut's economic development would continue well after the mandate and, as shall be seen, was the focus of great controversy among Syrian opinion makers, in spite of the ascendancy of their Arab nationalist brethren. This study will take up the matter of the Lebanese Arab stance towards these vehement criticisms, and investigate whether or not it was a source of discord between Lebanese and Syrian Arab nationalists.

Two decades before such questions came to the fore, the Syrian Revolt of 1925 shook the French order in the Levant. According to Khoury and Longrigg, the 1925 revolt was a major landmark in Syrian history. In the summer of 1925, it seemed that the French policy of *politique minoritaire* had succeeded in limiting opposition to the mandate. Yet within weeks, France was faced with an uprising of Syrian Druze and Arab nationalists. The revolt had profound repercussions for Syrian and Lebanese politics, as well as on France's policy towards Syria, throughout the next decade. The rebellion evoked strong feelings of patriotism and transformed Arab nationalism into a major ideology in Syria and the Arab world. The revolt pressured France to reconsider its policy in Syria. Franco-Syrian negotiations for independence commenced, fuelling the apprehension of Lebanese nationalists. They feared that, after the withdrawal of Britain and France, Lebanon would be overwhelmed by the Islamist/pan-Arabist tide that was already spreading throughout the region. They followed the Franco-Syrian negotiations closely, and became alarmed at any sign of French concessions, especially on Syrian unity.

Zamir argues that, at the time, Lebanese nationalists had the choice of joining the Syrians in demanding a treaty and independence, and thereby severing their traditional ties with France, or advocating continuation of the mandate, and thus arousing the hostility of the Arab nationalists in Lebanon and Syria. At this historic juncture, there were conflicting influences working on Lebanese nationalists. On one hand, France's internal and international weaknesses made an agreement with the Syrian and Lebanese Arab nationalist leadership more appealing for most Lebanese nationalists as a means of ensuring their country's independence and territorial integrity.[28] On the other hand, the Lebanese nationalist fear of being engulfed by an Arab unionist or Greater Syria scheme has remained a major component of Syro-Lebanese relations to the present day. Lebanese nationalist apprehensions were especially pronounced during the post-independence period and it would have a profound influence upon the making – as well as the fragility – of agreements concerned with the functional aspects of bilateral relations.

Raghid el-Solh's *Lebanon and Arabism*, Kais Firro's *Inventing Lebanon* and Zamir's *Lebanon's Quest* explain how three schools of thought emerged in the Lebanese Arab nationalist camp. There were those who accepted integration into the Lebanese state provided they were granted full equality; those who demanded immediate union with Syria; and those for whom the most pressing issue was neither equality nor borders, but securing Lebanon's independence by severing Maronite ties with France. According to el-Solh, the guiding principles of the Arab nationalist leaders who presided over several governments in Lebanon and Syria were full independence from France; no special status for France; forgoing the idea of Syrian unity; special relationship with Syria; a Lebanese state that would be part of an Arab order and had an 'Arab face'.[29] Zamir also puts great importance on how the ideological debate over Lebanon's national identity, its borders and ties with the West and the Arab Muslim world, especially Syria, became progressively entangled in the bitter 13-year struggle for the presidency between Emile Eddé and Bshara al-Khuri. The National Bloc and their Arab nationalist allies in Lebanon exploited the rivalry between the two men. It weakened the radical Lebanese nationalist camp. It also enabled Muslim politicians to exercise considerable influence on, and facilitate their integration into, the Lebanese political system. By the second half of the 1930s, Lebanese nationalists were less and less able to resist Syrian intervention as well as attempts by the High Commission to tighten its control.[30]

The debate among Lebanese Arab nationalists as well as the Syrian National Bloc strengthened the belief of the Khuri camp that the Maronites should relinquish their historic ties with France and forge an alliance with the Syrian Arab nationalist movement, both to affirm Lebanon's existence and guarantee their access to power. In talks held in February 1936, Riad el-Solh advised the leaders of the Constitutional Bloc, which was headed by Khuri, that the National Bloc would be willing to recognise Lebanon's independence and territorial integrity, provided that the Christians joined the struggle against France to achieve these goals. Later on, seven deputies from the Constitutional Bloc (excluding Khuri) presented the High Commission with a memorandum requesting that France grant

Lebanon the same rights it had given their 'Syrian brethren'. They demanded restoration of the constitution, replacement of the mandate with a treaty and Lebanon's admission to the League of Nations. They also asked permission for a Lebanese delegation to go to Paris to negotiate a treaty with the French government. Although rejected by the High Commission, the memorandum marked another stage in the Constitutional Bloc's attitude shift vis-à-vis the French Mandate. It enhanced Khuri's stature among both Muslims and Christians. To the Syrians and Lebanese Muslims, he was an anti-French Maronite leader, willing to join the national struggle for independence; to the Christians, he was a patriotic Lebanese statesman, demanding that France treat Lebanon on equal terms with Syria.[31]

Raghid el-Solh attributes this 'realignment' process among Lebanese Arab nationalists, Lebanese constitutionalists and Syrian Arab nationalists to the fact that political relations were conducted at a less formal – indeed, more personal – level. This was mainly because

> the majority of the Syrian and Lebanese Muslim leaders shared a similar social and cultural background. Many of them were bound by old friendships or family ties, as those between the Mardams and the Salams, for example, or the Solhs and the Jabiris, or the Karamis and the Haffars. These relations enabled the Lebanese Arab nationalists to secure a number of concessions from their Syrian counterparts.

By securing concessions from Syria, Lebanese Arab nationalists were able to consolidate their alliance with the constitutionalists and affirm their image as the local protector of Lebanese independence, thus eventually managing to neutralise and undermine the isolationist trend in Lebanese politics.[32] This state of affairs was to serve Lebanese and Syrian Arab nationalists in their struggle against France. However, as shall be seen, the kinship between the ruling elite of Lebanon and Syria did not suffice to ensure smooth bilateral relations in the post-independence period.

During the second half of 1936 Syria and Lebanon signed a 25-year 'treaty of friendship and alliance' with France. Numerous studies – among them Zamir's *Lebanon's Quest*, Najla Atiyah's *The Attitude of the Lebanese Sunnis Towards the State of Lebanon*, Firro's *Inventing Lebanon* and Michael Johnson's *Class and Client in Beirut: The Sunni Muslim Community and the Lebanese State, 1840–1985* – maintain that the conclusion of the Franco-Syrian treaty precipitated a shift in the Sunni leadership's stand on Syria and the Lebanese state. Many Lebanese, including supporters of Syrian unity, were disappointed with the National Bloc. Abandoned by Syria and with Lebanon on the threshold of independence, they believed that the Muslims' most urgent goal was to ensure their own rights in a Lebanese state. Hence, the Lebanese Muslim leadership was more willing to take part in the political haggling designed to lay down the rules of confessional office-holding in the country. Although their rhetoric still focused on Lebanese union with Syria, Muslim politicians had come to appreciate that, whereas they might be of first-rate importance in Lebanon, in a greater Syria they might at best be second-rate next to political leaders from Damascus and Aleppo.

Consequently these politicians, true to the traditions of the urban notability, rallied mass support by advocating unity with Syria, but used this support as a tool to gain political leverage within the Lebanese political arena. Beirut's burgeoning Muslim and Christian mercantile bourgeoisie, won over to the idea of Greater Lebanon as the best means of protecting its economic interests, further facilitated this process. Indeed, the affluent Muslim class to which the Lebanese leaders belonged came to appreciate the wealth that Beirut generated as a capital city, an administrative and trading centre, and an important gateway to the Arab hinterland.[33] The involvement of a number of Muslim merchants, and more than a few Christians, in the trans-shipment of Western manufactures from Beirut to the Syrian hinterland – and the importation of raw materials to Beirut for Western markets – created fear about the consequences of completely separating Lebanon from the Arab world – which might occur if Lebanon became too much of a French client state.[34]

The Franco-Syrian and Franco-Lebanese treaties stipulated that bilateral economic relations were to be decided in direct negotiations between the Syrian and Lebanese governments. By April 1938, discord regarding economic issues erupted into an all-out trade war. Reflecting on the April 1938 economic dispute between Lebanon and Syria, Raghid el-Solh emphasises that this development was only welcomed by hard-line radical Lebanese nationalists, a few Syrian merchants and a number of civil servants, who perceived the customs barrier as an additional source of income.[35]

After independence, the economic disputes of 1938 resurfaced throughout the late 1940s, driving Syria to dissolve the Syro-Lebanese economic union. In his *Lebanon: The Challenge of Independence*, Eyal Zisser focuses on the role of Bshara al-Khuri and his governments in the course of modern Lebanese history. Zisser attributed the dissolution of the Syro-Lebanese customs union in 1950 to the rise of the military to power in Syria, which caused great and irreversible damage to Syro-Lebanese relations.[36] Steven Heydemann's *Authoritarianism in Syria* adds that the rise of the military was accompanied by the rise of a capitalist class in Syria. He argues that the Syrian capitalists strove to Syrianise the economy by introducing measures principally aimed at reducing Lebanese participation in Syria's economy. These measures led to the dissolution of the Syro-Lebanese customs union.[37]

Attributing the dissolution of the economic union to a resurgent military and an affluent capitalist class raises a number of questions that this book will address. Were relations between Beirut and Damascus free of strain prior to the military takeover? After independence, was Syria's ruling elite disposed to separation from Lebanon? In addressing these issues, the book will focus on the political and economic factors that led the Syrians to favour separation over integration or cooperation with a neighbour upon which they had depended for much of their exports and imports.

In a paper entitled 'The Syro-Lebanese Customs Union, Causes of Failure and Attempts at Re-Organization', Elias Saba argues that the Syrian and Lebanese political elites put both states on the road to separation in 1943 by concluding an economic agreement that was – for reasons of political expediency – deficient in economic regulatory mechanisms. Saba proceeds to give an economic analysis of the 1943 Syro-Lebanese agreement's shortcomings without addressing local and regional factors that prevented the agreement from surmounting its failings and encompassing other aspects of bilateral relations. Antoine Hokayem's paper 'Al-'alakat al-lubnaniya al-suriya, 1918–1950', presents a brief survey of bilateral relations, focusing on the Alexandria Protocol and the dissolution of the economic union. In his conclusions, Hokayem stresses the need for a deeper investigation of relations between the two states after their independence until the break-up of the customs union.

Other scholars attribute the rupture of economic relations to Lebanon's insistence that their economy maintain its free-market, free-trade orientation. Nadim Shehadi and Carolyn Gates maintain that the Lebanese ruling elite's attitude towards Syro-Lebanese relations was rooted in the country's laissez-faire system.[38] Shehadi and Gates attribute a central role to a group of Lebanese economic and political elites that acted as the midwives of Lebanon's economic liberalism. The architects of Lebanon's laissez-faire system are identified as mainly belonging to the Christian community or the Lebanese nationalists. Hence, it is argued, that it was in their interests to safeguard Lebanon's free-market economy, even if this meant rupture with Syria, which remained adamant at safeguarding its protectionist economy.

This book will consider how and whether the Lebanese nationalists favoured the dissolution of the economic partnership or opted for maintaining it. Also frequently overlooked was the role played by Lebanese Arab nationalists in post-independence Syro-Lebanese relations and their disposition towards economic separation with Syria. It is noteworthy, aside from very few exceptions, the political leaders at the helm of the Lebanese Arab nationalists, such as Riad el-Solh, were not financiers or merchants. This book hopes to shed light on the circumstances that led to the convergence of their positions with those of the Lebanese nationalists, at least where Syro-Lebanese relations between 1943 and 1950 are concerned.

1 The Syrian Arab Nationalists: Independence First

A. THE FORGING OF A NEW ALLIANCE

With the creation of the Lebanese state, Syrian Arab nationalists regarded successive Lebanese governments, as well as the Lebanese presidency – regardless of Lebanon's incumbent head of state – as unconstitutional and lacking legitimacy. Syrians regarded the Lebanese parliament as unrepresentative, the Lebanese ruling elite as French pawns, and Lebanon as a French satellite. However, during the second half of 1942, Syrian attitudes and policies, particularly those of the National Bloc, witnessed profound change. This change may partially be attributed to political factors. This chapter shall focus on the alignment of Lebanese and Syrian nationalist movements against France and the manner in which this alliance influenced Syro-Lebanese relations.

The Syrian Arab nationalists' change of heart towards Lebanon was mainly due to an increased awareness that the struggle for independence could not operate solely at the Syrian national level. It was necessary to bring their policy into harmony with that of Lebanese nationalists. Jamil Mardam Bey, who had many personal friends among the Lebanese leadership, took the initiative and held a number of meetings with Bshara al-Khuri and even with leaders known for their loyalty to France, like Emile Eddé. There was an effort on the part of the National Bloc to find common ground for the termination of the French Mandate. The common ground was to constitute the restoration of a democratic constitutional regime (which meant the removal of the pro-French Lebanese leadership, as represented by Eddé, through the election of a new parliament) and the integration of Lebanon into the pan-Arab fold so as to limit French political and military influence. In Bshara al-Khuri the Syrian Arab nationalists found an eager partner who was willing to cooperate along these lines.[1]

At the end of January 1943, the French announced that constitutional life would be restored. Elections were conducted and a nationalist government came to power in Syria.[2] But with the *Troupes Spéciales* and the *Sûreté Générale* still in French hands, its influence remained great. Arab nationalists were fully aware that France could turn the tables on them at any moment. It was also feared that at war's end British troops would withdraw and be replaced by French forces, enabling France to impose a treaty on Syria and Lebanon, which would prejudice their independence.[3]

Even before the 1943 elections, France had demanded the issuance of a treaty prior to relinquishing control over the vital institutions and levers of power in Syria and Lebanon. To that end it had proposed a bargain to Shukri al-Quwwatly and his Nationalist Bloc associates. France would bring Quwwatly to power in exchange for a treaty along the lines of the agreement of 1936. Quwwatly refused, fearing that this would make the Nationalist Bloc extremely unpopular among Syria's general public. He refused to discuss the issue of the treaty, preferring instead to negotiate from a position of strength after the elections, which the Nationalist Bloc anticipated winning.[4] Indeed, the election results did enable the nationalists to claim to represent the Syrian popular will. The nationalist position was further strengthened by Lebanese–Syrian diplomatic cooperation, brought about by the election of a nationalist government in Beirut shortly after the Syrian elections.[5]

The emergence of a united Syrian–Lebanese negotiating front in the autumn of 1943 was the product of converging political attitudes in Lebanon and Syria on the future of their countries' relations, at least where the French presence in the Levant was concerned. Syro-Lebanese rapprochement was further facilitated in 1943, when an alliance of the Muslim and Christian commercial bourgeoisie brought the two major proponents of an independent Arab Lebanon to power – Bshara al-Khuri became President of the Republic and Riad el-Solh became Prime Minister.[6] The understanding among the commercial bourgeoisie, cultivated since the mid-1930s, also forged an unwritten agreement known as the National Pact (*al-Mithaq al-Watani*). A 'temporary' compromise formula among the different Lebanese sects – primarily the Maronites and Sunnis – it was designed to 'balance' and distribute posts and political positions in the newly independent republic. The attainment of the National Pact was further facilitated by the perceptions of most of the Muslim ruling elite, who, while using threat of union with Syria to enhance personal importance, were not wholeheartedly behind such a scheme. They realised that their position as leaders of a Muslim community in Lebanon was more important than the one they would hold in a Greater Syria.[7] The pact also planted the basic pillars upon which Lebanon's foreign policy was to rest, by assuring Lebanese Christians of independence and some sort of a Western orientation, while at the same time guaranteeing Muslims complete cooperation with Arab states.[8] As mentioned above, the pact's ascendancy was further reinforced by the results of the Lebanese parliamentary elections that brought Khuri and Solh to power.

Khuri's and Solh's ascent to power on 7 October 1943 was a clear victory to the Arab nationalist cause, taking place despite French attempts to alter the results of Lebanon's parliamentary elections to include a greater number of French loyalist deputies.[9] The nationalists in Syria were extremely pleased. The promises of friendly and close relations between Syria and Lebanon, stressed in Khuri's inaugural speech, were regarded as a good augury for Lebanese integration into a future Arab federation. The new Lebanese government was regarded as the strongest and most progressive cabinet in the history of Lebanon. It was also felt that Lebanese aspirations to greater control over their own country had a better chance of realisation than ever before. The Lebanese Premier was expected to announce a strongly nationalist policy. In this regard, in an interview prior to his appointment to form the government, Solh declared that the Lebanese flag – which had been the French tricolour with a Lebanese cedar on the white band – should be replaced by the Arab colours, the cedar alone being retained.[10]

Syrian opinion-makers wrote about the newly appointed Lebanese government with great enthusiasm. Khuri was described as a politically mature statesman and an example of honesty and honour. Riad el-Solh was characterised as a man of *jihad* and struggle for the independence and sovereignty of Lebanon, Syria and the Arab nation.[11] Syrian opinion-makers and Lebanese Arab nationalist circles were expecting the cabinet to follow a policy of closer cultural and economic relations with other Arab states, particularly Syria.[12] The nomination of Solh, and his visit to Damascus within 24 hours of the formation of his cabinet, was seen in Syria as an obvious sign of Lebanese politics' veering from isolationism to pan-Arabism.[13]

This was evident in Riad el-Solh's parliamentary declaration, made during a special session on 7 October 1943, in which he presented his government's programme. Solh emphasised Lebanese independence and the territorial integrity of Lebanon's present frontiers, but stressed the importance of negotiating an agreement with Syria for joint control of common interests and bringing Lebanon out of its isolation to cooperate more closely with Arab states. The Lebanese Premier declared that 'Lebanon is a country whose features are Arab but which desires to extract what is best from occidental civilization ... We do not wish Lebanon to be a colony [and] neither do [the Arab states] wish her to be a channel through which they themselves might be colonized.' The Solh government obtained an overwhelming vote of confidence.[14] The Arab nationalist sentiments in the Solh speech were anticipated. However, what irritated the French most was Riad el-Solh's commitment to revise the constitution with a view to eliminate certain provisions incompatible with independence, particularly those that recognised the right of authorities other than the legitimate representatives of the Lebanese people to participate in the administration. In parliament Solh also voiced his commitment to instate Arabic as the official language and to revise a number of conventions and regulations that the government considered prejudicial to Lebanese sovereignty, such as the *arrêtés* and *décisions* issued by the French.[15]

During the month of October, Riad el-Solh frequently visited Damascus. Syrian opinion-makers described his very first visit as the first instance in which Damascus received an 'independent Arab Lebanon'. There was optimism in Syrian political circles that, although the 'pains of the past prevented the unity of Syria and Lebanon in their relations and interests, hope in the future will undoubtedly unite us'.[16] Obviously, the new governments in Beirut and Damascus, backed by public opinion, were acting in close concert. For the first time in the history of these states, Lebanon had ceased to be a pawn played off by the French against the Syrians.[17] The emergence of the new national rule in Lebanon and its policy of independence and Arabism thus satisfied the Syrian ruling elite to the extent that they abandoned Syria's old claims in Lebanon. The Syrians saw Lebanon's association with other Arab states as an expression of this new policy and a guarantee for Syria and Lebanon's newly acquired freedom.[18]

Discussions between the Syrian and Lebanese governments focused on liberating their countries from French dominion. The Syrians stressed the need to prevent a direct confrontation with France but Solh's parliamentary declaration had the opposite effect. On 5 November the French Committee issued a communiqué in Algiers refusing to recognise the revision of the constitution.[19] The same evening, the Lebanese government replied with a communiqué stating that the government had submitted to the chamber a bill revising certain articles that had come to be seen as incompatible with complete independence. The government then called on parliament to vote on the administrative functions and the rights of the French, the omission of all reference to the mandate, the substitution of Arabic for French as an official language and the formal recognition of the present borders as final. Jean Helleu, French delegate general, took the unprecedented step of imprisoning President Khuri, Prime Minister Solh, three ministers, and one deputy. Strikes and demonstrations over the next two weeks united the country against France. Never before had Beirut remained closed for more than 48 hours and the unanimity with which closure was maintained testified to the strength of Lebanese public opinion. In Damascus, students, who regarded their government as having not responded firmly enough to the Lebanese crisis, went on strike.[20] Indeed, although on 15 November the Syrian general assembly demanded that the French reinstate the Lebanese government, Foreign Minister Jamil Mardam Bey alluded to the justification of Syrian inaction. Mardam Bey declared that the French Mandate was more 'theoretical than real' and thus no longer a threat to 'an established [de facto] independence'. Consequently, Damascus was happy to 'let the Lebanese pull the chestnuts out of the fire: it was only two months after the Lebanese crisis that the Syrian parliament passed a law amending the Syrians' constitution along the lines Beirut had sketched for them'.[21]

Britain quickly threw her support behind the Lebanese government and forced the French National Committee in Algiers to release the interned leaders. On 22 November 1943, in Algiers, the initial solutions to the crisis in Lebanon were announced. Khuri, Solh, as well as the rest of the prisoners were released. The Lebanese President returned to office and negotiations commenced with the aim of returning constitutional life to the country. During that time General George Catroux started negotiations with the Syrian and the Lebanese governments to coordinate the transfer of the directorates from the mandate to the national government.[22] In Syria the end of the Lebanese crisis was received with relief and a certain trace of reserve. It was generally realised that the release and reinstatement of the Lebanese head of state and the government was almost entirely the result of British pressure. This increased the Syrians' confidence in the British guarantee of Syrian independence and with it Syria's bargaining power with France. Consequently, the Syrian leadership was more than eager to identify itself with British policy. But there remained a lingering fear in Syrian political circles that a showdown with France was inevitable.[23] More importantly, Syrian and Lebanese steadfastness and coordination was instrumental in turning the tables on the French.

The Lebanese crisis of November 1943 not only signalled the end of the French Mandate but reinforced the attitudes of the Lebanese and Syrian leaderships regarding their future relations with the French.[24] The attitude of the two governments towards the coming negotiations with the mandatory Power was firmly defined by the formal declarations of policy, which had been made by the Lebanese and Syrian Prime Ministers in their respective chambers. Following the line they had previously adopted in their public declarations, both Solh and Mardam Bey repudiated the mandate and insisted upon the immediate transfer of the various directorates of the Common Interests that were in French hands. Both emphasised the right of the Levant states to complete independence, in accordance with Allied pledges and the Atlantic Charter and subject to the exigencies of the war alone.[25]

Meetings between Syrian and Lebanese leaders were stepped up, especially during December, to ensure agreement and logistical readiness for the takeover of the directorates of Common Interests between the two states. Great care was taken to relate to the public and the Great Powers that Beirut and Damascus were in full agreement over matters related to the Common Interests.[26]

B. THE HIGHER COUNCIL OF THE COMMON INTERESTS

The department of the Common Interests (or Intérêts Communs) was formed in 1928. It was the creation of the French administration in Syria to administer the income and expenditure of the departments of the Common Interests. This department managed customs, postal and telegram services and antiquities and supervised the concessionary companies. The income of these institutions was at the sole disposal of the High Commissioner, who directly administered the Common Interests' budget, the bulk of whose revenues (95 per cent annually) came from customs receipts. Since the states under the French Mandate lived within a single customs zone, it was difficult to equitably distribute revenues from the Common Interests among the different state budgets. It was also difficult to establish ratios for state budget contributions to the Customs and Cadastral Survey administrations, and to the Ottoman public debt. Lebanon and Syria were unable to reach an agreement among themselves. Lebanon demanded a 70 per cent share of customs receipts owing to her higher standard of living and hence to her greater consumption of imports, whereas Syria demanded a 70 per cent share on demographic and territorial grounds. As a result, the High Commission imposed its own terms in the Customs Union Accord of 1930. Receipts were to be distributed on a quota basis, the coefficient being calculated on estimates of consumption of imported products. Although much contested by both parties, the agreement granted Syria (including the Alawite territory and Jabal Druze) a 53 per cent share and Lebanon a 47 per cent share. Yet each state had to contribute roughly 50 per cent of its total annual receipts to the unproductive defence and security sector.[27]

It should be noted that by May 1943, the heavy expenditure upon the armed forces was one of the main reasons for price rises in Lebanon and Syria. Growing scarcity of goods caused by import reduction was the other. Increased expenditure and the rise in prices and wages in Lebanon and Syria led to an increase in bank deposits and notes in circulation, which, along with wholesale prices, rose to heights unparalleled elsewhere in the Middle East. Notes in circulation had risen about five times and wholesale and retail prices nearly seven times. British and French military commands were unwilling to reduce military expenditures. The prospect of the Lebanese and Syrian governments resorting to direct taxes was non-existent, since neither government had the necessary machinery for assessing and collecting direct taxes on a large scale. More importantly, they were unwilling even to take the necessary steps to enforce existing laws, owing to strong opposition from the commercial classes and landowners. The treasuries of Beirut and Damascus relied mainly upon indirect taxes and licensing fees for revenues.[28] For Beirut and Damascus such issues were of secondary importance. Priority remained liberating all the directorates and departments of the Common Interests.

On 22 December 1943, a meeting took place in Damascus between General Catroux and representatives of the Syrian and Lebanese governments. The result was an agreement that saw the Common Interests, together with their personnel, transferred to the states of Syria and Lebanon, along with the right to enact laws and regulations, as of 1 January 1944. Lebanon and Syria also agreed upon the share of revenues from the Common Interests. The agreements were submitted to the Lebanese and Syrian chambers, which were passed unanimously and with great enthusiasm.[29] Commenting on the Syro-Lebanese spirit of cooperation, Prime Minister Sa'adallah al-Jabiri stated that, in the past Syria used to hold on to its rights facing an occupied Lebanon, 'today, on the other hand it welcomes all the demands of the Lebanon of tomorrow'.[30] Noteworthy was the fact that Riad el-Solh was able to influence al-Jabiri to adopt a new stance towards Lebanon and, subsequently, the agreement.[31] For the time being, the Syro-Lebanese differences on customs union revenues were conveniently shelved.

Commenting on the aforementioned talks between France, Syria and Lebanon, it was noted that it was the first time in 25 years that the Lebanese and the Syrians met on one side, with the French on the other. This was characterised as a significant new development in the policy of Lebanon, compared to the Lebanese position of 1938. At that time France had told Syria to reach an agreement with Lebanon first, after which it would transfer the Common Interests. The Lebanese government under the presidency of Emil Eddé then created insurmountable obstacles, which resulted in the Common Interests remaining in French hands. Political circles in Damascus believed that, had not the Lebanese government postponed issues of shares and figures in 1938, the directorates of the Common Interests would have been in Syrian and Lebanese hands much earlier. Lebanese intransigence provided France with the justification for retaining control over these vital directorates. It was due to Khuri and Solh that the negotiations were not trilateral but bilateral, involving the nationalist and imperialist camps. Opinion-makers in Damascus were convinced that there was agreement among the leadership of both states to take control of the Common Interest first without expressing differences over numbers and shares.[32] Lebanese Arab nationalist circles held similar views but emphasised that the Syrian government of 1943 was not that of 1938.[33]

Late in the evening of 29 December 1943, the Syrian Minister of Finance and the director general of the ministry returned to Damascus after two days of talks in Beirut with representatives of the Lebanese government and French officials. They came away with an agreement on a modus operandi for the transferral of the Common Interests.[34] The two governments had also agreed to establish a Higher Council of the Common Interests. This higher council would oversee the accounts of the Common Interests as well as the distribution of revenues between the two states.[35]

At noon, on 4 January 1944, a ceremony took place in Beirut in which representatives of France, Syria and Lebanon signed an agreement marking the transfer of the Common Interests. The Syrian and the Lebanese delegations were headed by the Minister of Finance, Khaled al-'Azem, and Prime Minister, Riad el-Solh. On the occasion, the Lebanese Prime Minister gave a speech in which he addressed the concerns of the radical Lebanese and Arab nationalists. Solh emphasised that Lebanon and Syria were two independent states and that cooperation with Lebanon's Arab brothers or the West did not diminish the sovereignty of the two states. Addressing the Arab nationalists, he noted that 'Lebanon is a nation with an Arab face and does not hesitate to cooperate with the west for its benefit, and I believe that that is the intention of Syria as well'.[36] Opinion-makers regarded the signing of the agreement as having elevated the country's independence from a theoretical to a practical level. Opinion-makers were convinced that

Lebanon and Syria would closely cooperate in administering the various 'liberated' directorates.[37]

Coupled with the signature of the protocol, close consultations were taking place between Beirut and Damascus about finalising the Higher Council of the Common Interests (HCCI). An October agreement outlining the mandate of the HCCI was to be put into effect by the end of January 1944. Even the thorny issue of dividing the revenues of the Customs Directorate was temporarily resolved.

The ink had not dried on the agreement when the Maronite Patriarch, Mar Antoine Butrus 'Arida, sent a memorandum to the Lebanese President in which he asserted that the HCCI agreement infringed upon Lebanese sovereignty and was contrary to Lebanese interests. The patriarch saw that the mandate given to the HCCI granted it independence from Lebanon's legislative and executive branches of government. Consequently, 'Arida demanded that the Lebanese President terminate the agreement. He also called upon parliament not to ratify it.[38]

Radical Lebanese nationalist circles rallied behind the patriarch and campaigned against the Syro-Lebanese Agreement. They protested that the HCCI's mandate conflicted with the Lebanese constitution since it created two legislatures in one state. Lebanese Arab nationalists rejected these assertions and wondered how Lebanese sovereignty was threatened if Syria and Lebanon were cooperating in putting customs duties. Lebanese Arab nationalists were campaigning for the ratification of the agreement in parliament.[39] Syrian opinion-makers were closely following the debates in Lebanon. Their dailies widely disseminated a statement by Jamil Shehab, a Lebanese delegate to the HCCI, in which he had declared that 'I am a Lebanese Christian and it is impossible that I might go against the interests of Lebanon. There is nothing in the agreement that we conducted with our Syrian brothers that undermines Lebanese sovereignty and independence, on the contrary, Lebanese rights are safeguarded in every way.'[40]

In response to 'Arida's memorandum, President Khuri issued a statement in which he affirmed that there were some ambiguities regarding the legislative authority of the HCCI. The presidential statement revealed that the government had sent a bill to parliament that removed all 'vagueness' and noted that only the Lebanese government had the right to legislate. The presidential statement concluded by announcing that the Syrian parliament had ratified a bill similar to the one that was sent to the Lebanese parliament.[41]

The public exchange between the Lebanese presidency and the Maronite patriarchate did not end there. Hardly had a day passed after the publication of Khuri's response when 'Arida issued a number of declarations in which he clarified that his objection to the agreement was not confined to his previous memorandum. He continued to denounce the agreement as an infringement upon the sovereignty of the Lebanese state. Referring to article four of the agreement, which stipulates that Syria and Lebanon form one unified customs region where goods move freely, he asked if it would harm Syria if it took a transit fee on all the goods passing through her territory. Similarly, Lebanon would charge a transit fee on Syrian imports passing its territory. In that manner all grounds for differences would be removed. He added if the French Mandatory decided to combine the interests of both states, Lebanon – after gaining its independence – did not have to follow the same policy. He reiterated his demand for the liquidation of the HCCI, describing it as a government within a government, with the primary function of achieving union between Syria and Lebanon. 'Arida dismissed any schemes of Arab unity, stressing that 'we want the independence of Lebanon, we do not want unity because we would melt in it, thereby losing our existence and entity'.[42]

In an attempt to allay the patriarch's fears, Riad el-Solh paid a visit to Bkirki, the seat of the Maronite patriarchate. Over dinner, Solh outlined the benefits of the agreement. After the meeting the Prime Minister commented that 'everything is in order and I left the meeting with the patriarch in full agreement with him'. The patriarch presented the Prime Minister with a box of Damascene sweets as a symbol of their consensus.[43]

Solh was able to convince 'Arida by suggesting the redrafting of article three of the agreement. The phrase 'putting the necessary legislation for all the directorates of the Common Interests' was rewritten to 'drafting or preparing the necessary legislation'. Before his meeting with the Maronite Patriarch, Solh had secured the agreement of the Syrian Minister of Finance, al-'Azem, on the amendments. Opinion-makers aligned with the radical Lebanese nationalists commented that the amendments safeguarded the constitution, since the legislative authority of each state remained within the hands of their respective parliaments.[44]

The amended draft of the agreement was sent to the Lebanese parliament to be reviewed by the Foreign Affairs Committee. The committee published a report in which it affirmed that the agreement fell within Lebanese interests. More importantly, the committee's findings decreed that the immediate separation of the Common Interests was a logistical impossibility, since Syria and Lebanon had neither the administrative apparatus nor the necessary legislation for the sound operation of the different directorates. The report noted that what took 25 years to accomplish could not be undone with a day's notice.[45]

The Lebanese chamber convened during the first days of February. In his address to the assembly, Solh went to great lengths to thank the Syrian government for the position it took during HCCI negotiations. The Lebanese Premier pointed out how Syria used to have a constant difference of opinion with the previous Lebanese governments on the issue of customs revenue. He stressed the fact that, with his government, Damascus made the maximum concessions and conceded to equal distribution of revenues. Hamid Franjieh took the floor and, addressing the critics of the agreement, declared that, even if the government and people had wanted separation, it would not have been possible, highlighting the findings of the parliamentary Foreign Affairs Committee.[46] The radical Lebanese nationalist deputies, led by Alfred Naccache and George 'Aqel, objected to the agreement and maintained that article three was an infringement to the constitution and that the introduced amendment did little to rectify the situation. 'Aqel argued that, if an expert in international law were consulted, he would have observed that this project was aimed at forming an economic federation between the two states. Ayub Tabet, who was also aligned to the radical Lebanese nationalists and was a former President of Lebanon, defended the agreement, insisting that it was the best that could be reached under the existing circumstances. Tabet recommended that the final agreement should be based on financial and economic considerations or facts. He noted that the assembly could judge the agreement after two years had passed and then decide whether to extend it or not. The amendment was ratified.[47] The parliamentary debate revealed how radical Lebanese nationalists differed among themselves concerning cooperation with Syria. The assumption that Lebanese nationalists were unanimously opposed to Syro-Lebanese cooperation is thus inaccurate.

Syrian commentators quoted the statements of Solh and Franjieh, emphasising that for 25 years France had assured the union of Syro-Lebanese economic interests. It was emphasised that Syria and Lebanon complemented each other in trade, agriculture and industry. While Syria was a producer of grain, with Lebanon as its main customer, the geographical location of Lebanon had turned the Lebanese into formidable importers and merchants, and the Syrians into their customers. Opinion-makers in Syria wondered why a Syro-Lebanese economic council was perceived as a peril to Lebanese sovereignty.

> Why is this danger not seen in the *Majless al-Mira*, for example, which imposes the price of grain on the producer and consumer, and specifies the amount of cereals, barley, corn in the bread of the Syrian and the Lebanese... The Higher Council of the Common Interests only includes Lebanese and Syrians. Is this a hazard to Lebanon? The *Majless al-Mira*, which includes foreigners as well as Lebanese and Syrians, does not pose a danger to Lebanon?[48]

On 18 March 1944, Khuri signed a decree establishing the HCCI.[49] The organisation of the different customs departments, their supervision and the jurisdiction of their officials, and the implementation of the agreement between France and the two national governments (with regard to the former and current civil servants and their salaries) were to remain unchanged until six months after the end of the war.[50]

As seen above, the Lebanese government was able to disarm local opposition to the agreement with Syria by avoiding the establishment of any permanent joint Syro-Lebanese institution that retained independent executive power or authority. The agreement was limited to the customs union only and left other aspects of the economic union to the arbitrary decisions of independent governments, without any formal contractual obligations on either party.[51] Nevertheless, Lebanese Arab nationalists reaped great political capital from

Syrian concessions on the agreement to further their image among the Lebanese nationalists as the protectors of Lebanese independence.[52] The hastily conducted agreement between the two governments released the Lebanese and Syrian leadership to concentrate on their negotiations with France for transfer of the remaining directorates of the Common Interest.

C. THE TRANSFER OF THE CONTESTED *TROUPES SPÉCIALES*

During the second half of 1944, France transferred most of the directorates of the Common Interests to the national governments, except the *Troupes Spéciales* and the *Sûreté Générale*.[53] To the Lebanese, and to the Syrians in particular, the transfer of the army and police was of utmost importance. To official thinking and public opinion alike, it was the acid test of both governments' success in their seven-month-long negotiations to have the attributes of sovereignty transferred to independent Lebanon and Syria.[54] The strikes and demonstrations clearly indicated the popular appeal of founding a national army. It was glorified as the symbol of independence and national sovereignty. The Lebanese and Syrian cabinets submitted a bill to their respective chambers in which they allocated the sum to establish their national armed forces – 15 million and 5 million Syrian-Lebanese liras (liras), respectively. The Lebanese force, officers and soldiers, was envisaged to stand at 5000 – around one-third of the 13,000-strong Syrian army.[55] For their part the French were in no hurry to transfer authority over the army and police, demanding that a treaty or a *Convention Universitaire* be concluded first.[56]

Beirut and Damascus were adamant in not undertaking any international commitments until the end of the war. A deadlock ensued.[57] Unable to confront France militarily, Lebanon and Syria began to mobilise international support while their political leadership quietly encouraged public demonstrations against the French presence in Damascus and Beirut. On 10 January 1944, schools closed and students demonstrated to demand conscription.[58] Meanwhile, negotiations continued but to no one's satisfaction. By that time, the French National Committee had moved its headquarters to Paris after the liberation of the city and had established itself as the provisional government of France. Having returned to Paris, the French were not keen to give in on any issue affecting their position in the Levant. Meanwhile, and to the great irritation of Beirut and Damascus, the French delegation general in Beirut continued to issue *arrêtés*.[59]

The first week of October 1944 the political scene in Lebanon and Syria was in a state of suspended animation. The Lebanese and Syrian leadership, as well as most of their Arab counterparts, were gathered in Alexandria attending the 'Arab Unity Conference'. On 7 October 1944, seven Arab states signed what came to be known as the Alexandria Protocol. These states undertook to establish the Arab League, which could best be described as a group of sovereign states associated according to a set of accepted principles, the most important of which forbade the members to conduct policies detrimental to the League. Also important was the principle of non-intervention in the domestic affairs of other members.[60]

The return of the Lebanese delegation from Alexandria was coupled with the public dissemination of the protocol. French and pro-French circles attacked Prime Minister Solh for the commitments he had made, and considerable pressure was brought to bear on his government to intimidate it into signing a *Convention Universitaire*. General Beynet, the French representative, met with President Khuri and informed him that Lebanon's stand at Alexandria precluded the signing of a treaty and pointed out that, as a result, the Catroux declaration of Lebanese independence might have to be reconsidered. Beynet stressed that the protocol clearly envisaged the conclusion of such a treaty. The chamber responded to French pressure in a resounding vote of thanks to the Premier and his government for their work. Thereafter, when it became clear that the government would not yield on the matter, attacks shifted from diplomatic issues to internal matters, in particular the rising cost of living.[61]

Public dissatisfaction at the failure of the government to check the rise in the cost of living and to improve the efficiency of the administration toppled the Solh government on 7 January 1945. More importantly, a substantial section of Lebanese nationalists had been persuaded by the government's opponents that the Alexandria Protocol would place the Lebanese Christians under Muslim domination.[62] The controversy surrounding the Alexandria Protocol did not end with the formation of a new government.[63]

The issue resurfaced a month later when, on February 1945, Camille Sham'oun, the Lebanese minister delegated by the Syrian and Lebanese governments to negotiate with the British government in London, gave a statement to the press. Speaking in the name of both states, Sham'oun's statement highlighted the sensitivities of radical Lebanese nationalists about Lebanese sovereignty and independence vis-à-vis its Arab neighbours, especially Syria. Sham'oun's statements received wide exposure, particularly in the Syrian press, where one headline read, 'The Syrian-Lebanese Position from Signing a Treaty and the Takeover of the Army: A Dangerous Political Statement by a Lebanese Minister.' Lebanese Arab nationalist opinion-makers sang Sham'oun's praises with exhilaration. In his statement, Sham'oun stressed that the transfer of the army was not only a Syro-Lebanese matter but an issue concerning the entire Arab world. Sham'oun outlined the numerous agreements between France and the Syrian and Lebanese governments concerning the transfer of the army and police, which dated back to 1936. The Lebanese minister revealed that, since then, France had repeatedly undertaken to transfer control over the armed forces, the last of which was a commitment by General Catroux on 24 December 1943. At that point Beirut and Damascus preferred to wait until the financial aspects of the transfer could be worked out. Unexpectedly, the French then left negotiations, announcing that the local armies and police force would not be transferred to Syrian and Lebanese control until they entered treaty negotiations. This was followed by a declaration by Charles de Gaulle that France intended to retain a special position in the Levant. Sham'oun insisted that Lebanon and Syria could not agree to French designs, particularly concerning the treaty. The Lebanese minister pointed out that Lebanon was bound to the Alexandria Protocol, according to which Beirut must consult with the Arab states to obtain agreement to sign any treaty. 'We do not wish to start our "international life" by folding on our commitments,' he added, 'therefore we cannot be bound to any treaty that endangers our cooperation with the Arab states.'[64]

Radical Lebanese nationalist circles were outraged by Sham'oun's assertions, declaring that the Lebanese minister went 'too far' and that he should be silenced. The Lebanese government was called upon to furnish an explanation. Proclamations were made on Lebanon's right to sign treaties and adopt policies in line with its own interests.[65] The Lebanese government quickly intervened and issued a communiqué clarifying the statement of its representative in London. The communiqué, which included an outline of a section from the Alexandria Protocol dealing with treaties, stressed that it was not required that an Arab state seek the approval of League members before signing a treaty.[66] Soon afterwards during his address on Mar Maroun Day (while in the presence of Prime Minister 'Abdel Hamid Karameh), Beirut's Maronite Archbishop Ignatius Mubarak declared 'in the name of the whole Lebanese people, regardless of their religion or sect, that they wish to preserve their independence'. Mubarak concluded his address by thanking Karameh and his government of the precaution taken, which was the official refutation of Sham'oun's statement.[67]

Political circles in Syria were irritated by the Lebanese government communiqué. They were surprised that a Lebanese government – headed by 'Abed Hamid Karameh, with Henri Phar'oun as Foreign Minister – would be the author of such a statement, one that only served to weaken the position of the Lebanese minister who was speaking in the name of Syria and Lebanon, 'defending their independence, honour and sovereignty'. Opinion-makers in Damascus reminded the communiqué's authors that the recognition of Lebanon only came after Lebanon accepted the Arab League Charter and on the condition that it remain independent of any foreign country: 'Is it not important that the Alexandria Protocol recognized the borders of Greater Lebanon, putting an end to the 25-year-old debate of where the borders of Greater or Smaller Lebanon should be drawn?'[68]

On 10 February 1945, Sham'oun issued another statement, confirming that the Alexandria Protocols did not obligate the Lebanese government to consult Arab states prior to signing a treaty with a foreign country. His first statement, he said, only meant to say that all states that were party to the Alexandria Protocol were obliged not to sign any treaty or agreement that went against the spirit of the protocol or against the interest of any member state of the Arab League.[69]

The underlying fear of all Lebanese nationalists of eventual Syrian encroachment on Lebanon remained strong. These fears were reflected in the proposals carried by the Lebanese delegation that left for Cairo during February 1945 to take part in deliberations on the Arab League's statutes. The delegation was headed by Foreign Minister Phar'oun, who carried the new Lebanese proposals. They were the following:

1. The absolute recognition of the independence of each Arab League member.
2. The freedom of each member to withdraw from the League.
3. The right of each independent state of the Arab League to sign agreements with any party.
4. The decisions of the League should not be binding unless a consensus is reached.[70]

However, in spite of government assurances, which materialised in the Lebanese proposals to the Cairo conference, radical Lebanese nationalists were convinced that unity schemes were being secretly harboured. They substantiated their claims by a number of statements, made by Syrian and Arab politicians such as Jamil Mardam Bey, who declared that an Arab state was in the making. These declarations were coupled by the incessant demands of Prince 'Abdallah for a Greater Syria. Opinion-makers affiliated with the radical Lebanese nationalists asked how, in such an environment, the Lebanese could feel at ease about their independence. The Alexandria Protocol was dismissed as an effective protection. Instead, a treaty with France was the ideal means to preserve Lebanon's independence. The Lebanese government was called upon to take advantage of Lebanon's 'special status, which had put it in a special strategic position vital for [Western] nations which were looking towards the east'.[71]

The situation was further aggravated by Syrian Prime Minister Faris al-Khuri's parliamentary address of 4 April, announcing his government's resignation. Aside from listing his government's achievements during his tenure, the outgoing Premier made a few remarks concerning Lebanon. Faris al-Khuri maintained that a Greater Lebanon was no threat to Syria and reminded his audience that Syria only renounced its claims in Lebanon on the condition that Lebanon remain an Arab state independent of any foreign control. 'It is on this basis alone that we conceded to the existence of the Lebanese nation (*kiyan*).'[72]

Khuri's remarks even angered Lebanese Arab nationalist circles. Jubran Tweini, criticising Faris al-Khuri's observations, pointed out that it was not in the interests of Arab unity to deepen the wounds of Lebanon with such statements, and 'to inform the Lebanese on every occasion that we recognized your nationhood conditionally'. Tweini, addressing Faris al-Khuri, asked which of the Arab states was completely sovereign and not under the influence of foreign powers. He warned the Syrians of continuing to use such methods, which only served to antagonise the Lebanese, regardless of their political orientation. Tweini concluded that Lebanon's free acceptance of the Arab League Charter gave Lebanon the right over those who were antagonising Lebanon and who were killing all good intentions.[73]

It was generally believed among political circles in Beirut that the Syrian public disagreed with its government over the recognition of Lebanon, which triggered the statement of the outgoing Syrian Prime Minister. Commenting on the numerous statements made by a number of Syrian deputies, who demanded the return of the four *qadas*, radical Lebanese nationalist circles – described some Syrians and their leaders as extremists. Regardless of the fears and objections of the Lebanese nationalists, the Lebanese parliament ratified the Arab League Charter.[74] However, Syrian statements did charge the atmosphere in Lebanon towards Syria.

Aside from his remarks on Lebanon, the outgoing Syrian Premier declared that his government had refused to negotiate a treaty that would undermine Syrian sovereignty. He then announced the cabinet's decision to resign on the grounds that, following the signing of the Arab League Pact and the invitation to the San Francisco conference, Syria's isolation had come to an end. A new stage in the life of the nation had been reached. A few days after his address to parliament, Faris al-Khuri was appointed to form his second government.[75]

In the same month, Beirut and Damascus were receiving reports that an Anglo-French understanding was being negotiated, whereby British forces would evacuate Syria and Lebanon. British intentions to leave Lebanon and Syria prior to settling their disputes with France recalled memories of the British withdrawal of 1920. At that time, Faysal was left alone to face French invasion. Mardam Bey realised that, with the French unwilling to compromise on the *Convention Universitaire*, a clash with France was inevitable. If it had to happen it was preferable that it happen while British troops were still in Syria, and while the United Nations were assembled in San Francisco. On 19 April, Mardam Bey had a meeting with Count Stanislas Ostrorog, the acting French High Commissioner, who reiterated France's willingness to negotiate an overall settlement if only Syria would agree to sign a revised text of the *Convention Universitaire*. The French government would be greatly encouraged if the Syrians were to conclude the cultural agreement, the only demand France insisted on. Immediately after his discussion with the count, Mardam Bey left for Shtura to meet Lebanese Prime Minister Karameh, and informed him of the latest developments and of the new draft of the *Convention*, which he considered as unacceptable. The Lebanese Premier concurred. The *Convention Universitaire* had become a national issue for France as much as the transfer of the army had become a national issue for Syria and Lebanon.[76]

Although there was Syro-Lebanese agreement on the position to be adopted vis-à-vis France, on the economic side there was disagreement. The Syrians had published an order that all goods destined for Syrian merchants should be imported through Syrian customs posts. The Lebanese vehemently objected to this, holding that this would deal a blow to Beirut's entrepôt trade. The Lebanese also protested strongly against the manner in which the Syrian government was implementing the textile agreement. The Lebanese claimed that while all Lebanese cotton yarn due under the agreement was being delivered to Syria, the Syrian cloth delivered to Lebanon in exchange was of such poor quality as to be useless. The Lebanese threatened that, if its quality was not improved in a week, they would cancel the whole agreement.[77] The agreement was in fact abolished without much controversy. Recriminations were limited to the papers. At that time, Beirut and Damascus did not want to risk creating a controversy over yarn and textiles, preferring to present a united front against France.

On 14 May, the Lebanese government learned that a French ship carrying troop reinforcements had sailed from Tunis and was bound for Lebanon. A few days later, French troops landed in Beirut. Their landing was coupled with the arrival of new proposals from Paris. Shortly afterwards, Lebanese and Syrian representatives met with French delegates amidst disturbances and strikes in major cities and towns in Lebanon and Syria. In the meeting, the French presented the Syrians and Lebanese with an aide-memoire, containing unchanged French demands, outlining France's special position in the two states, including safeguards for the financial interests of their nationals, their companies and their cultural as well as religious establishments.[78] The Lebanese and Syrians refused to enter negotiations based on the document presented, and instead wished to address the matter of the newly arrived French troops. The French side evaded the issue altogether. Immediately after the meeting, which took place in Damascus, Mardam Bey and Phar'oun went to report to the Syrian President, who contacted his Lebanese counterpart. A meeting was arranged in Shtura.[79]

Five days later, the Syrian and Lebanese Presidents and their heads of government met at Shtura. The meeting examined Franco-Lebanese and Franco-Syrian relations as well as France's latest aide-memoire. It was decided that neither side would enter talks with France without prior consultations. The Syrians informed the Lebanese that they were determined to assume command of the *Troupes Spéciales* whenever circumstances permitted and urged the Lebanese to follow suit. Both sides agreed to draft memoranda addressed to the heads of Arab states and the Great Powers informing them of the latest developments. The texts of the memoranda were to be identical so as to impress on the Great Powers that Lebanon and Syria were firmly united. At the end of the meeting, a communiqué was issued condemning the troop landing as constituting an infringement of sovereignty. The communiqué regarded the French aide-memoire as containing proposals in direct contradiction to the spirit of independence. The communiqué concluded that Lebanon and Syria had agreed to suspend negotiations with France.[80] Shortly after the communiqué, the Lebanese Foreign Minister released a statement, in which he emphasised that 'the French troops' arrival is unwelcome ... Lebanon will not negotiate under coercion.'[81]

Lebanese public opinion was mixed on the matter. Moderate Arab nationalists commended Beirut and Damascus' refusal to negotiate in an atmosphere of threats and coercion. It was recalled how in 1936 France forced a treaty on Lebanon that parliament passed while French troops were waiting outside. Though the wording had changed, France's 1945 demands were no different from those of 1936.[82] The views of the radical Lebanese nationalists differed. They followed with great concern Mardam Bey's statements that the Arab League Charter prevented its members from granting any foreign Power a privileged position on its territory or signing any treaty that would infringe on its independence. Inquiries were made whether Arab leaders had hidden a secret clause in the charter. It was argued that, if there was indeed such a clause, it should be made public. Otherwise, there was nothing preventing the Lebanese government from signing a treaty with France, since 'we owe France our culture, administration and judicial system … there are no grounds for Syrian reservations'.[83]

Toward the end of May, anti-French activities had spread all over the mandate. People went to the streets shouting that Maysalun would not be repeated.[84] Within ten days law and order had completely broken down. Between 29 and 30 May the French military command shelled and bombed Damascus. This time, however, the newer, modern quarters received the brunt of French punishment, suggesting how far the urban political protest had shifted in 20 years.[85] Describing French military measures, Syrian Speaker Sa'adallah al-Jabiri stated that 'Damascus is a battleground and the city is not only cut off from the outside world but, is cut off from every street … Tanks are positioned everywhere and bullets are being fired from every corner … At 6:55 on Tuesday [30 May 1945] evening they started firing at the parliament building.'[86] The British intervened. French actions had the potential to upset Britain's overall Arab policy.[87] The British ordered French troops back to their barracks and assumed military control until the Syrian government could resume its normal functions.[88]

In June, the Syrian and Lebanese ministers in London communicated a *note verbale* to the British government, which stated that the two states were 'not willing to concede any influence to France or conclude any treaty with her' and that they were determined to establish their relations with France only on 'the bases of international law which ordinarily govern the relations between two states'. At the same time, the Arab League Council met in Cairo to discuss the French aggression against Syria and passed resolutions supporting Syrian and Lebanese demands for the evacuation of all foreign troops from their territories.[89] On 21 June the Syrian and Lebanese governments held a meeting in Damascus, after which they issued a joint communiqué, which called for the implementation of the Arab League decisions, the dismissal of French officials working for the two governments, complete withdrawal of French forces from Lebanon and Syria, and the transfer of the *Troupes Spéciales* to the Syrian and Lebanese governments. The two governments reiterated their position that they did not intend to grant any state special status or privileges.[90]

While engaged in military operations to suppress Syrian national aspirations, France strove to create sectarian divisions among the Lebanese in a desperate attempt to break the Syro-Lebanese alliance. The focus of French pressure was particularly directed at the Maronite Patriarch Antun 'Aridah. At the early stages of the crisis he had expressed his approval of the government's position, but since then had reverted to a pro-French stand and even strove to secure the backing of the entire Maronite community. 'Aridah's sudden change of heart was attributed to considerable French pressure, which consisted of repeated warnings that without French protection the Christians of Lebanon must expect to be dominated and persecuted by the Muslims, and that the true solution of the problem lay in the formation of a French-protected Christian 'Smaller Lebanon', which would permit the Muslim areas of Lebanon to revert to Syria. Pressure on the Maronite Patriarch was also coming from the Vatican, where the Pope had expressed the desire that France maintain its pre-eminence in the Levant.[91]

The Lebanese and Syrian governments countered French moves by exerting every effort to prevent the sectarian question from developing into an inter-communal crisis. In Syria, the seriousness of the situation caused President Quwwatly to convoke a meeting of Christian leaders in order to assure them personally that their position in Muslim society was secure and that their fears of Muslim persecution were unfounded. The Syrian President further ordered that sermons advocating Muslim–Christian goodwill should be delivered in all mosques.[92] Moreover, the Greek Orthodox Patriarch of Damascus issued a communiqué in which he denied the right of others to speak for the Greek Orthodox community, and emphasised that the Orthodox Church had always stood at the forefront of the struggle for the full independence for Syria and Lebanon. The president of the Presbyterian synod of Syria and Lebanon issued a similar communiqué.[93]

Nevertheless, Syrian public opinion was wondering why there was calm in Lebanon while the French army was bombing Syrian cities. Although in the diplomatic arena Lebanon was strong in representing Syria, there was a feeling that the Lebanese had cheered from the sidelines. They had never put up such a struggle that France felt uncomfortable concentrating all its forces in Syria.[94] Reports circulated that Lebanon had changed its alliance with Damascus and had agreed to conduct a treaty with Paris. These reports prompted Lebanese Foreign Minister Phar'oun to hold a press conference, in which he categorically denied that there was a schism between the Lebanese and Syrian leaderships. He attributed the calm in Lebanon to the Lebanese government's efforts to restrain the public.[95]

At the same time, Lebanese relief efforts were widely publicised. The government allocated 100,000 liras to assist Syrian relief efforts. The Lebanese Prime Minister took the sum of money to Damascus in person. The municipality of Beirut allocated 20,000 liras for the same purpose, in addition to sending firefighters to assist in putting out the fires, which flared up all over the Syrian capital. A Lebanese medical delegation headed to Damascus with two carloads of medical supplies.[96] Every effort was made to ensure that an image of solidarity with Syria was transmitted to local and international public opinion. Moreover, on almost every occasion, the Syrian and Lebanese leaderships were engaged in alleviating the fears of Lebanese nationalists regarding Lebanon's sovereignty, which was seen as being threatened by the Syro-Lebanese political alliance against France. After Faris al-Khuri resigned his premiership, Sa'adallah al-Jabiri was called upon to form a government. Among the first statements al-Jabiri made was that his policy towards Lebanon would be based on mutual respect of each state's independence.[97] The same was true in Lebanon, with the formation of the new government by Sami el-Solh. Addressing parliament, Sami el-Solh declared that the cooperative relationship with sister Syria was dictated by the common interests existing between the two states and that the relationship with Arab countries was based on the Arab League Charter.[98] When there was renewed talk of Greater Syria, Sami el-Solh confirmed that Lebanon entered the Arab League on the condition that its current borders and sovereignty were respected and the issue of Greater Syria was not open to discussion.[99] Similarly, President Bshara al-Khuri, in a speech given while touring the south, affirmed that the concept of Greater Syria went against the vision of the Arab League, which guaranteed the borders of all independent Arab states.[100]

By July, France had agreed to transfer control of the much-contested *Troupes Spéciales*. During that time, the Syrians were keeping their contacts with the French to a strict minimum, mainly through their minister in Paris. Locally, they relied on Lebanese intermediaries. It became evident in most diplomatic circles that France had no future in Syria. Even a cabinet crisis, provoked by parliament when the legislature charged the executive branch with an inept administration, caused two government reshuffles but did not change the Syrian stance towards France. Although there was yet another cabinet change in Damascus at the end of August, all Arab nationalists, whether in the government or not, were watching and awaiting events while British and French statesmen were debating their future imperial positions in the Middle East. The result was the Bevin–Bidault agreement.[101]

Following the Bevin–Bidault Agreement concerning France and Britain's respective 'interests' and 'responsibilities' in the Middle East, in December 1945 the Syrian and Lebanese delegations to the United Nations received instructions to take their case to the Security Council. After examining the Syro-Lebanese complaint, the United States representative at the Security Council introduced a resolution calling upon foreign troops stationed in Syria and Lebanon to withdraw as soon as possible. Shortly afterwards, an Anglo-French communiqué was released in which it was stressed that the two Powers 'wish to see a completely independent Lebanon and Syria, practising their independence, which was announced by France 1943'. The communiqué also stressed the acceptance of Syria and Lebanon within the United Nations, saying that with the end of hostilities it was decided to study the redeployment of its forces in the region in order to expedite withdrawal. French and British military experts met in Beirut on 21 December 1945 to initiate withdrawal.[102]

2

The Functional Aspects of Bilateral Relations

A. DISCORD OVER CUSTOMS REVENUES AND TAXATION POLICIES

With France yielding to international pressure and announcing its intention to withdraw its troops from the Levant, meetings between the Lebanese and Syrians intensified to ensure consensus on the distribution and the administration of the numerous directorates of the Common Interests. Of particular sensitivity was the Customs Directorate. A temporary agreement was reached at the end of January 1944 whereby each state would receive 40 per cent of the customs revenue, the remaining 20 per cent being divided on the basis of each state's total import consumption. Until import consumption figures could be determined, these funds remained on account. The customs' major source of revenue was import and export taxes. The Lebanese Ministry of Supplies retained wide jurisdiction over these issues, and import and export trade laws – which were closely coordinated with Syria – were applied to the letter.[1]

In 1944, the Lebanese and Syrian leadership were primarily concerned with the liberation of their countries, so consequently the HCCI agreement was hurriedly drawn. Later, however, it began to look as though Lebanese merchants were manipulating the hastily assembled HCCI agreement to their own advantage. Upon exhausting their import licences, for instance, they would purchase the licences of their Syrian counterparts or utilise Syrian importers. Imported goods would pass through Beirut port and customs, where the paperwork would indicate a Syrian destination for the merchandise. Consequently, the freight would be taxed in favour of the Syrian account at the directorate. After being released from customs, the commodities would be transported to the nearest Syrian border checkpoint – or, in some cases, simply driven to the outskirts of Beirut – after which the trucks would return to

Beirut to unload. The goods were consumed in Beirut, although officially a Syrian merchant imported them to Syria and the tax revenues from the merchandise were registered in the Syrian account at the Customs Directorate. Lebanese officials feared that, when calculations were conducted to divide the disputed 20 per cent, accountants would find that Syria consumed many more imports than the Lebanese, and that Syria would thus receive the lion's share of customs revenue. It was feared that this state of affairs would affect Syro-Lebanese relations.[2] At the national level, the abuse of import licences and the sale of accompanying dollar exchange were very profitable in local markets. This, in turn, led to higher import costs, profiteering on the part of especially favoured persons and a loss of public confidence in official institutions in both Syria and Lebanon.[3]

In December 1945, the Lebanese and Syrian governments reached an agreement that would facilitate the coordination of imports and exports between them.[4] This agreement was followed up by a meeting in Beirut, on 28 December 1945, between Lebanese Prime Minister Sami el-Solh and his Syrian counterpart Sa'adallah al-Jabiri. Discussions focused on the division of the revenues of the Common Interests in light of the temporary agreement of January 1944. In order to resolve this issue once and for all, Jabiri demanded 55 per cent of the shares for Syria while Lebanon would receive the remaining 45 per cent of the total revenues. A provisional agreement was reached in which Lebanon and Syria divided the customs revenues by 44 and 56 per cent respectively. In this manner the contested funds were unfrozen and officials in Beirut were confident that a better division would be reached during 1946.[5]

In Damascus, opinion-makers were not satisfied with Syria's 56 per cent share, since it was believed that Syria's greater size and population predetermined the dispute in her favour. Aside from the issue of customs shares, Syrian merchants were increasingly voicing criticisms of their own government for having failed to upgrade its Customs Directorate services and facilities. The absence of customs storage facilities, except for a small wooden hut, compelled merchants to amass their merchandise in the open air – exposing them to sun and rain – until the authorities cleared them. Under such circumstances, Syrian merchants preferred to settle their customs affairs in Beirut, which had the proper facilities already in place. Commenting on the plight of the merchants, opinion-makers in Damascus wrote that

> at the present time, and in spite of independence, Syria had become a subordinate to Beirut in most of its economic matters … if the Common Interests, including the Customs Directorate, are between the Lebanese and us, and if the revenues are divided after the expenses of running the Common Interests are deducted, is it not our right to demand the establishment of a warehouse and proper customs administration in our capital?

Syrian merchants also complained about the malfeasance in the Syrian customs department, its tedious procedures and uncooperative bureaucrats. This contributed to the further transfer of large amounts of trade and official transactions to the Lebanese capital. As one Syrian commentator asked:

> To what suspicious end are customs officials striving? Do they mean to transfer all official transactions, so that Damascus loses and Beirut profits? It should be kept in mind that the municipality of Beirut levies a fee of 1 per cent of the value of the goods that are released from its customs, regardless of whether the goods are bound for Damascus or remain in Lebanon, to which the revenues made from the fees of the port, transport and bureaucratic procedures should be added.[6]

On 30 January 1946, the Lebanese cabinet met to discuss the issue of abolishing taxes on imports. The abolition of the *taxes de ravitaillements* or supplies tax, which in the Lebanese government's view was critical for lowering the cost of living, met with opposition from Damascus. The Syrian government had initially agreed on removing the *taxes de ravitaillements* but changed its position shortly before implementation. In addition, the Syrian representatives to the HCCI requested that taxes be imposed on certain items that were being imported, particularly those that were available in Syria. Among these goods were flour, cotton and yarn that were at the time exempted from customs. Lebanon was opposed to these proposals.[7]

Political circles in Lebanon found themselves in a difficult position. On one side, the Lebanese leadership did not wish to anger the Syrians, and on the other the interests of Lebanon would be better served if the *taxes de ravitaillements* were abolished and Syria's insistence on imposing other taxes on imports were resisted. In Beirut, Syria was seen as a producing country whose espousal of protectionism was inevitable. In contrast, Lebanon produced very little, particularly where vital consumer items such as grain was concerned. Radical Lebanese nationalists thought it absurd that the Lebanese government should restrain the flow of such goods into Lebanon by enforcing taxes. They also realised that a separation of the Common Interests was unlikely and difficult.[8] Significantly, Lebanese Arab nationalist opinion-makers were in agreement with the radical Lebanese nationalists. Although they were strong advocates of uniting taxation policies in Lebanon and Syria, Lebanese Arab nationalists did not favour imposing restrictions on imports. Instead, they argued, unrestricted import policies provided the Lebanese and Syrian consumer with cheaper goods. They emphasised that both states should not confine themselves to imports from the United States or Europe but should also encourage trade with their Arab neighbours.[9]

Despite a Syro-Lebanese agreement – reached on 29 December 1945 – to remove the *taxes de ravitaillements* by March 1946, Lebanese appeals to their Syrian counterparts to remove the tax were to no avail. The tax was seen as serving the interests of Syria at the expense of Lebanon. It was common knowledge among Lebanon's political and economic elites that the Syrian government's budget predicted revenues of 18 million liras from these taxes. In forming its budget the Lebanese government, on the other hand, did not take these taxes into account as a revenue source since they were to be abolished. Removing the taxes would strain the Syrian budget and the political and economic solidarity between the two states put pressure upon Lebanon to concede to Syrian demands. Beirut made this concession, taking into consideration the government's need to secure Lebanon's grain requirements after 31 March 1946, when the *Mira* would be replaced by a Syro-Lebanese administration. Lebanese participation in this institution was essential, since the Allies made it clear that Syria and Lebanon constituted an economic unit that was self-sufficient in grain. Nevertheless, Lebanese opinion-makers called upon their government to seek a formal and definitive commitment from the Syrians. 'Sa'adallah al-Jabiri would find it difficult, without allied military assistance, to control the revenues of Jazira and Houran where large landowners, with their conspiring tribal chiefs, would smuggle their harvest across the borders to Turkey, Iraq or East Jordan [for greater profit].'[10]

Dissatisfaction grew among Lebanon's general public following another increase in bread prices to 125 piastres a kilo in Beirut, against 80 in Damascus and 50 in Palestine, and delayed distribution of rationed bread. Many working-class families in Lebanon paid their entire daily wage for one meal's worth of bread. Inasmuch as bread was the chief staple, the price increases affected many more people than did price fluctuations for imports. Lebanon's Minister of Finance exerted great efforts to persuade labour leaders to defer general strikes and street demonstrations. According to industrial circles, unless Beirut's cost of living – particularly for bread and clothing – were reduced, serious labour demonstrations were expected. The Lebanese government attempted to address the deteriorating economic situation with deflationary tactics – tighter bank credit, decreasing currency circulation and increasing imports. These measures were obstructed, however, by the Syrian government's failure to reduce both the high cost of grain exported to Lebanon and delays in delivery. The issue was causing strains on the Syro-Lebanese economic union. Lebanese merchants urged the government to arrange alternative grain imports to break or threaten Syrian grain profiteering. Lebanese allegations of Syrian deviations from agreements were countered by Syrian charges of Lebanese evasions. According to official Syrian circles, the Syrian government had invited its Lebanese counterpart to draft grain-control regulations for the period following the dissolution of the *Mira*. Nevertheless, an economic agreement was impeded by the Syrian allegation that Lebanese merchants and government were being excessively responsive to French influences and that they opposed Syrian insistence on reducing the concentration of foreign commercial agencies in Beirut and distributing them equitably in Damascus.[11]

This Syro-Lebanese conflict of interests was not allowed to influence bilateral relations. In London and Paris Syria, Lebanon, and France were negotiating the latter's military withdrawal from the Levant. There were differences on the timing of French withdrawal.[12] On 10 March 1946, a meeting took place in Shtura between the Syrian and Lebanese Prime Ministers. The Lebanese briefed the Syrians on the

Paris negotiations of 2–6 March 1946 between French and British military representatives studying the French withdrawal from Lebanon.[13] To the annoyance of the Syrians, the exact date of French troop withdrawal from Lebanon remained vague. This prompted Syrian opinion-makers to remark that the Lebanese government's silence on the timing of the French withdrawal was causing great doubt 'in the hearts (*nufus*)'. Syrian doubts were reinforced by Reuters and BBC reports that France and Britain had agreed that the former would not withdraw her troops for a year, and that the British withdrawal would be completed by June 1946. According to Syrian political observers, the likelihood of an Anglo-French agreement was corroborated by the fact that the Lebanese delegation in Paris issued no statement and made no official denial of the news reports. The Reuters/BBC reports were further reinforced by the fact that after the Syro-Lebanese summit in Shtura (on 10 March 1946) the official communiqué made no reference to the withdrawal issue. Political circles in Damascus concluded that France would remain in Syria's vicinity for another year. A lot of things could happen in a year.[14]

In the same regard, Faris al-Khuri, who was heading the Syrian delegation to the United Nations, stated that the Syrian and Lebanese governments were in solidarity on the question of foreign troop withdrawal. He emphasised that two issues in French and British withdrawal plans were unacceptable: the time-frame and the preparations for withdrawal, which did not ensure the simultaneous departure of French and British forces. Khuri stressed that withdrawing British before French forces could lead to disturbances. He proposed that, in the event that France was unable to withdraw prior to their designated time, the Lebanese government could ask Britain to postpone her evacuation.[15]

On 13 March 1946, the Lebanese government met to consider the British memorandum informing it that French and British military experts had agreed that troop withdrawal from Syria would be completed by 30 April 1946. This would also be accompanied by the withdrawal of a thousand soldiers from each army stationed in Lebanon. British military experts informed their French counterparts that British forces would depart from Lebanese territories before the end of June 1946. French experts informed the British that they would be unable to complete their Lebanese withdrawal before April 1947. Accordingly, the Lebanese government issued a communiqué in which it rejected the French military's schedule for withdrawal. The Lebanese sent an official delegation to Paris to resolve this matter.[16]

Upon his arrival at Beirut International Airport, a few days after the release of the Lebanese communiqué, Faris al-Khuri declared that he was against any official Syrian or Lebanese visit to Paris. Nevertheless, after the Lebanese delegation decided to travel alone, it would have been preferable for the time-frame of the negotiations to have been agreed upon, in order to prevent negotiations from dragging on endlessly and preventing Lebanon from presenting its case to the Security Council. Khuri demanded that the Lebanese delegation in Paris return soon.[17] Shortly after

Khuri's statement, Lebanon and France reached an agreement in which the latter undertook to withdraw a major part of her troops by the end of June, and the remainder before the end of August 1946.[18]

During the Shtura summit of 10 March 1946, the Syrian Minister of Economy Hassan Joubara and Lebanese Minister of Finance Emile Lahoud hoped to reach a quick solution regarding the taxation of imports. The issue, which appeared to have been resolved, faced sudden complications when the Syrians made new demands. In order to obtain a Syrian commitment to supply Lebanon's grain needs, Lebanon had agreed that the taxes remain in force on certain items that were consumed in both Syria and Lebanon. But the Syrians came to Shtura with new proposals, mainly that the *taxes de ravitaillements* remain in force for an indefinite period of time. The tax should also encompass other items. It was only his fear of not reaching an agreement that saw Lahoud agree to refer the issue to the HCCI. What had transpired in Shtura was not well received by Lebanese opinion, particularly Syria's extension of the *taxes de ravitaillements* to include other goods, some of which Lebanon consumed in greater amounts. The general perception that the Syrian government was adjusting its budget at Lebanon's expense was only reinforced.[19]

Indeed, radical Lebanese nationalist circles complained that the Lebanese people were increasingly paying the costs of Arab solidarity and Syro-Lebanese brotherhood. They saw the newly promulgated customs duties as adding up to a list of Lebanese concessions and sacrifices for the cause of political and economic collaboration with Syria. The Lebanese government's acceptance of Syrian conditions to secure Syrian grain – which saw the Lebanese consumer paying an extra charge that ended up in the Syrian treasury – only confirmed this impression. Radical Lebanese nationalists were also very critical that Lebanon was purchasing Syrian grain at very high prices.[20]

In Beirut on 5 April 1946, Syrian, Lebanese and British army representatives took part in negotiations focused on ensuring ample grain supplies for Syria and Lebanon during May and June. The deliberations reflected on the protocols of the *Mira*, which were put down in 1942 and amended in May 1945. From the two texts a new agreement was formed in which the Lebanese managed to add a provision granting the Lebanese government the right to import grain from the international market, provided that necessary funds were available and that the quantity of imported grain be deducted from the quota of Lebanese grain from Syria. The delegations agreed on the text of the protocol.[21] Accordingly, the two governments formed a draft of the bill, which was sent to their respective parliaments, and received passage at the end of June 1946.[22]

The long deliberations and the delay in the passage of the bill through parliament was a consequence of a Lebanese cabinet crisis. Despite internal bickering, the weak Sami el-Solh government managed to stay in power until it became evident that the Bloudan Arab League conference would be postponed. The moment the postponement was announced, the opposition acted. The most vigorous and powerful group in the chamber, Karameh's Party of Independence, held a caucus on 16 May and resolved to withdraw its members from the government. Next day, Sa'di al-Munla and Ahmad al-As'ad resigned from their posts. Rather than face a long-deferred vote of confidence, Sami el-Solh submitted his resignation on 18 May. Four days latter, Sa'di al-Munla was asked to form a government. He retained the Ministry of National Economy, Philip Takla was given the Foreign Ministry and Emile Lahoud headed the Ministry of Finance. With their eyes fixed on the upcoming parliamentary elections, almost all of Lebanon's political 'heavyweights' preferred to delegate the country's economic problems and differences with Syria to a compromise cabinet – at least until such time as public demand again summoned them, together with the candidates on their electoral lists, to save the situation.[23] A cabinet reshuffle was also taking place in Syria at the end of April, when Sa'adallah al-Jabiri took a respite from the load he had been carrying as Prime Minister and Ministers of Foreign Affairs and Defence. Jabiri was able to secure a large majority in the chamber, however some of the most influential deputies voted against the government or abstained from voting.[24]

The politicians' preoccupation gave way to speculations and debates among the general public and Lebanese as well as Syrian opinion-makers. Aside from the public anger and outrage over the publication of the Anglo-American Committee on Palestine's findings – which recommended the immediate admission of 100,000 Jews into Palestine – the demand that Lebanon purchase her grain from a source other than Syria became increasingly vocal. This debate became particularly heated when, in spite of the good harvest in Syria, Damascus insisted on selling grain for 47 piastres a kilo instead of 46 piastres – the previous year's price. Consequently, a ton of Syrian-imported grain would cost Lebanon £53.25 or 476 liras. Then it became generally known that the Syrian government intended to sell 200,000 tons of grain to the United Nations for £20 a ton. These grain supplies were destined for famine-stricken Italy, Greece, Yugoslavia and Czechoslovakia. In this regard, radical Lebanese nationalist commentators held that 'we understand that the fate of these people aroused the conscience of Mr al-Jabiri but, after all, the Italians are not the Arab brothers of the farmers of the Jazira and Houran. And since the privilege of this brotherhood should be primarily directed to us, would it not have been better if this act of good faith were bound to us?' There were calls for removing the restrictions on the import of grain and that the agreement of 30 May 1946, which determined that Lebanon be supplied with 120,000 tons for £53.25 a ton, should be reviewed, or abolished, even if such a measure strained Syro-Lebanese relations. Moreover, *L'Orient* reported how Syria was selling Lebanon grain for 476 liras per ton, while the Syrian government was purchasing it from farmers for 350 liras a ton. In the black market in Aleppo, according to *L'Orient*, a ton of grain was being sold for 300 liras.

> This year's harvest was the best in Syria's modern history and was estimated to have exceeded the 400 thousand-ton consumption needs of the Syrian population. Of the surplus, Lebanon was to receive 90 thousand tons. A 100 thousand tons would go to the Syrian poor and the remaining amount, in case the United Nations did not purchase, would decay – since this year smuggling grain into Transjordan, Turkey and Iraq would not be profitable because these states had surpluses themselves.

L'Orient concluded that the measures of the Syrian authorities had been taken to protect the interest of some 20 landowning families.[25]

Significantly, indignation against Syrian grain prices was not only limited to the radical Lebanese nationalists. Lebanese Arab nationalist opinion-makers voiced their criticisms against the Syrian government's grain policy towards Lebanon. They declared themselves unable to support such a policy under existing conditions, where the Lebanese consumer was being victimised for the sake of Syrian acquiescence. Lebanese Arab nationalists called upon the Lebanese Premier to review the grain agreement with Syria in the hope of receiving better prices, especially since Lebanon was receiving good offers from the international market. Like the Lebanese radical nationalists, Lebanese Arab nationalists expressed their indignation at the Syrians selling grain to the United Nations for 20 piastres per kilo while Lebanon had to pay 47 piastres. Lebanese Arab nationalists urged the two heads of state to conclude a proper agreement that would safeguard the Lebanese consumer from shouldering such high prices. They warned that should this state of affairs continue, the economic union between Lebanon and Syria would be compromised.[26]

Najib al-Raiyyes' *al-Qabass* led the Syrian Arab nationalist response. In an extensive editorial Raiyyes claimed that the grain Syria sold to Lebanon was the same price as the grain the *Mira* was selling to the Syrian consumer. He asserted that it was purely for political reasons that some members of the Lebanese press were raising the grain issue in the aforementioned manner, with fabricated claims by certain dailies such as *L'Orient* and *al-Bashir*, whose political affiliation to France was generally known. The owner and editor-in-chief of *al-Qabass* pointed out that these newspapers had taken it upon themselves to carry on the mission on behalf of France, with the sole intent of creating animosity and suspicion between the two states. Raiyyes insisted that the *Mira* was the Syrian people's most dreaded directorate, which was imposed by France and Britain, who feared that grain supplies would be monopolised by a few Syrian merchants and sold in Lebanon at exorbitant prices. He concluded his editorial by emphasising that the sole reason the *Mira* was established was to ensure that the Lebanese receive grain 'for the price of sand' and that

> we are not exaggerating if we say that the grain farmers, during the past five years, have been the victims of the Lebanese consumers. If there are states that offer their grain for less than what Syria is demanding, we say, in the name of the Syrian

farmer, that Syria welcomes any offer that is made to the Lebanese government. At least, in this manner we are able to rid ourselves from the directorate of the *Mira*, which is depriving the Syrian farmer of profit.[27]

L'Orient responded to *al-Qabass* by stating that

at a moment in which we are burdened with our obligations and duties on the national level and when we have passed half way towards reconciliation with yesterday's enemies [Syria], and now that we are willing to cooperate with them, only because it serves our national interests, we are branded as traitors... we have enough of these accusations against the Lebanese national press... It is surely not Mr. Najib al-Raiyyes and his *al-Qabass* that will guide us in pursuing our national interests.[28]

Syrian opinion-makers went to great lengths in justifying the price of Syrian grain destined for Lebanon, which was described as a matter of covering the costs and expenses of the Syrian farmer on one side and the *Mira* directorate on the other. It was argued that the Syrian government purchased the grain for 340 liras and sold it to the Lebanese government for 470 liras. The difference between the purchasing and the selling price went to covering large expenses such as the salaries of the civil servants and other operational costs. The Syrians admitted that the price of grain in countries such as the United States, Canada, Egypt and Iraq was lower than theirs, attributing this to production costs, which was in Syria seven times higher than that in the mentioned countries. They also compared the cost of labour and machinery employed for grain production in different countries. The Egyptian labourer received a daily wage equivalent of 90 Syrian piastres a day, while his Syrian counterpart received between 5 to 7 liras a day, aside from his food. The American farmer who used machines for the harvest paid 110 piastres for 20 litres of fuel, while the Syrian farmer who utilised the same machines paid 8 liras in Damascus and Aleppo, and as much as 9 liras in the Jazira area.[29]

While the debate on the price of grain continued, strict control measures were being applied on the Syrian side of the border with Lebanon. These measures drove the Syrian and Lebanese public to complain of the long hours of delay at the border checkpoints, while waiting to be searched and cleared. In order to alleviate the suffering of the travellers, the Syrian Ministry of Interior exempted personal cars from being searched. This was met with relief by Syrian commentators, who justified the ministry's decree by the fact that personal vehicles cannot possibly carry more than a few kilos of fruits, vegetables and bread upon which fees had already been levied in the city. It was believed that the export of these small quantities did not harm the treasury in any way but the searches at the borders for these items did inconvenience the traveller without any gain for the government. However, the ministry's decree remained unheeded. Private vehicles continued to be thoroughly searched at the border and officials confiscated whatever they found, regardless of whether it was a kilo of bread, a kilo of bulgur or other similar items.

This drove Syrian opinion-makers to rebuke the government:

> We understand the need to confiscate large quantities of smuggled grain but there is no wisdom in confiscating people's possessions and fining those carrying a few kilos of bulgur, bread, even cookies and pastries... it should be left to the discretion of the people to purchase their needs in Syria or Lebanon... These strict border controls should be abolished so that the traveller from Syria to Lebanon will feel that he is still in his country, and that there is no border nor are there differences between Damascus and Beirut.[30]

Increasingly, Lebanese and Syrian citizens were beginning to feel that there was a border between the two countries. These barriers were not the making of France or Britain, but Syria, where an Arab nationalist government resided in Damascus. The controls introduced by the Syrian authorities came in light of disagreements between Beirut and Damascus on the prices of grain as well as taxation on locally produced commodities. Lebanese Arab nationalists voiced strong objections against the Syrian government that was claiming to promote inter-Arab cooperation. Arab nationalist dailies in Lebanon went to great lengths in exposing Syrian unilateralism in their economic relations with Lebanon. 'In recent days, Syria has applied a one-sided economic policy without cooperating, consulting or even contacting the Lebanese government... This one-sidedness will gravely undermine the economic union.'[31]

On 28 June 1946, a Syro-Lebanese conference took place between the Syrian Minister of Economy, Khaled al-'Azem, and his Lebanese counterpart, Emile Lahoud, to solve outstanding issues concerning the *Mira* and grain. 'Azem presented Lahoud with two proposals. Lebanon would commit to purchasing all its grain needs from Syria for an extended period of time. Under such a scheme, the treasuries of both states would share in the profits and losses. The alternative proposal was for Lebanon to receive all its grain needs for one year, during which Syria would commit itself to supply its grain for the same price as the Syrian consumer (47 piastres per kilo). The Lebanese rejected this offer and suggested that Lebanon purchase its grain for a whole year for the price of 34 piastres and that Lebanon's grain needs would be specified as 110 tons a year. The Syrians refused.[32] Another meeting between the two Finance Ministers took place in Shtura on 24 July 1946.

Both governments were preoccupied by events in Palestine, it being the month when the King David Hotel was blown up by a Zionist terrorist organisation. There was a feeling in Beirut and Damascus' political circles that events in Palestine were moving to a climax and the Syrians were determined to be in on the final accounting. Palestine thus influenced the 24 July Shtura meeting and agreements were made quickly. It was decided that a common committee be created with the aim of solidifying economic relations between the two states. It was also decided that the *Mira* agreement be amended, so that the ton of grain in Aleppo would be set at 423 liras, including transport costs. The trucks would proceed from Aleppo directly to the Lebanese station in its vicinity. The total amount of Lebanese purchases from Syria would be 100,000 tons of grain. There was also agreement to ensure conformity in the two states' import-export regulations, as well as measures taken to combat high prices.[33] It was noteworthy that the Syrians took great care to tie the issue of grain to broader aspects of bilateral economic relations, and the import-export question in particular.

Nevertheless, radical Lebanese nationalists continued to insist that it was cheaper for the Lebanese government to purchase Turkish grain. At that time, a Turkish grain offer was turned down by Lebanese authorities because of the lack of hard currency. In reality, it seemed that Beirut did not wish to antagonise the Syrians by buying its grain supplies elsewhere.[34] A summit of Syro-Lebanese government heads, in Saufar on 13 September 1946, did not stem the tide of Lebanese agitation. Although a communiqué was issued indicating that agreement had been reached regarding the *Mira*, fuel taxes, hard currency, common economic policy, import and export policy and car registration, the Lebanese and Syrian public were not impressed. The Lebanese and Syrian leadership continued to demonstrate the collaborative spirit required to sustain the economic bond between the two states, while diplomatic circles reported to their capitals that the outlook was not encouraging. At that time it was becoming increasingly clear that both states lacked a clear economic policy as well as a modicum of expert administrators able to adjust economic policies for their mutual benefit. Instead, bitter accusations and recriminations were exchanged, while the press became more 'chauvinistic, intemperate and obstructive of real accommodation'.[35]

By that time, the Lebanese public was convinced that the *Mira* agreement was not safeguarding the country's interest. Moreover, Lebanese public opinion was certain that, if restrictions on the free trade in grain had been lifted and the *Mira* system liquidated, the price of grain would have been 60 per cent less. The Lebanese consumers felt that high grain prices had been forced on them by Syria. The high price had also added to higher living expenses. Lebanese Arab nationalist opinion-makers held that the *Mira* was primarily sustaining itself on the largest consumer and customer, Lebanon, 'which refuses the exorbitant prices forced on it. Without Lebanon, the *Mira* entity loses its purpose.'[36]

B. THE COMMON INTERESTS AND LEBANESE SENSITIVITIES

Grain was not the only sore point in Syro-Lebanese relations. By the second half of 1946, the economic crisis was worsening, characterised by increasing unemployment and labour troubles. Moreover, by that time Lebanese and Syrian hard currency reserves – particularly dollars and sterling – had been depleted for astonishingly large orders of non-essential consumer goods. Customs warehouses and ports were congested because of money shortages and prospects of losses resulted from excess supply. It was reported that Beirut customs warehouses contained enough toothbrushes, shoe polish and tennis balls for the next decade.[37]

Against this backdrop the question of the Common Interests was raised again, especially the issue of the customs union. There was wide speculation that the various directorates of the Common Interests were going to be liquidated and that the two states were to run their respective administrations independently. At the same time a report was circulating in Beirut stressing that the termination of the Common Interests would gravely harm the Lebanese economy, since Syria was working on organising its economic and trade system in a manner that would positively influence Lebanon. The report recommended the cancellation of the HCCI should its authority remain limited to only determining customs fees. The Lebanese cabinet convened a special meeting to deliberate on these matters.[38] After consultations with their Syrian counterparts, the Lebanese authorities requested the mandate of the HCCI be enhanced to include the study of bilateral economic problems. The Lebanese also wished that the HCCI lay down a plan to incorporate various directorates.[39] Lebanese Arab nationalists strongly supported the views of the Lebanese government regarding the HCCI and maintained that the Syro-Lebanese union was an important trial with long-term repercussions. They held that the Arab states were watching closely and that their drive to unite would be greatly influenced by the success of the Syro-Lebanese union.[40]

Damascus preferred the creation of a 'Higher Economic Council' instead of expanding the mandate of the HCCI. To that end numerous meetings took place between the representatives of the two governments. The Syrian Minister of Economy, Khaled al-'Azem, commenting on the results of these discussions, indicated that the two governments had to establish a united financial and economic policy (*tawjih*) to prevent differences in decision-making that could have harmful ramifications for Lebanon and Syria. By the end of August, the Syrian Ministry of Economy had concluded the studies necessary to draw up the mandate of the Higher Economic Council. The Syrians envisaged the council to be composed of prominent Lebanese and Syrian businessmen and factory-owners. Based on the findings of the Economic Higher Council, the two governments would adopt a unified economic strategy, the primary aim of which would be to combat the high prices of staples. The Syrians hoped that this would enhance the purchasing power of its citizens. Also among the priorities would be the protection of locally produced industrial as well as agricultural goods.[41] Earlier, during the month of April 1946, the Lebanese and Syrian governments were seriously considering establishing a 'Joint Economic Council'. A Syrian initiative, the Joint Economic Council was to emulate the British-run Middle East Supply Centre, which the Allies were phasing out. The Joint Economic Council was to coordinate and supervise major economic projects between the two states.

The Lebanese economic and financial community was not thrilled with these initiatives. The predominant view in Beirut was that the envisaged Economic Higher Council would only be inferior if not equal to the HCCI. Commentators described the new scheme as 'a humiliating manifestation of the anarchy and chaos' dominating Syro-Lebanese relations.[42] Opinion-makers in Lebanon went even further. Listing the numerous councils and joint committees: the Higher Economic Council (*Conseil Supérieur Economique*), the Higher Council for the Common Interests (*Conseil Supérieur des Intérêts Communs*), the Joint Economic Council (*Conseil Economique Commun*), the Commercial and Monetary Commission for the Exchange with the Sterling Zone (*Commission Monétaire et Commerciale Pour les Echanges avec la Zone Sterling*), they pointed out how Lebanon and Syria had more higher councils, commissions and sub-commissions than they had problems. Radical Lebanese nationalists were especially critical of the Joint Economic Council scheme, reminding the Lebanese public how the Middle East Supply Centre used to favour Damascus and Aleppo over Lebanon, since the allocation of resources was based on the number of the population in each state. Consequently, Syria used to receive the major share of aid. Opinion-makers in Lebanon were convinced that the Middle East Supply Centre attempted to turn Syria into an agricultural and industrial country with Lebanon as its satellite and that the Syrian government wished to continue with this policy. The Syrian proposal was regarded as an attempt by the Jabiri government to force the Lebanese leadership to adopt an economic plan that would reduce Lebanon to a Syrian vassal. 'If this council is created, Lebanon will not be able to decide on issues related to exports and imports, customs, railroad tariffs...without the consent of Syria. The experts, who reviewed the Syrian proposal, observed that there is an obvious trend towards turning Lebanon into a Syrian satellite and that the Council is one step before political union.'[43]

There were also questions about the role of the HCCI in light of the Syrian scheme. Syrian policy-makers were reminded that the Lebanese leadership only agreed to the establishment of the HCCI because it had a two-year mandate, which was extended until the end of 1947. In contrast, the Joint Economic Council was being presented by Damascus as a permanent body, which to the radical Lebanese nationalists was unacceptable. In light of the strong Lebanese nationalist opposition, Lebanese political circles advised the Syrians not to insist on the scheme, since stability in Syro-Lebanese economic relations would suffer. Instead, it was recommended that the HCCI continue with its mandate unaltered. Lahoud rejected the Joint Economic Council scheme and during his negotiations with 'Azem had adopted an intransigent attitude in that regard.[44]

Lebanese Arab nationalist opinion-makers continued to voice their support for strengthening the economic union by expanding the mandate of the HCCI. They called upon both governments to ensure objectivity and even-handedness in bilateral relations.[45] The radical Lebanese nationalists kept up the pressure to discredit the Syro-Lebanese economic partnership. Taking advantage of a minor border incident, one of their prominent mouthpieces, *L'Orient*, published an extensive editorial in August on a shooting incident at the Syro-Lebanese border that had occurred in March. The incident was an exchange of fire between Syrian smugglers from the Sha'laan clan and Lebanese customs police, which resulted in the smugglers' deaths. The Lebanese authorities were pressured by Damascus to return the confiscated goods to the clan and pay 30,000 liras to the families of the dead smugglers in compensation. Although the border incident was minor in nature, it was used by *L'Orient* to describe the customs union as a typical bad marriage. The daily called upon the Lebanese government to take the decision to end the union. The matter should have been addressed months ago, it said, but the paper refrained from tackling the issue, not wishing to poison the relationship with Syria until the border incident. *L'Orient* alleged that Damascus was unwilling to stem the smuggling trade that was originating from Transjordan, where customs fees were relatively low compared to Lebanon and Syria.

> We categorically object to the government paying 30,000 liras. Does not the government see that our markets are flooded with smuggled goods from Transjordan? How long will our government accept to pay 56 per cent of the Common Interests' revenues when the Lebanese provide most of the customs revenues?[46]

Naturally, Syrian opinion-makers, led by Najib al-Raiyyes, were irritated by the editorial of *L'Orient*. They refuted the editorial's allegations, describing them as malicious propaganda. The Syrians insisted that Lebanese customs authorities provoked the incident and that the goods were destined for the Syrian border town of 'Adra, not Lebanon.

> *L'Orient* and its fellow newspapers do not cry over the 30,000 liras but *L'Orient* cries on the past glory when France ruled over all the customs revenues, funds or posts, when it used these funds to pay high monthly salaries to its political protégés and spies at the expense of Syria and Lebanon.[47]

Raiyyes asked the Lebanese government whether it was in agreement with *L'Orient* concerning customs separation. He also asked if Lebanon considered herself to have been treated unjustly when it had to pay 30,000 liras. Raiyyes reminded the Lebanese that Syria had not demanded the millions of liras that made up its rightful share of the customs revenue. He also reminded the Lebanese that the Syrians had declined from demanding their quota of civil servants at the HCCI administration, noting that if the share of Syria was 56 per cent then it should have this percentage of Syrian employees – whereas the number of Syrian civil servants did not exceed 5 per cent of the total workforce.

> We have not seen a Syrian newspaper demand customs separation despite all the injustice that Syria faces because of this partnership. We believe that the Lebanese

government does not agree with the mentioned newspaper views concerning the separation because it is fully aware of the damage that Lebanon would face in the event of separation.[48]

Raiyyes' editorial was widely read in Lebanon, prompting a response from radical Lebanese nationalist circles, which maintained that the economic union between Lebanon and Syria was against nature. Both states could not adopt the same policy, since Syria was an industrial and agricultural country while Lebanon relied on services. Consequently, while Syria was compelled to impose taxes to protect its nascent industry, this policy was incompatible with Lebanese interests. The Syro-Lebanese economic union may be assisting the Lebanese in securing their grain supplies, regardless of the unfavourable price and condition, but this benefit did not balance the cost of the other inconveniences Lebanon was forced to bear. Radical Lebanese nationalists were convinced that Lebanon was becoming poorer while Syria was enriching itself; for every year Lebanon paid Syria a 'solidarity' tribute of not less than 80 million liras.

They insisted that the Syrian authorities were facing difficulties in containing smuggling, especially on the Syrian–Transjordanian border. At that time, taxation in Transjordan was less than 11 per cent, while in Syria and Lebanon it ranged between 40 and 60 per cent. This state of affairs encouraged large-scale smuggling, resulting in reduced Syrian customs revenues, thus reducing her contribution to the Common Interests while Lebanese contributions to the HCCI were systematically increasing. As a result, it was concluded that the Treasury of the Common Interests was nearly exclusively funded by Lebanon while Syria's 56 per cent of the revenues had become a Lebanese present to the Syrian Treasury.

Lebanese nationalists claimed that they had a weak government in Lebanon, which did not know how to protect the country's interests, while in Syria they had a businessman in the position of Prime Minister who knew how to separate economic problems from political and moral issues. They described the incumbent Lebanese Prime Minister, Sami el-Solh, as an ideologue who had recently converted to Arab nationalism, and confused morality, politics and economics. Under such conditions, Lebanese nationalists were not hopeful that the situation could be rectified. Addressing al-Qabass, L'Orient wrote that 'Raiyyes affirmed that Syria is sacrificing a lot to please Lebanon. We do not wish that Syria bleed to assist Lebanon. We are deeply touched by the favours of Syria, but this bleeding has to cease. For once we agree with al-Raiyyes in calling an end to this marriage that is causing problems to both states.'[49]

The sharp debate between Lebanese and Syrian opinion-makers compelled the Syrian Premier, Jabiri, to intervene in order to allay the fears of Lebanese nationalists, which he described as exaggerated. Jabiri stressed that Syria was taking great care that the partnership between the two states was in the interest of both parties. The Syrian Premier noted that the two states were adamant about assuming control over the different directorates of Common Interests as quickly as possible. To that end, temporary regulations for their administration were agreed upon between Lebanon and Syria. He said Syria preferred to make any sacrifices from its share of the revenues from the Common Interests, rather than seeing them separated. Jabiri believed that it was only natural that each government wished to safeguard its interests and to promote its interests over that of its partner. Where Syria was concerned, Jabiri declared that Damascus preferred to make large concessions and to add them to Lebanon's interests, since Syria had political considerations, placing great importance upon remaining in complete understanding with Lebanon. Commenting on Jabiri's statement, Arab nationalist circles in Lebanon held that the Syrian Prime Minister was speaking with complete sincerity and dedication, giving the impression that the Syro-Lebanese differences on some issues would not result in the break-up of the partnership.[50]

Echoing Jabiri's statement, Syrian commentators reiterated that the relationship with Lebanon was never driven by the desire for material gain or inaccurate counts of what Syrians and Lebanese consume in their respective states. As far as the Syrian ruling elite was concerned, Syro-Lebanese relations would continue to be dedicated to a common purpose – the complete independence of Syria and Lebanon. Disagreement over revenue shares or on who would head the Customs Directorate was no reason to break up the Syro-Lebanese partnership and turn away from the Syrian national priority – which was above all other concerns. Syrian opinion-makers were very critical of radical Lebanese nationalists who were pleased with Beirut and Damascus' disagreements and who demanded the break-up of the Syro-Lebanese partnership – this in spite of the fact that, from an economic perspective, a break-up would harm Lebanon.

> But this group of people, when demanding the break-up and insisting upon it, bear a message that is pleasing to a known foreign power. This foreign power is looking forward to being asked to intervene and proclaim that 'Lebanon, which is being unjustly treated by its persecuting neighbour', requires strong protection. We believe that the nationalists in Lebanon, especially those in power, and the parliamentary majority, will not allow this vicious melody to continue in the Lebanese press.[51]

Syrian opinion-makers declared that the relationship with Lebanon should not be a material and commercial affiliation. Disagreements between the Syrian and Lebanese negotiators should not be based on the calculation of figures alone. Instead they recommended that disagreements be dealt with in a generous manner, encompassing the political spirit. A narrow economic perspective on negotiations was dismissed, since agreement with Lebanon was not based on customs shares, the number of Syrian and Lebanese employees in the directorates of the customs. Agreement with the Lebanese was based on complete independence and the withdrawal of foreign forces. It was maintained that both Lebanon and Syria had adhered to their agreement, under the auspices of the Arab League, and that 'the number of positions, shares and figures will not divide us, whatever the losses and the profits, because the agreement on independence and sovereignty needs to remain, regardless of the price each of us has to pay'.[52]

These commentaries allude to a series of meetings that took place between the heads of Syrian and Lebanese governments. Described by the press as stormy negotiations, the meetings cumulated in a summit in Soufar on 13 September 1946. Again, the first issues to be discussed between Lahoud and 'Azem were grain and the *Mira*. During the deliberations, Lahoud was overheard saying that the Lebanese were the 'small fry' at the summit. Lahoud demanded that the Syrians lower their prices of grain. 'Azem then tabled a price list and read it in a low voice. Lahoud repeated his insistence that Syrian prices were too high. Jabiri intervened and stated in a loud voice, 'Do what you wish but I am not leaving here before a complete understanding is reached.' The Lebanese suggested that Lebanon's share of the grain of the *Mira* be 180 tons. The Syrians agreed, but insisted that the price for this amount remain at 13 million liras. 'Azem demanded immediate payment in cash. Lahoud retorted that this was not possible since time was needed to raise the necessary funds and, in any case, in view of the fact that the supplies would be received in instalments, payment should be made accordingly. 'Azem refused and insisted that payment be immediate and in cash. The debate became heated to such a degree that Minister Lahoud asked for an aspirin while refusing the Syrian demand. The Syrian and Lebanese Premiers, Sa'adallah al-Jabiri and Sa'di Munla, mediated an understanding in which the 13 million liras would be paid in two instalments – the first being due at the end of September, the second at the end of October 1946. Deliberations turned to the Customs Directorate. The debate became heated again, especially over the question of which state was to head the administration of the directorate. Jabiri demanded that the directorate be placed under a Syrian national who would be assisted by a Lebanese director. The Lebanese director would have the same jurisdiction as his Syrian counterpart. The Lebanese disagreed, maintaining that two directors with the same jurisdiction would only hamper the administrative function of the institution. Instead, the Lebanese proposed that a Syrian general inspector be appointed beside the Lebanese director. The Syrians refused. The meeting was adjourned with the understanding that the disagreement be presented to the respective cabinets to decide on them.[53]

The discussions continued on 15 October 1946, taking place in the Syrian summer resort of Zabadani, before moving to Damascus. The delegations were comprised of the Syrian and Lebanese Presidents, Prime Ministers, and Ministers of Finance and Foreign Affairs. The two sides agreed on designating a Syrian co-director to assist the Lebanese director in running the Customs Directorate. The Syrians demanded the abolition of the Higher Council of the Common Interests that proposed that it be replaced by a Syro-Lebanese ministerial committee. The Lebanese refused on the grounds that they needed to consult their cabinet on such a delicate matter. They also held that the different Common Interests directorates should be supervised by a permanent administration, not a ministerial entity that was likely to resign at any moment. Moreover, the Lebanese delegation asserted that a minister would not have enough time to devote to the proposed organ. Besides, the Syrian proposal would cause uproar among radical Lebanese nationalists, since they would fear that such a body would inevitably lead to a federal council. Nothing conclusive was reached at the Zabadani and Damascus summits.[54]

According to diplomatic observers, Syro-Lebanese economic relations reflected political attitudes more than economic matters. The nature of the meetings was to clarify political relations. The Lebanese tended to emphasise the role of Beirut as the natural port for both states and the role of the Lebanese as the natural importers for both peoples. The Syrian recognition of Lebanon's 'natural' role depended on the degree to which the Syrians felt confident of Lebanese agreement and support in the political sphere. Syro-Lebanese political relations were described as vague because both states had one unresolved political issue: Christian autonomy versus Muslim hegemony. Strain came from Lebanese elements distrustful of Syrian Muslim extremists and from Syrians sceptical of Lebanese Christians' sincerity vis-à-vis the Arabist agenda.[55]

There were strong misgivings about the appointment of a Syrian co-director to the Customs Directorate. Lebanese nationalists were under the impression that the metamorphosis of the HCCI and the introduction of the [Syrian] co-director general were intended to reduce the influence of Lebanese officials. However, the new scheme was accepted as a temporary solution that removed a dispute between the two governments. Lebanon's official position in rejecting the liquidation of the HCCI was widely supported. Aside from the political ramifications in Lebanon, it was thought that the HCCI did not have absolute authority on vital issues, since its higher authority rested with the two governments, who retained the right to overrule any decision or solve any difference of opinion between the delegations. Consequently, a ministerial committee was regarded as useless. Moderate and radical Lebanese nationalists hoped the Syrians would withdraw their proposal since the interests of two independent states were above the interests of governments and their politics.[56]

After a visit to the Syrian capital by Emile Lahoud, it was decided that both governments ought to study how customs unions were being applied in other countries, such as Belgium, the Netherlands and Luxembourg. The purpose was to investigate how their system could be applied to Lebanon and Syria as well as the manner in which the revenue of the customs could be fairly divided.[57] The study of the Benelux countries prompted L'Orient to ask if the removal of the tariff barriers between Belgium, the Netherlands and Luxembourg – where such arrangements were supposed to lead to the formation of a union – whether such designs harboured eventual political union.[58]

Finance Ministers in both countries kept up discussions. By November there was still no agreement. Difficulties arose from the failure to agree on an appropriate system to administer customs. The functioning of the HCCI – which had been reduced from six delegates to two – was also a source of difference. In response to inquires by parliamentarians on the negotiations, Lebanese Prime Minister Sa'di al-Munla declared that

> neither Lebanon nor Syria have presented a proposal for the abolition of the Common Interests, however both parties have agreed that we should base the system on solid foundations and that this be the core of the discussions with the Syrians. There are only questions of formality, for example as to whether the council should be formed of three Syrian and three Lebanese delegates or whether it would constitute one delegate from each state. As you see this change does not touch on the essence of things.[59]

Contrary to the statements of the Lebanese Prime Minister, both governments decided that the Higher Council of the Common Interests be terminated at the beginning of the new year. Taking its place would be the Lebanese and Syrian Ministers of Finance, who would be acting in the capacity of permanent secretary-general. It was even reported that the Lebanese government had started to search for new positions for the members of the council who would lose their postings.[60]

Political changes in both capitals put the whole issue on hold as Jamil Mardam and Riad el-Solh were appointed to form new governments in Damascus and Beirut. Shortly afterwards the radical Lebanese nationalist daily L'Orient reported the appointment of the Syrian co-Director of Customs, Fayez Dalati. More important, though, the Syrians were also asking to renegotiate the agreement on replacing the HCCI with a new entity of two delegates. The Syrians wanted these delegates to be ministers, preferably both countries' Ministers of Finance and Economy, thereby increasing the new entity's composition to four members.[61]

Cabinet changes in Beirut and Damascus brought optimism about the future of Syro-Lebanese relations, which were strained by the Sha'laan border incident and the subsequent resignation of Musa Moubarak, the president of the Higher Council for the Common Interests.[62] More importantly, the downfall of the Sa'di al-Munla government was also hastened by the excessive price of grain his government was willing to pay the Syrians.[63] At that time, differences over the management of the Customs Directorate remained unresolved. There was strong divergence over what kind of economic policy to embrace. Syria espoused a protectionist model, while a laissez-faire approach was more popular in Lebanon. Syrian protectionism was causing high prices in Lebanon, particularly in vital supplies such as grain. Moreover, Syrian opinion-makers kept alluding to Lebanon not being a political entity but a result of foreign imperialism. Such declarations reinforced the insecurity of Lebanese nationalists, driving them to scrutinise the economic relationship with Syria and to dismiss any arrangement that had the potential of Syro-Lebanese federation or unification.[64] The expiry of the Higher Council for the Common Interests was another challenge to bilateral relations, particularly since this issue was going to take centre stage, as the nationalist struggle against France was drawing to an end.

In spite of the aforementioned challenges, radical Lebanese nationalists were hopeful, especially since Jamil Mardam had regained power. In their view, Mardam was unlikely to impose an arrangement that would not satisfy the Lebanese. In addition, the fact that Riad el-Solh formed a national union government, which enjoyed the support of most Lebanese, facilitated a Syro-Lebanese modus vivendi on all disputes. This would be further facilitated by the prestige that Riad el-Solh had in the Arab states, including Syria. Solh and Jamil Mardam Bey were described as speaking the same language. Solh was expected to extend the mandate of the Higher Council of the Common Interests and 'for the time being we can not ask for more'.[65]

In his last editorial of 1946, Najib al-Raiyyes was not as optimistic as his radical Lebanese nationalist rivals. Disregarding the political events in Beirut and Damascus and the ongoing debate concerning the Customs Directorate and the HCCI, he reported that Syrian merchants and importers were complaining about the Syro-Lebanese partnership, which was supposedly established to serve Lebanese and Syrian interests. In this partnership, he maintained, Lebanon was playing the role of a rival who would sign an agreement and then breach it. Raiyyes related the example of the Syrian olive oil harvest. In 1946, Syrian authorities prohibited the export of olive oil. In spite of the directions of the Syrian authorities, Lebanese merchants headed to Syria and purchased the entire harvest, which they exported via the port of Beirut. Thus, the Lebanese rendered the Syrian decision meaningless. A similar example was the Syrian prohibition of cotton imports. Lebanese merchants imported cotton goods, which were smuggled to Syria, thus harming the cotton producers and farmers and nullifying the precautions of the Syrian government. Raiyyes described Lebanon as a rival partner who seemed to oppose each action that served to protect Syrian interests. Arguing along the same lines, 'Aref al-Laham, the secretary of the Syrian chamber of commerce, described the situation as follows:

> The fact is, Syria is actually living in a house with one door whose key is with Lebanon. It is not possible for Syria to take a decision if Lebanon has not taken the same decision, or else everything that Syria decides is futile. Something has to be done to ensure stability and save Syria from economic deterioration.

Raiyyes emphasised that everything related to trade and industry, imports and exports, was in the hands of Lebanon. As a result, he argued, Lebanon could oppose every Syrian government decision or action. He called for the establishment of a port in Latakiya so that 'the house key' would return to Syria. Syria would be able to take charge of her economy and to protect her decisions and actions. Raiyyes concluded with the following remarks:

Syrian trade is no longer in Damascus, Aleppo or any other Syrian city but most of it has relocated to Beirut. All the agents and distributors, importers and exporters have transferred to Beirut because Beirut is the port and has the key to the house, which we have closed upon ourselves. We call upon the government to proceed with establishing a port of which studies and plans have already been put down.[66]

Clearly the aforementioned editorial was a call to arms for the Syrian ruling elite to secure Syrian interests in light of the new reality: France was safely out. 'The burden of independence' was upon them.[67]

3 *The Customs Union: The Cause of Discord*

The early days of 1947 were a time of celebration in Lebanon, for they marked the withdrawal of the last foreign troops from its soil. Lebanon and Syria were finally free. At that time, all Arab capitals were sending their compliments to Beirut and their representatives took part in Lebanese festivities marking independence. So were the Syrians. The Syrians perceived their participation in the Lebanese celebrations as essentially different from all the other Arab states. They firmly believed that the withdrawal of France from Lebanon completed the withdrawal of France from Syria. Damascene opinion-makers emphasised that Syria's independence would have remained threatened as long as Lebanon was under occupation or pseudo-occupation.

Syrian opinion-makers contended, with evident remorse, that the price of France's withdrawal was Syria's relinquishing the four *qadas* to Lebanon. From the Syrian perspective, after the loss of Alexandretta, the country came to depend on the ports of Beirut and Tripoli. Consequently, the whole of Syria, including Damascus, had been reduced to a mere customs area subordinated to Beirut. Syro-Lebanese customs union was perceived to be a Syrian concession to Lebanon. 'No member state of the League of Arab States has sacrificed as much as Syria. We hope that they will be satisfied with mentioning, in future independence celebrations, what an exorbitant price Syria has paid for Lebanon's independence.'[1]

Syrian sentiments found strong opposition among the radical Lebanese nationalists.

> The Lebanese have had enough of being bullied ('*antariyat*) [by the Syrians]. All those in Damascus should understand that we are not prepared to receive lessons in patriotism from anyone, especially from a number of Ottoman *vilayets*, which have no territorial claims, especially in Lebanon.[2]

These polemics drove Prime Minister Riad el-Solh to make a formal protest to his Syrian counterpart, Mardam Bey, with a request that pressure be applied at once to 'cease this senseless battle'.[3]

Diplomatic circles in Lebanon attributed the skirmishes among Lebanese and Syrian opinion-makers to worsening relations between Beirut and Damascus. The Lebanese were angry over the price of grain, and the Syrians were angry over the role the Lebanese were increasingly playing as middlemen for the distribution of commodities in Syria. Syrians were convinced that the high prices were due to the Lebanese wholesale mark-up before distribution to retailers. Diplomats explained that the recriminations were symptomatic of age-old rivalries between two fundamentally different peoples – one a desert people, subject to all of the prejudices and judgements of nomads who earn a precarious living in relatively forbidding surroundings, the other a coastal people living in lush Mediterranean surroundings, who had developed a legendary mania for close and ruthless business dealings in the ancient custom of the Phoenician bazaar.[4]

Diplomats also attributed the tense atmosphere between Beirut and Damascus to the post-war depression afflicting the general public of both countries. Lebanese and Syrians were tired of the high prices they had to pay for their food, consumer goods, rents and services. Succeeding governments had made half-hearted efforts to ameliorate the mounting economic crisis but no promising economic reforms had been initiated.[5] Throughout 1947, these reforms would prove the point of contention between Beirut and Damascus.

A. TAXATION POLICIES

As noted above, recriminations came amidst continued economic deterioration in Syria and Lebanon. The major share of commercial and industrial activity was attributed to the small merchants, shopkeepers, artisans and small manufacturers, while the educated urban middle and lower middle class grew rapidly. By 1947 the number of civil servants had increased more than three times from the 1939 level and their salaries now consumed more than half of the state budget. A great expansion of education after 1944, coupled with urbanisation, modernisation and the extension of state services, offered many new employment opportunities to middle-class young people. However, not much of post-war prosperity trickled down to workers and poor peasants. Wartime inflation, following on the drastic fall in real wages in the late 1930s, had severely reduced the living standards of Syrian workers. With the influx of foreign imports that began in 1946, wage cuts were frequent. Working conditions in the new factories were as primitive as in the old. Post-war growth in the construction industry created some jobs, but a large number of workers were either unemployed or underemployed.[6]

The 1946 annual report of the *Banque de Syrie et du Liban* revealed how Syrian and Lebanese merchants were threatening to undermine the Lebanese and Syrian economies through continued imports and the stockpiling of goods. These goods were sold at outrageous profits. Moreover, the report revealed that the main threat to the independence of Syria and Lebanon was preserving the equilibrium in the two governments' balance sheets. Ironically, the cause for the disequilibria was the withdrawal of foreign troops from the Levant. The expenditure of the mandatory power during the years of 1920 to 1941 had left a surplus, which was reinforced by the expenditures of the Allied armies in 1941 and 1946. However, independence, the end of the war and the withdrawal of the French and British armies deprived the two states of vital sources of income.[7] Aside from the anxiety of keeping the books balanced, the Lebanese and Syrian governments' major preoccupation was combating the high cost of living and the continuous rise in the price of staples.

On 1 January 1947, most members of the Lebanese cabinet were in Damascus congratulating the newly formed government on receiving the vote of confidence from the Syrian parliament.[8] But more important, the Damascus meeting was part of a series of previous meetings held at the end of 1946 devoted to laying mechanisms to combat the rise in the prices of basic food and fuel necessities. The most sensitive issues facing Syro-Lebanese deliberations were the measures to be taken by the two governments to lower the price of grain and the appointment of a Syrian director to the Common Interests to serve beside the Lebanese. Also high on the agenda was the reduction of taxation on certain vital goods. Luxury items were to be taxed instead. Outlining Syrian concern to achieve uniformity of economic policy between Beirut and Damascus, Syrian Prime Minister Jamil Mardam Bey stated after the meeting, 'We are two states composing one economic union, hence it is not possible that there is diversity in economic, supply and trade matters.' In Damascus, it was decided to hold another meeting in Beirut that would focus on Lebanese proposals, which entailed lowering the prices of basic consumer items such as grain, combustibles (petrol, diesel and kerosene) and building material (especially cement). The Lebanese government also advocated the marketing of low-quality fabrics (*aqmisha sha'biyya*) for the poor and the low middle classes as well as lowering taxation of primary goods.[9]

On Thursday 2 January 1947, Mardam Bey, heading a Syrian delegation, arrived in Beirut. The two governments agreed to lower the price of grain and to lower customs fees on petrol, sugar, tobacco and kerosene, as well as other major necessities. It was expected that these measures would soon be adopted by the two states, especially since studies revealed that prices of similar goods in neighbouring countries were much lower.[10]

Syro-Lebanese discussions did not merely deliberate on taxation policies. There were serious differences on the nationality of the director of the Customs Directorate. The directorship was seen as a vital and sensitive post, which not only collected revenues on imports and exports but, more importantly, set the sum of fees and the type of goods to be taxed. Moreover, a report put forward by the Syrian Merchants Association indicated that public officials charged with releasing goods from customs were predominantly Lebanese, as were most of the high-ranking and highly paid officials of the Customs Directorate. The report emphasised that it was the Lebanese who retained exclusive control to release the goods bound for the two states from customs. The report alleged that Lebanese authorities deprived Syrian customs officials of their rights.[11]

In order to change this status quo, the Syrians were keen on putting a Syrian national as head of the Customs Directorate – a post that, since independence, had been occupied by a Lebanese. The Lebanese refused to entertain the Syrian request. In 1946, the Syrians reduced their demand to the appointment of a Syrian beside the Lebanese director. The debate between the Syrians and the Lebanese became heated, prompting the director general of Customs, Jamil Shehab, to request a leave of absence. The duration of his leave was not known. In the midst of the Syro-Lebanese economic crisis, the 'leave' of a key civil servant was not beneficial; nevertheless the dispute continued for a month. In fact the Syrian government proceeded to appoint a director to assume a post beside that of the current Lebanese head of customs. However, Prime Minister Riad el-Solh eventually managed to alter views in Damascus and convinced the Syrian leadership that two directors would threaten uniformity and undermine the economic union. Moreover, the unification of the two states' political position was given precedence, for Syro-Lebanese political conformity would induce the alignment of economic policies. Hence, the proposal of appointing a Syrian co-director was abandoned. Instead the mandate of the Higher Council of the Common Interests was broadened, to enable the council to cooperate with the Customs Directorate in order to ensure the two states' respective interests. In this regard, on 27 February 1947, the Lebanese President of the Republic received Jamil Shehab (who had returned from his leave) and Musa Moubarak, the head of the Lebanese delegation to the HCCI, and instructed them to facilitate all affairs between the two states.[12]

It has been noted how, in 1946, successive Lebanese governments attempted to convince their Syrian counterparts to alter their taxation policies. During the beginning of 1947, the Syrian public also began to be very critical of Damascus' taxation policies. As in Lebanon, the Syrian public attributed the high price of necessities to the taxation policies. It was argued that, had the government been satisfied with only partial profit from its monopolisation of vital consumer goods such as sugar, petrol and kerosene, the cost of living would have been at least 50 per cent less. Moreover, the public received Syrian and Lebanese official declarations regarding the reduction of tariffs with great doubt. Syrian economic circles sceptically asked how their government could agree with Lebanon to lower tariffs while it was insisting on retaining them in the budget. Although it was expected that the Syrian government would ask parliament to review the budget, the manner in which the government planned to cover the expenditure resulting from the loss in revenue remained vague. These views were accompanied by an appeal to the two governments to lower tariffs by 50 per cent, even if this would result in a budget deficit. It was thought that lower tariffs would lower the high cost of living, and consequently would positively affect important elements of the economy such as labour wages and transportation fees.[13]

While the Lebanese ministry of economy was studying ways to engineer a lower cost of living, Lebanon's general public was demanding a reduction in the price of bread. Bread, aside from being a nutritional staple, was characterised as a benchmark of Lebanon's price index. In parliament and in the press, the Lebanese government was facing mounting pressure as regards the price of bread. It was maintained that the cost of Lebanese bread was quite disproportionate to world prices of grain and flour and that 'many offers are reaching the Lebanese government, namely concerning flour of higher quality CIF at 20 piastres per kilo, while the Lebanese population continues to pay 45 piastres a kilo for a flour of mediocre quality'. There was a growing demand for a revision of the Syro-Lebanese grain agreement. Lebanese Premier Solh was called upon to make use of his personal prestige among the Syrian leaders to obtain this revision because 'we are very much willing to accept and even prefer to purchase our grain from Syria at a 10 to 15 per cent mark-up than the international market value but we obstinately refuse to pay 120 per cent more than their normal price'.[14]

Policies related to grain drew the attention of Syrian commentators as well. The Syrian Prime Minister had declared in parliament that he intended to present a bill that would continue to restrict the trade in grain to the *Mira*. However, a majority of the Members of Parliament as well as the director of the *Mira* lobbied to ensure that the government continued to purchase grain directly from the farmers – this at a time when the price of grain in the free market was 20 per cent lower than the price of the *Mira*. As a result of mounting public opposition, Jamil Mardam Bey reconsidered and announced in parliament that, starting January 1947, transportation and trade in grain would be unrestricted and free. Najib al-Raiyyes, an old and strong advocate of free trade in grain, welcomed Mardam Bey's decision and in his editorial expressed the hope that communiqués be issued to the precincts, production sites and to all those who were concerned with the grain trade, informing them that trade and transportation in grain had been permitted 'so that the poor and those in villages will not be victims of the ill intent of some civil servants who will ignore the government's decision if word does not reach them officially. They will continue to receive bribes and commissions with the excuse that the old restrictions are still in force.'[15] Raiyyes was addressing the various groups, composed of landowners, merchants and civil servants, who had a vested interest in retaining the precarious situation for their personal profit.

There were calls on the Syrian authorities that restrictions on the trade and transport of grain should also be lifted for Lebanon, since both states formed one economic union. The grain trade should proceed according to the principles of supply and demand. The owner and editor-in-chief of *al-Qabass* predicted that only then would grain prices fall, pointing out that Lebanon, which had bought a 100,000 tons from Syria, had reduced the price of grain, from 48 to 33 piastres a kilo. He explained that this was due to the grain surplus, which had filled Lebanese stores and villages, and had resulted in the majority of consumers not being in need of the supplies of the *Mira*, prompting the Lebanese government to greatly lower the price. Raiyyes concluded his editorial by saying that permitting free trade and transport inside Syria would not result in the intended benefits [lowering the price of grain], if the decision to authorise the trade and transport of grain did not include Lebanon. 'Otherwise,' he warned, 'smuggling will generate bribing and corruption among the civil servants. Syria and Lebanon are one state, one land, one people, which are not bound by geographical, political or regional borders; it is absurd to restrict transportation between them to permission or licences.' Raiyyes dismissed the claims of the *Mira* officials who were advocating that lifting restrictions on the transport and trade in grain would cause price rises in Syria. He argued that such claims would have been justified had Syrian grain prices been low, since this would have tempted smugglers to sell to neighbouring countries and overseas. Raiyyes pointed out that this was unlikely to happen since grain prices in the neighbouring countries were lower than in Syria. Syrian grain prices exceeded Egypt's by 50 per cent, Turkey's by 40 per cent and Iraq's by 60 per cent, and even Lebanon, which purchased her grain needs from Syria. In another editorial Raiyyes added that the Syrian government had offered its grain to Europe, but it was turned down. Europe preferred to purchase from Iraq, Turkey and Egypt, whose prices were 30 per cent less than Syria's.[16]

Syrian political circles rejected Raiyyes' arguments. It was feared that, aside from the loss of badly needed revenues, such a measure would needlessly surrender a strong political card with which to pressure Lebanon. Why was Lebanon buying from Syria, they asked, if she could fulfil her grain needs from countries where grain was cheaper? They also maintained that lifting restrictions would encourage grain merchants to make larger profits by exporting the larger part of Syria's grain supplies abroad – through Beirut Port and mainly to Europe – thereby exposing Syria to famine. Moreover, landowners continued to support the *Mira* because an excellent crop was expected, and a free market would drive prices down.[17]

Opposition to the *Mira* came from those deputies who were not cultivators of grain. They claimed that the arguments of the Syrian civil servants and cultivators were unfounded, particularly since, under the *Mira* agreement, Lebanon was prohibited from importing grain during the harvest from any country but Syria. This, despite the fact that during that time Lebanon had already contracted Syria to supply her with 120,000 tons of grain – a quantity that Lebanese authorities requested be reduced by 40,000 tons. Moreover, the Lebanese *Mira*, which had purchased grain for 48 piastres a kilo from Syria, was selling grain to the Lebanese consumer at 30 piastres a kilo. The Lebanese consumer was unwilling to purchase grain at 48 piastres, since there were ample supplies of smuggled Syrian grain in Lebanon, despite the transport restrictions. The quantities that were smuggled to the Lebanese market from Syria were estimated to be double that purchased from the Lebanese *Mira* from its Syrian counterpart. Even then the Syrian consumer preferred to purchase his grain from the free market, instead from the *Mira*.[18]

While the discourse over grain continued, a number of dailies, described by *al-Qabass* as Lebanese 'isolationists', were criticising the Syrian government for refusing to cut its trade ties with Palestine. Syria, to the annoyance of the Lebanese, was importing its citrus needs from Palestine. The Syrians claimed that Lebanese citrus fruits were exorbitantly priced. They also claimed that there were so many obstacles preventing their export to Syria that they had become almost rare items in the Syrian markets. The Syrian press alleged that Lebanese 'isolationists' were aiming to sever the primary revenue of the Palestinian people, revenue desperately needed in their struggle with the Zionists. The radical Lebanese nationalist press compared Syria to a brother, 'who conditioned the partnership to suit his personal interests. He imposes on his little brother to purchase grain at double the market price and refuses to buy his citrus fruits because he prefers to buy Arab citrus fruits to Lebanese citrus fruits.' In Syria, these sentiments were described as being inspired from the depth of 'Phoenicianism', which was reincarnated during the days of the 'tender mother' (France) in her struggle against pan-Arabism. Damascus saw radical Lebanese nationalists as never hesitating to utilise any opportunity, no matter how insignificant, to stab Arab cooperation, and Lebanese cooperation with the Arab states, in the back.[19]

In the midst of these polemics, the Premiers of the two states were scheduled to meet in Shtura on 9 January 1947. Syrian public opinion was increasingly critical of their leadership's courteous and indecisive policy towards Lebanon. It was hoped that the coming meeting in Shtura would not be similar to previous meetings that were characterised by being courteous, inconclusive and dominated by a continuous drive to create subcommittees to study issues of disagreement. Decisive action was called for since finding a solution to the economic situation of both states could be postponed no longer.

By that time, the predominant view in Syria was that Syro-Lebanese economic relations were abnormal and ambiguous and the belief in one Syro-Lebanese economic union was restricted to Syria. The Syrian impression was reinforced by a number of instances in which decisions reached by the Lebanese and Syrian governments to limit imports were neither respected nor executed by Lebanese authorities. Banned from importation, foreign goods such as cotton, grain, fruits, olive oil and timber would usually end up in the Syrian markets. Lebanese authorities were also preventing Syrian merchants from exporting Syrian grain via the port of Beirut, this, although restrictions on grain exports were lifted. Syrian public opinion was convinced that Lebanese customs officials did not wish to facilitate the export of Syrian goods by sea. Moreover, the continuous mistreatment of Syrian nationals at Beirut Port and airport received wide press coverage. 'We hope that the Lebanese government will realize that there are mutual economic interests and that the Lebanese will mend their ways after the withdrawal of French troops.'[20]

Radical Lebanese nationalists rejected the existence of an economic unity between Lebanon and Syria, regarding it as an artificial one. In their view, the Syro-Lebanese economic union was established by the mandate to serve French and Syrian interests. They prophesied that the economic union was starting to collapse and that Syrian greed and envy for Lebanon's resources, in addition to Syria's desire to subjugate Lebanon to her loaf of bread, would destroy the economic union. 'The nature of our country is different from yours, our way of life is different than yours and our resources are different than yours, where is union then?'[21]

Regardless of the tense atmosphere, the Syrian and Lebanese prime ministerial delegations arrived in Shtura on Thursday 9 January 1947. Discussions were again dominated by lowering taxes on basic consumer goods. It was decided to lower taxes on combustibles by 30 per cent; taxes on diesel were completely abolished since this fuel was heavily used in agriculture and transportation. It was also decided to put off tackling the issue of the Higher Council of the Common Interests. After the meeting, Prime Minister Mardam Bey noted that there was consensus on the removal of economic barriers and indicated that during the last meetings preliminary steps had been taken in that regard. He also stated that measures against rising prices would come into effect during the month of February.[22]

The public was not as optimistic as the Syrian Premier. Syrian taxi drivers went on strike to protest high petrol prices. In solidarity, their Lebanese counterparts refused to drive passengers to Damascus.[23] This prompted the secretary general of the Syrian Chamber of Commerce, 'Aref al-Laham, to address the issue of combustibles and taxes. Laham argued that it was not sufficient to lower tariffs in order to induce economic prosperity. Instead, he called for a complete revaluation of all the tariffs imposed by the authorities, especially taxation on combustibles. Laham concluded that, due to high tariffs, Syrian exports were suffering greatly since they were not able to compete on the international markets. This was threatening Syria with bankruptcy.[24]

The concerns of the Industrial Economic Conference echoed those of the Syrian Chamber of Commerce. The conference, in which leading Syrian and Lebanese industrialists and textile factory owners took part, demanded that tariffs on primary materials (silk, cotton and wool thread) be lifted while customs remain on imported finished clothing items.[25]

It was estimated that each person in Syria was paying the government an estimated 100 liras per year in taxes. Aside from the high government taxes, the weakness of the national industry was its want of primary resources. Other important factors were the exhaustion of fabrics and food supplies and the termination of rationing and price fixing.[26] Monopolists took advantage of this state of affairs by retaining the freedom to charge exorbitant prices. Finally, there was chronic monetary inflation, caused by the local currency in circulation, which jumped from 35 million liras to 350–400 million liras, thereby contributing to high prices. High prices lowered the standard of living, the cost of living becoming particularly unacceptable to the poor. The poor were getting poorer and the rich getting richer. Labour demanded higher wages, which in turn harmed the local industry and agriculture.[27]

B. DIVERSE PERCEPTIONS ON THE FUTURE OF THE CUSTOMS UNION

The Syrian public did not limit their criticism to their government. With much greater clamour, they blamed the economic union with Lebanon as the major cause of their economic plight: 'Syria is an exploitation farm and a milk cow for Lebanon and we prefer economic separation a thousand times more than maintaining the union' read the headline of the Damascene daily *al-Nasr*. Syrian opinion-makers reasoned that the economic union could only be fruitful and durable if the interests of the two states were guaranteed with justice and equity. Syria's status in the economic union with Lebanon was perceived not to differ from that which existed under the French Mandate.

> The French have made Syria an exploitation farm and a milk cow to fatten Lebanon; and our government, after having assumed the economic affairs of the country, has continued to follow the same policies. It reveals itself soft and conciliatory before the demands and whims of the Lebanese, giving them everything at the expense of the impoverished Syrian taxpayer.[28]

Increasingly, Syrian public opinion was demanding that their government adopt a more assertive stance towards Beirut. The Syrian government was also called upon to abandon duties of affection, parental ties and good neighbourly relations when negotiating with Lebanon:

> Only interests should be the basis of a partnership. If Syria maintains this state of affairs, its economy will head towards disaster…The agricultural and industrial renaissance, which Syria is currently experiencing, cannot develop and bear fruit. On the contrary, this renaissance is meant to die if we continue with the present customs policy, which is transforming Syria into a milk cow for Lebanon. Consequently we prefer economic separation a thousand times more than maintaining a union that only tends to pressure Syria in favour of Lebanon.[29]

Economic circles in Lebanon perceived things differently from the Syrians. They believed that it was a mistake to pretend that France had only created the economic union for the benefit of Lebanon, when in fact the union had always operated for the profit of Syria, especially since it was Syria that produced and Lebanon that consumed, at high prices. The economic union had been instituted because France found it cheaper to have only one customs administration and one economic policy for all states. Such a system also facilitated the High Commissioner's control of the two economies. The Syrians were reminded that back in 1938, when Syria taxed all merchandise coming from Lebanon, the Lebanese authorities drew up a five-year plan to make Lebanon self-sufficient in grain. The project was on the verge of realisation when the High Commissioner intervened and opposed, forcing Lebanon to continue to buy from Syria at exorbitant prices.

Most members of Lebanon's economic and financial elites were convinced that it was Syria that was pursuing a unilateral economic policy that diverted all the profits of the partnership in favour of her own production and to the detriment of Lebanon. In Lebanese eyes, the striking examples of Syria's unilateral economic policies were as follows:

1. Contrary to the 1943 Syro-Lebanese convention of the Common Interests, Syria was collecting from the Lebanese consumer an ad valorem tax of 15 per cent on grain coming from its territory. The Lebanese *Mira* paid an additional tax of 10 piastres to the Syrian cultivator. The mentioned taxes on grain amounted to 32 million liras, paid annually by Lebanon to Syria.

2. The Syrian government had also taken similar measures on different products such as rice, butter, cheese, etc. ... Moreover, since 1944 and at several times, Syria had prohibited the export of numerous products from its territory towards Lebanon. The export licences were only given to Syrian merchants, who sold those products to Lebanese consumers at very high prices.

3. Although the Lebanese held 80 per cent of foreign commerce, the distribution of import quotas was distributed according to the population of each state in such a manner that the imports made by Syrians could not be completely sold in the Syrian market and were thus sold back in Lebanon at a profit to the Syrian merchant.

4. Since 1945, ad valorem taxes ranging from 20 to 50 per cent had been imposed on imported products. The Syrian government had often reduced these taxes, for the benefit of the Syrian importer.

Lebanese nationalists were convinced that ever since the institution of the mandate, Lebanon was forced to heed the interests of the Syrian producer and purchase Lebanese provisions in Syria at high prices – 'That is what our Damascene colleagues mean by living as a parasite from Syria ... A parasite that brings profit.'[30]

Radical Lebanese nationalist circles strove to capitalise on the raging debate and advocated that economic separation should be studied by the two states objectively. They even listed the advantages of economic separation, which would allow each state to freely pursue its economic interests. It was maintained that separation would limit Syro-Lebanese friction and disputes, thus positively affecting political relations. Lebanon would be able to fully develop its commercial and tourist abilities and improve its agricultural production without fear of Syrian censure. Syria could, on the other hand, freely intensify its production of grain, cotton and other industries. In other words, by developing their respective natural resources harmoniously, Syria and Lebanon would be working towards the best of their common interests.[31] It was also argued that Syria was seriously considering establishing its own independent port. Syrian ambitions for an independent port were an indication that they expected the end of the partnership or at least desired it. Consequently, there were calls on the Lebanese government to commence immediate preparations for economic independence.[32]

Significantly, the aforementioned views did not predominate among Lebanese nationalists. Quite the contrary, Lebanese nationalist opinion-makers voiced strong criticisms against the recriminations raging between the Syrian and Lebanese pundits. In this regard, Khalil Gemayel wrote in *Le Jour* that during the previous 25 years, Lebanon and Syria were (due to the mandate) living under identical conditions with similar economic legislation. He held that after independence a new basis for Syro-Lebanese relations had to be found, one that took into consideration new post-war developments. 'We are neither for the maintenance of the current state of affairs in our economic relations with Syria nor are we for separation. Nevertheless, sterile controversies poison the atmosphere and create a detrimental state of malaise.'[33]

The heated discussions between Lebanese and Syrian opinion-makers was beginning to affect public opinion, prompting Lebanese Prime Minister Solh to intervene. He held a press conference in which he assured the public that the Syrian representatives had proven to perfectly understand every aspect of Lebanese interests. He singled out Syrian readiness to collaborate with the Lebanese on any issue related to the reduction of the high cost of living. The Lebanese Prime Minister explained that the controversy that had sprung up between a number of Lebanese dailies and their Syrian brethren was based on nothing but misunderstandings. Solh requested that the Lebanese newspapers put an end to the squabbling without delay, indicating that he had put in a similar request to the Syrian government to intervene with the Syrian dailies. He emphasised that such an environment was harmful to the interests of both states.[34]

Between 6 and 8 February 1947, a Syrian-Lebanese economic conference convened in Beirut in which prominent economists and financiers from both states participated. Among the key recommendations, unanimously adopted, was the pursuit of economic collaboration between the two states within the framework of economic and customs unity. The strengthening of the general economic relations on the basis of equilibrium between Syrian and Lebanese interests was also recommended. The liquidation of the *Mira* system was sought and it was noted that any export of grain could not be undertaken without the approval of the Higher Council of the Common Interests. It was also noted that the grain trade between the two states should be unrestricted. The conference expressed its wishes that these suggestions be followed literally, especially as regards the policy of imports and exports in Syria and Lebanon. It highlighted the fact that the exchange of goods between the two states should not be subject to arbitrary abuse.[35]

The evening before the conclusion of the economic conference a banquet in honour of the participants was held at the Saint George Hotel by the Société Libanaise d'Economie Politique.[36] Gabriel Menassa, a prominent Lebanese political economist and head of the society, presented a paper he had put forward at the conference. The paper was also distributed to Lebanese and Syrian officials as well as numerous economic and political institutions. In the presence of the Syrian delegation to the HCCI, Menassa drew a very pessimistic picture of the future economic relations between the two neighbouring states. He maintained that the Syro-Lebanese economic partnership forced the Syrians and Lebanese to work in close affiliation for their mutual benefit, which was not the case. The partnership was much more in favour of Syria than Lebanon.

Menassa based his reasoning on the balance of payments of Lebanon with Syria in 1939 and 1946, listed below:

BALANCE OF PAYMENTS IN 1939 AND 1946
(IN MILLIONS OF LEBANESE-SYRIAN LIRAS)

	1939		1946	
	Credit	Debit	Credit	Debit
Grain and cereals.........	-	5	-	55
Agricultural products.........	1	1	4	7
Fat (*Samneh*), Cheese and oil.........	-	2.5	-	13
Livestock.........	-	2	-	10
Industrial products.........	1.5	1.5	11	15
Balance of Lebanese Commerce in Syria.........	5	-	7	-
Balance of Syrian costs in Lebanon and of Lebanese costs in Syria.........	1.5	-	6	-
Remittances of Syrian and Lebanese immigrants and Revenues from Syrian capital Exploited in Lebanon.........	2.5	-	-	-
Balance of diverse benefits.........	0.5	-	2	-
General Balance.........	12	12	30	100

Menassa pointed out that if the Lebanese balance of payments with the outside world – an estimated deficit of 65 million liras in 1946 – was also considered, the gravity of the Lebanese situation became increasingly acute. According to Menassa, the cause of Lebanon's economic plight was the sale of Syrian grain to Lebanon at exorbitant prices in comparison to world market prices. He added that the numerous restrictions imposed on the Lebanese merchant and the high cost of living in Lebanon, which Menassa depicted as a corollary of the cost of bread, was also to Lebanon's detriment. The political economist emphasised that a high cost of living in Lebanon was an obstacle to the trade in 'services', particular to tourism. He concluded his presentation by underlining that, if she did not wish to go bankrupt in a few years, Lebanon could not accept such a state of affairs for long. Consequently, he invited the Syrian delegates to investigate the situation during their stay in Lebanon in order to base their own conclusions on real data.[37]

Referring to Gabriel Menassa's affirmation that Lebanon's balance of trade favoured Syria by 70 million liras, Raiyyes criticised the fact that, aside from citing Lebanese commerce in Syria, Menassa's paper only referred to Syrian exports to Lebanon, without mentioning Lebanese exports to Syria. Raiyyes expressed great scepticism in the accuracy of the figures, particularly in the absence of customs offices that could give an idea on the exports and imports between the two states. He stressed that Syria and Lebanon formed a monetary and an economic union and that this partnership was among one people of the same blood ties, religion and race.

> We can say to Mr. Menassa and to all those who are floating in imaginary numbers that between Damascus and Beirut are economic ties, and continuous movement of trade and agriculture, travel and tourism, a hundred times more than the case between Damascus and Hama. This fruitless argument should end, either we accept the current situation without any complaints or we establish census offices.[38]

Radical Lebanese nationalists who viewed the Société Libanaise d'Economie Politique as a particularly serious body, which enjoyed the esteem and general consideration of the Lebanese, joined Raiyyes in demanding the establishment of a census office at the HCCI. They asserted that without such an organ, each side would continue contesting the numbers presented by the Société or by other private institutions.[39]

It was clear that the lack of reliable data on Syro-Lebanese trade only served to increase speculations as to which side was abusing the other in the customs union. With no effective measures to mend this state of affairs, permanent mistrust was ensured. However, it is important to note that these speculations were not only confined to Syro-Lebanese relations but were also the source of doubt at the national level. A striking example was the publication of the revenues of the Common Interests during mid-January 1947. These revenues, estimated at 35 million liras for 1947, were discussed in the Syrian parliament, where most of the Syrian deputies judged the reported figure as unrealistic. Justifying their views, they compared the figure of 1947 with that of 1945, which was 48 million liras. It was seen to be odd that after 1945, during which Lebanon and Syria witnessed 'dramatic' increases in imports and a surge of customs revenues, the Common Interests performed so badly.[40]

By mid-February 1947, the efforts of the Syrian and Lebanese governments to reduce the high cost of living had failed. This was primarily attributed to the Syrian government's refusal to lower grain tariffs, despite popular demand. The general perception among economists and intellectuals was that the reduction of customs on combustibles and cement, without lowering the prices of grain, was futile.[41]

Amidst the Syrian and Lebanese governments' inability to stifle rising prices, as well as the raging discord between Syrian and Lebanese opinion-makers, Syrian President Shukri al-Quwwatly visited the Lebanese capital on 22 February 1947. Quwwatly's visit to Lebanon was welcomed by Syrians and Lebanese alike, regardless of their political affiliation – Arab nationalist, Syrian unionist or Lebanese nationalist. The historical ties binding the two states were strongly emphasised in all the commentaries. Speeches were exchanged between the Lebanese President and his Syrian guest, which reiterated their commitment to the democratic-republican systems of government and their political and economic solidarity within the framework of the charter of the League of Arab States.[42]

Lebanese nationalists stressed that, beyond the divergences, the mis-understandings and the polemics, there was an indestructible bond between Lebanon and Syria, which was their geographic bond. It was highlighted that independence did not mean isolation. Objection to the Greater Syria scheme and the need to maintain the status quo were said to fall within the interests of Lebanon and Syria as well as constituting an essential condition to the maintenance of Middle East stability. Quwwatly and his government were depicted as the first defenders of this common cause. A breach in the Arab League Charter, it was believed, would lead to disorder: 'Syrians and Lebanese meet on solid grounds: they are inevitably neighbours and all [geopolitics] dictates that they remain good friends.'[43]

The Syrian President's visit to Lebanon was regarded as an endorsement of Lebanese independence and a rejection of the Greater Syria scheme, which was being advocated by King 'Abdallah and his followers at that time. In spite of the fact that Quwwatly was approached by numerous Lebanese politicians and economists, complaining about Syria's restrictive policy concerning grain shipments to Lebanon, bilateral economic relations were left for the already well-institutionalised Shtura discussions between the concerned ministers. The Lebanese were particularly annoyed that while they were negotiating the purchase of grain from Iraq, the Syrian Ministry of Economy approved the export of 6000 tons of grain by auction. Moreover, the Syrian government was studying a Greek request for the purchase of *Mira* reserves of grain. Damascus was also considering selling part of its grain reserves to Italy, after a request made by the latter.[44] This decision was made despite assurances from Damascus that Syria would not sell its grain surplus before the needs of Lebanon were met.[45] But Syria's need for hard currency, a budget deficit reduction and import-export balance superseded brotherly relations.[46]

Aside from having to cope with Syrian intransigence, the Lebanese government faced numerous domestic challenges. Apart from imminent general elections, a number of politicians hoped to take advantage of Fawzi al-Qawuqji's return to Lebanon to further their popularity. Qawuqji, a leader of Palestine's Arab revolt in 1936, proceeded to Tripoli on 9 March, thus instigating clashes between the supporters of Karameh and their opponents. Sixteen people were killed and the Palestinian leader left Tripoli for a mountain village at the request of the government. The return of Qawuqji coincided with the return of Antun Sa'ada, leader of *al-Hizb al-Suri al-Qawmi* or the Syrian National Party. Although some members of his party warned Sa'ada to avoid provocative declarations upon his return, he ignored this advice. In one speech he spoke in uncompromising terms of his belief 'in natural Syria of which Lebanon was a part'. Sa'ada was summoned by the police but went into hiding. Confrontations ensued between the followers of the Syrian National Party and the radical Lebanese nationalist Phalange and the Lebanese internal situation deteriorated considerably. The deterioration was accentuated by dissensions within the cabinet, in which Kamal Jumblatt figured prominently. His advocacy of closer economic cooperation with Syria – proposing that the Syro-Lebanese union should be developed into full economic union – led to lively controversy. Jumblatt followed this up with sensational revelations to the press regarding 'the rottenness' of the Lebanese administration, which put him in serious difficulty with the President.[47]

Internal differences also faced Mardam Bey's cabinet, with two ministers – Hikmat al-Hakim and Adnan al-Atassi – threatening to resign over differences with the Prime Minister about the appointment of senior government officials. More importantly, since 18 February, Jabiri had been seriously ill. Jabiri retained the largest individual following among the National Bloc leadership. His absence from the political scene exacerbated a power struggle within the National Bloc that saw the movement split into groups whose following was based on individuals rather than any particular programme. With elections in mind, Mardam Bey was among the leading individuals to embark on the formation of a new party whose core would be members of the old National Bloc.[48]

C. SYRIAN TRADE ESCAPES TO LEBANON

In spite of the internal nuisances besetting both governments, the Syro-Lebanese Shtura summits continued. On Saturday 8 March 1947, the Syrian and Lebanese Prime Ministers, accompanied by their usual entourage, met in Shtura. The meeting ended without any decisions or measures being taken to treat the states' economic ills. The fact that the official communiqué only stated that the two governments had common views was interpreted by political and economic circles to mean that Damascus and Beirut were waiting for the Syrian–Lebanese Higher Economic Council's prescription for the countries' economic maladies.[49]

Speaking on behalf of the Syrian and Lebanese governments, the Syrian President and Prime Minister assured the members of the Higher Economic Council that all its recommendations would be realised. It was stressed that the two governments had decided to rely on those who had the expertise. The statements of Quwwatly and Mardam Bey were seen as the political umbrella needed for the eventual realisation of the Higher Economic Council's recommendations. Even in Beirut, Minister Kamal Jumblatt threatened to resign from government if the Lebanese cabinet did not adopt the recommendations. For the Syrian public, the Higher Economic Council was an opportunity and a test of the merit of Syrian and Lebanese men of economics – as opposed to the economic partnership represented by the Higher Council of the Common Interests, which was described as knowing nothing except erecting tariffs and making sterile laws that acted as an obstacle to the economic activities of the Syrians and the Lebanese.[50]

Between 7 and 10 March 1947, the Higher Economic Council convened its meetings in the Syrian capital. Four days of deliberations among Syrian and Lebanese economic, business and financial experts resulted in eight recommendations and decisions. Among these recommendations were the formation of a census directorate under the Common Interests and the unrestricted movement of agricultural goods between the two states.[51]

However, only a few days after the recommendations of the Higher Economic Council were published, the Syrian Minister of Economy issued decree number 58, which prohibited the movement of grain and flour outside Syria. Members of the Higher Economic Council protested, maintaining that there was no justification to ban the movement of grain to Lebanon since both states formed one economic entity. Nevertheless, the decree stood.[52]

The Syrian government's attempts to tighten its grip on the Syrian economy had repercussions on Syria as well as Lebanon. On the orders of the Syrian Minister of Finance, Sa'id Ghazzi, government officials or inspectors were instructed to control Syrian imports. Tight control over imports resulted in shortages of foreign goods in Syrian markets. Consequently, within the Syro-Lebanese customs union, trade in foreign goods became restricted to Lebanon. Ironically, the Syrian decision was invigorating Lebanese trade. Moreover, while the Syrian Minister of Economy was drawing up rationing laws and requiring permits from Syrian merchants, his Lebanese counterpart decided to cancel tariffs on imports.[53]

Syrian economic circles were very critical of their government's economic measures, which were regarded as rendering great service to the Lebanese merchants. Syrian merchants held that it had been more than two years since the war had ended and that Lebanon was among the first states that cancelled all restrictions, stimulated and facilitated trade and created competition among importers. In

Syria, however, merchants were not only complaining about import fees, which were still in place, but on the new government restrictions. The new regulations were seen as paralysing trade activity. Syrian merchants and economists were publicly asking what became of the Syro-Lebanese Higher Economic Council's recommendations – which both governments had undertaken to implement. Syrian policies were also regarded as undermining the economic union and the uniformity of the laws with Lebanon. They looked with envy at Beirut, which they described as being a city of free trade, while Damascus was, in their eyes, a small market, compared to the volume of trade in Beirut.[54]

Voices of protest were growing among Syrian merchants concerning the obstacles they were confronting in the various departments of the Ministry of Economy and in the Customs Directorates as well as the Hard Currency Bureau. Exporters and importers alike were subject to numerous difficulties, described by merchants as trade barriers. Reports indicated that the barriers faced by the Syrian merchant in Damascus were practically non-existent in Beirut. The Syrian merchant, it was reported, travelled to Beirut, where all required facilities were found. Goods were released from customs in less time and effort than in Damascus. The Syrian merchant was made welcome and his affairs facilitated. In Damascus, on the other hand, merchants complained of outdated laws and the 'silliest' regulations, in force since the war, which were unnecessarily complex. These regulations were put in place simultaneously in Lebanon and Syria, but the Lebanese authorities abolished them when they became considered obsolete. *Al-Qabass*, commenting on the plight of the merchants, wrote that

> those who are responsible for the economic departments in Lebanon are conscious of the interests of their country as well as the profits the Lebanese treasury earns from importers and exporters. Wars are made between states for markets, but in our directorates and departments we are combating any economic activity, and we put everything that is stagnant and ignorant in our heads, only to lose the export battle to the Lebanese.[55]

Reports appeared in the press detailing how Syrian business was suffering from delays originating in various government directorates. When Syrian merchants applied for export licences, it was only natural that they took great care to transport their goods with the least possible delay in order to minimise, if not prevent, depreciation in the value of their merchandise. The days Syrian merchants spent chasing after export licences encouraged Lebanese merchants to travel to Syria and purchase all these goods. As they did not require a licence, the Lebanese transported these goods from Syria to Lebanon with ease. In a few days, or hours, the Lebanese merchant exported these goods to Europe, the Americas, Palestine and Iraq while their Syrian counterparts were still waiting for their export licences. Consequently, the Syrian merchant encountered a sudden drop in the price of his merchandise or his clients simply changed their minds, having found a better offer.[56]

The situation was similar with Syrian importers, who preferred conducting their business in Beirut. In Lebanon, import licences were easily granted through the Lebanese Ministry of Economy and goods were effortlessly released from Lebanese customs. Lebanese merchants were thus able to sell their goods in the Lebanese markets, before the Syrian directorates had the opportunity to grant or reject import licences. Syrian merchants complained that in numerous instances they had imported merchandise from America and Europe, only to face the Syrian trade directorate's refusal to grant them import licences. These goods usually ended up in Lebanon. The Syrian food-canning industry was particularly hard hit by these practices. These factories purchased sugar at a high price while smuggled sugar was not only cheaper but also widely available. The same factories were also prohibited from buying necessary machinery, spare parts, wood and glass (jars) because the monetary bureau refused to supply them with the hard currency needed. Lebanese factories, on the other hand, were flooding the Syrian market with cheaper products. Lebanese merchants were also supplying the American and Australian canned food items that competed with similar Syrian-produced goods for the Syrian consumer.[57]

Another subject of growing criticism was the lack of Syrian government spending on development projects, particularly the improvement of such infrastructure as the airport and railways. Damascus – with its empty hotels, narrow-gauge railways and empty airport – was compared to the capital of a province and not that of a country. It was maintained that as long as Damascus was isolated by sea and air, the provincial capital of Aleppo was far better off economically. Beirut was a source of great envy, where passengers arriving from Europe to Iraq, Iran and India disembarked if they were travelling by air or sea. Nothing connected Beirut with Damascus except an old railway suitable for the transport of coal and stone. After spending some time in Beirut, travellers preferred to continue to their final destinations. The advantage of independence was questioned in the absence of any government attempts to improve Syria's economic standards; politicians and economists were blamed for the deteriorating situation of the Syrian capital. Government officials were asked for the reasons behind Lebanon's advancement in the absence of the French Mandate. Moreover, the Syrian government's 30-million-lira expenditure on a telephone network and radio network was widely criticised. Instead of facilitating 'chatter' and the hearing of songs, the funds should have been devoted to connecting the capital by rail or air to Beirut or establishing a seaport on Syrian territory so that Syrian independence would be complete.[58]

Further complicating matters for the Syrian business and industrial community was a shortage of hard currency. Again their eyes shifted with envy to Lebanon, where a limited supply of hard currency, especially the American dollar, was available. This was attributed to the Lebanese government's efforts to encourage exports of olive oil, beans and wool to the United States in return for dollars.[59] On the other hand, Syrian newspapers angrily reported Syrian authorities' export restrictions and confiscation of dollars from the market.

We have cursed this nation with a type of economic ministers and civil servants, who put barriers before any opportunity that comes along. If an expatriate visits his native land carrying a few dollars in his pocket, we order the customs department to confiscate those dollars. Lebanon, on the other hand – despite the hard currency bureau and its regulations – allows its expatriates to enter with all the dollars in their pockets. The Lebanese interior minister himself supervised the visit of expatriates to Lebanon and permitted them to take with them what they carried by way of funds – in other words he allowed them to sell their dollars on the black market.[60]

At that time France, which still controlled *Banque de Syrie et du Liban* (BSL), was reluctant to provide Lebanon and Syria with the needed dollars. French authorities were very critical of Lebanon and Syria wasting dollars on non-essential imports and contended that the French situation was too difficult to spare dollars except for the actual needs of Lebanon and Syria.[61]

Syrian officials at the Ministry of Economy were openly criticised for banning the export of olive oil, despite the existence of a 5000-ton surplus. These measures came in agreement with the Lebanese government. However, Lebanese merchants were heading to Syria and purchasing all the olive oil, which they exported from Lebanon to the US. The Syrian press reported with annoyance that in Lebanon Lebanese merchants were not informed that the export of olive oil was forbidden. Ironically, the Lebanese civil servants' innovation (in finding means to facilitate exports) was praised in the Syrian press. For instance, Lebanese authorities allowed the export of olive oil, with the understanding that the merchants imported vegetable oil. In the United States, the Lebanese merchants received payment in US dollars and was also able to import goods other than vegetable oil. The Lebanese merchants also took the opportunity to sell the badly needed vegetable oil on the Syrian market, thereby increasing their profits.[62] Similarly, Lebanese business circles related how Lebanese cement, although in painfully short supply, was being exported in large quantities to Turkey and Iraq. The sterling and dollars obtained from these transactions went to Lebanese private individuals.[63] Hence, to a degree, the badly needed dollar was available in Beirut while becoming scarce in Damascus.

While Syrian merchants were leaving to purchase foreign imports in Lebanon, Syria's unwillingness to lift trade restrictions with Lebanon on certain agricultural goods encouraged smuggling. This, in turn, contributed to higher prices in Syria. There were Syrian goods that were prohibited from entering Lebanon but, having been smuggled into Lebanon, lowered prices there. Between the years 1944 and 1946, for instance, Lebanon's only source of sugar was that smuggled from Syria. Something similar was true of large quantities of Syrian flour and semolina. In addition, it was estimated that 50,000 tons of Syrian grain were smuggled to Lebanon. This illegitimate but established situation ensured that ample supplies of these goods were available on the Lebanese market. When approached by Syrian officials, Lebanese government representatives openly declared that Syria's tightening of restrictions would not end smuggling but end in the termination of trade restrictions that affected the freedom of movement. They also argued that it would only be then that the prices would be similar in both states and as such put smugglers out of business.[64]

Aside from the tensions between the Lebanese and Syrian governments over economic policy and the manner in which to combat high prices, a new source of friction between Beirut and Damascus was emerging – the pipeline of the Trans-Arabian Oil Company. Towards the end of 1946, the Arab-American Oil Company (Aramco) had begun consultations with various Arab governments, including the Lebanese and Syrian leadership, to construct the Trans-Arabian Pipeline (TAPLINE) that would stretch over 1000 miles from the Persian Gulf to the Mediterranean.[65] It was clear for the Syrian and the Lebanese leadership that the country that had the outlet of the pipeline on its coast would benefit more than the state forced to settle for transit fees in return for allowing the pipeline through its territory. Thus began the race between Lebanon and Syria to secure the TAPLINE's terminal.

4 *Oil and Grain*

I n the spring of 1946, Aramco representative William Lenahan informed the US legation in Beirut that he would come to the Lebanese and Syrian capitals to negotiate transit rights for a pipeline and a refinery concession. Prime Minister Jabiri was non-committal to American advances; he was at the time disturbed by the US attitude towards Palestine and indicated merely that he would receive Lenahan. The Lebanese government, on the contrary, was eager to do business and upon discovering that Lenahan was in Amman negotiating with King 'Abdallah, invited him to come to Beirut and lay down his terms.[1]

Lenahan submitted his proposals to the Lebanese and Syrian governments in July 1946. The Syrians were not that enthusiastic and intimated that it would be impossible to do business until after Ramadan. Lenahan thereupon concentrated on the Lebanese. After the bombing of the American embassy in Beirut, the US ambassador induced the Lebanese cabinet to sign the Pipeline Convention. A few months passed while Lenahan remained in Beirut, awaiting a response from Damascus. None was forthcoming until the US embassy arranged a meeting between the Aramco representative and Syrian officials. The Syrian terms proved unacceptable to Lenahan, who was recalled to the US at the end of November 1946. Aramco decided to give the Syrians the 'silent treatment', hoping that they would come around with more favourable terms. By the end of December, Damascus reconsidered and sent positive signals to Aramco. Earlier, in August, the Lebanese chamber had ratified the TAPLINE agreement.[2]

At that time the Syrian leadership was particularly irritated with the British, who were increasingly interfering in Syrian internal affairs. Moreover, Damascus felt the British were using the Greater Syria plan to threaten Syria. Syrian Minister of Defence Ahmad Sharabati told an American diplomat that President Quwwatly wished to counterbalance British influence by granting the TAPLINE concession to Aramco. Quwwatly also related this information to his Lebanese counterpart. All indications pointed to the fact that the Syrians were susceptible to an agreement. Consequently, Lenahan returned from the United States in early February 1947, accompanied by a large Aramco delegation including company president Bert Hull. However, the Syrians proved very difficult, to the extent that Lenahan told US embassy officials that the Syrians could 'go to hell'.[3]

The difficulties Aramco faced spilled over into Lebanese internal politics, in turn straining relations with Syria. Deputies Alfred Naccache, Youssef Salem and Adib Firzli first raised the matter during the Lebanese parliamentary session of 13 March 1947. They criticised Damascus' position of not allowing the pipeline to pass through Syrian territory unless the pipeline terminal was built on the Syrian coast. Naccache emphasised that the Lebanese Treasury would be deprived of potentially large revenues (estimated to be 10 million liras annually) because of its economic union with Syria. Salem insisted that the Syrian government did not offer Aramco the facilities necessary to facilitate the connection of the pipeline to Lebanon. Minister of Finance 'Abdallah al-Yafi responded that the Syrians were free to make their own demands of Aramco, just as the Lebanese government was free to make its demands. Yafi stressed that, regardless of Syrian or Lebanese demands of the American company, an agreement had to be reached between Damascus and Beirut first. Significantly, Lebanese leaders, representing all political and commercial groups, took it upon themselves to prevail upon the Syrians to accept Aramco's proposals, but to no avail. The American legation in Beirut was flooded with inquiries and expressions of frustration at the 'intransigence of the greedy Syrians'.[4]

These debates were followed in Damascus with great annoyance. The criticisms of the Lebanese parliamentarians were regarded as interference in Syrian internal affairs. Among the Syrian ruling elite there was wide objection to the fact that members of the Lebanese parliament were questioning an action of the Syrian government – particularly since the pipeline and its terminus, which was to be on the Lebanese coast, would pass mostly through Syrian territory. There was great dismay with Lebanese insensitivity to Syrian interests. In response to Lebanese allegations that the Syrian government was undermining Lebanese interests, Syria's Minister of Public Works openly declared that the previous and current Lebanese government refused to reveal any information on its negotiations with the company. 'They should allow us to say to the members of the [Lebanese] cabinet, parliament and press that the country that owns the land through which the pipelines passes, retains the sole right to work for its interests within its borders.'[5]

In Lebanon, the TAPLINE debate was not restricted to the Lebanese parliament. Radical Lebanese nationalists were convinced that Syrian stubbornness was going to force Aramco to seek an alternative route. It was a well-known fact that Aramco was threatening both governments that it would lay its pipeline through Palestine and Jordan, even if this meant incurring an extra cost of £9 million.[6]

Ever vigilant, the Maronite Patriarch adopted the cause of the radical Lebanese nationalists. He sent a memorandum to the Lebanese President urging him to intervene with the Syrian leadership, and even wrote to the American consul in Beirut, pressing him to intercede with Washington. In an interview widely circulated in the Lebanese and Syrian press, the patriarch declared that Quwwatly gave Aramco a free hand in Syria on the condition that the pipeline and its outlet would not be on Lebanese soil.[7] He emphasised that the Syrian President's position came in spite of the fact that technical studies conducted by American engineers found that the terminal could not but be on the Lebanese coast. The patriarch concluded his interview by pointing out that Quwwatly's position was contrary to the brotherly relations between the two states, as expressed in the warm welcome the Syrian president received in Lebanon. The Syrian press, in turn, questioned the source of the patriarch's information, maintaining that 'Syria does not accept that its President is subject to speculation, not by the press nor by any religious authority (*maqam*). If the Maronite Patriarch has got used to attacking Lebanese governments, to interfere in their affairs, to override the legislative and the executive branches of government, he has no right to do the same in Syria, neither directly nor by allusion.'[8]

Damascus blamed Beirut mainly for putting it in an embarrassing position, arguing that the issue of the Saudi pipeline was either a Syrian or a Lebanese affair or it was part of the Common Interests. But since the former Lebanese cabinet had conducted an agreement with the American company without consulting the Syrian government, the matter was prevented from falling under Common Interests. It was in fact the government of Sa'di al-Munla who concluded the agreement with Aramco. This in spite of efforts on the part of the Syrian government to prevent the signature of any agreement before it had come to terms with the company.

Although Damascus considered any agreement between Aramco and the Lebanese government meaningless – without Syrian consent that the pipeline pass through its territory – it regarded the unilateral agreement between the Lebanese government and the American company as an attempt to present Damascus with a fait accompli. Moreover, the Syrians were adamant in wanting to prevent a repetition of their experience with the Iraq Petroleum Company (IPC), which, in Syrian eyes, had won favourable concessions from Arab governments to lay pipelines from Kirkuk (in Iraq) to the Mediterranean. The terminus of the IPC pipeline was in the northern Lebanese city of Tripoli. During the construction of the IPC pipeline, the Syrians had vainly attempted to ensure that the pipeline had an outlet on the Syrian coast. To add insult to injury, the Syrians were charged with guarding a 1500-kilometre-long pipeline for a fee that – in their eyes – was insufficient to rent 'a storehouse in Beirut' or 'a medium size farm in Syria'.

Previously, the French government had forced Syria to agree on conditions that made the Iraqi oil pass through our land to Tripoli for the sole benefit of Tripoli.

We did not gain anything by relinquishing 1500 kilometres of our land for a very low [transit fee] … Thus we turned into desert guardians. We alone in Syria own our land, we own the longest coast on the Mediterranean and enjoy the best of geographical advantages.[9]

Hence, where the Syrians were concerned, the priority in negotiating with Aramco was to ensure that the TAPLINE must have a terminal on its shores. The pipeline was expected to run 600 kilometres through Syrian territory. In return, Aramco had offered 1.3 piastres for every ton of oil that passed through Syria. In exchange, Syria was expected to be responsible for the security and safety of the pipeline. Damascus found this offer unacceptable, particularly since the outlet was to be on the Lebanese coast, where, in Syrian eyes, such American investment as buildings, installations and employment opportunities would be concentrated. It seemed the Lebanese were to be the sole beneficiaries from the TAPLINE project.[10]

The Syrians remained adamant in their demands: 'If the oil company wishes that its black gold reaches the Mediterranean, it has only to conclude an agreement with Syria in which the pipeline passes through Syrian territory with its terminus either on its coast, or in which half the oil goes through Lebanon and the other half through Syria, with each state retaining a terminus.'[11] American experts found that financial and technical difficulties prevented them from diverting the pipeline to a Syrian port. Moreover, the Syrian demand would require an extra $50 million, which Aramco was not willing to pay. The American company's representatives considered it best that the entire issue be regarded as a Syro-Lebanese affair, which should be settled between the two concerned states.[12]

On the other hand, Syrian Minister of Finance Sa'id Ghazzi stated publicly that, since Aramco was not sensitive to Syrian circumstances, the government had discontinued negotiations. He indicated that negotiations would resume after Aramco met Syrian demands.[13] Syrian intransigence took American negotiators completely by surprise.

In these negotiations it became apparent that the Syrians jealously hate the Lebanese far more than we had imagined and that they were determined that the Lebanese should not derive any benefit greater than they might receive. Also apparent was the stupid and baseless pride and infatuation with their own achievements in acquiring an independence not yet enjoyed by Egypt or by Iraq which has made the Syrians so difficult of late to deal with.[14]

In a last attempt, Lenahan attempted another round of talks with the Syrians, who remained insistent that the terminal be shared equally with Lebanon. Lenahan telephoned this last compromise to Hull, who rejected it. Thereupon Lenahan made his final farewell. Sharabati's last words were: 'I tell you to remember this, Damascus is the capital of the Arab world.'[15]

Towards the end of March 1947, the Arab League convened a meeting of Arab heads of state in Cairo. The meeting provided an opportunity for the Lebanese and Syrian Prime Ministers to discuss the TAPLINE affair. Premier Solh went to great pains to brief his Syrian counterpart on the Lebanese government's negotiations and agreement with Aramco, thereby hoping to mend fences.

Conveniently, the Lebanese and Syrian governments agreed that the Munla government was to blame for conducting the agreement with Aramco without consulting Damascus. Still, there were questions looming in the Syrian capital, particularly with regard to Syria's transit fee of 1.3 piastres for every ton of oil that passed through its territory, while Lebanon was promised 7 piastres. Another matter of contention was the 80 million liras of customs fees on machinery and equipment that Aramco needed to enter Syria. The American company demanded to be exempted from these fees.

Lebanese officials, who found themselves mediating between Aramco and the Syrian government, held that the TAPLINE issue was a Syro-Lebanese financial and economic matter. Official circles in Beirut suggested that these matters best be regarded within the framework of the Common Interests institutions. In this regard, it was proposed that Syria's fee of 1.3 piastres and Lebanon's fee of 7 piastres should be added and equally divided between the two states. Alternatively, it was also suggested to divide the revenues according to the percentage of shares in the Common Interests of each state.[16] Syrian opinion-makers were favourably disposed towards Beirut's suggestions. They held that the economic union between the two states compelled the Syrians to insist that this issue become part of the Common Interests. They advocated that if the Lebanese government refused to consider the matter as part of the Common Interests, the current economic union or the common interest would be jeopardised. 'Syria has endured a lot of losses, for political and non-political considerations, in order that the interests of the two states are one. However, if they wish to separate, the time has come for Syria to say, we trust in God and let us separate.'[17]

It was unthinkable for the radical Lebanese nationalists to turn over the TAPLINE to the Higher Council of the Common Interests, 'because it would be absurd in spite of the solidarity and fraternity [existing between the two states], to hand over to Syria a gift of 56 per cent of revenues that are rightfully ours'.[18] The radical Lebanese nationalists firmly believed that, 'until separation becomes possible, the interests that remain in common between the two states are those which the French mandate had created and which are at the present time impossible to separate. What is the point, then, of subjecting new interests, which are separate in their nature, to the old partnership?'[19]

By mid-April 1947, Lebanese public opinion shifted to the government's arrangements to secure the country's supplies of grain for the coming year. It is noteworthy that these concerns were reflected in all the Lebanese press, regardless of political affiliation. Moreover, by that time, the subject as well as the timing – grain and the spring season – had become a standard feature of Syro-Lebanese relations. Clearly disappointed that, for three years running, the grain issue had strained Syro-Lebanese relations, Michel Chiha pointed out that Damascus should treat Lebanon differently, in order to keep her as the largest consumer of Syrian vegetables and agricultural products. 'So there is for Lebanon the matter of Syrian grain or the end of a pipeline. We have the right to see friendly and reassuring behaviour from the Syrians because, no matter what, together we will be weakened or strengthened, enriched or impoverished.'[20]

While the Syrians were contemplating how to sell their coming harvest, Lebanese opinion-makers demanded that the government start negotiations early with Damascus, in order to avoid having a price forced on Lebanon. However, inquiries made by the Lebanese government on the matter were met with vagueness by Damascus. Syrian officials claimed that the future of the harvest was unknown and that, consequently, the Syrian government was unable to make any commitments.[21]

On 10 April 1947, a Syro-Lebanese summit took place in Shtura, headed by Presidents Quwwatly and Khuri. Premiers Jamil Mardam Bey and Riad el-Solh and numerous ministers also took part in the talks. In spite of the high-level attendance of the summit, a vague communiqué was released three hours after the meeting. It mentioned that numerous issues were addressed and that agreement was total. The communiqué only served to add fire to an already heated debate between Syrian and Lebanese opinion-makers.[22] Lebanese nationalists were convinced that, with regard to issues of grain and the TAPLINE, Damascus was pursuing a strictly unilateral Syrian policy. Consequently it was up to Beirut to follow a purely Lebanese policy.[23]

Even Lebanese Arab nationalist circles, generally sentimentally predisposed towards Syria, found themselves voicing their reservations against Damascus. They held that the Syrian position regarding grain was vague and not forthcoming, causing delay in solving this vital issue. While they described the Lebanese predicament as that of a man worried for his daily bread and wanting to secure his needs for the coming year. In Shtura the Syrians argued that they could not enter into any negotiations concerning grain because, should heavy rains not fall, the harvest would be compromised. Consequently, the Syrian delegation argued that it could determine neither the amount nor the price of grain they would be able to offer Lebanon. Lebanese officials, not seeing any justification for their counterparts' non-committal position, responded that they could not postpone the finalisation of such a vital issue and insisted that the amount of grain Syria could supply be determined immediately. Lebanese negotiators pointed out that in the worst seasons, according to statistics, the Syrian harvest produced 400,000 tons of grain – sufficient for both states.[24] The Lebanese added that the international price for grain ranged between 12 and 14 piastres per kilo. Thus Syria should sell Lebanon its grain at that rate. Lebanon supported its point of view with international grain maps, which set Syria and Lebanon in one region, indicating that both states were self-sufficient with their own harvests without importing from abroad. The Syrians expressed their readiness to supply Lebanon at the international market rate (12 or 14 piastres per kilo), but on the condition that the payment would be in Ottoman gold lira (one Ottoman gold lira was the equivalent of 13 liras).[25]

In an interview, Jamil Mardam Bey stated that there were ample quantities of grain in Syria but that these quantities would only be sufficient to feed the Syrian people if not a single ton of grain was exported. The Syrian Prime Minister added that if rain were to fall, the Syrian government would be likely to change its position. Commenting on Mardam Bey's statement, the Lebanese Arab nationalist daily al-Nahar wrote, 'We do not know if the Syrian harvest was poor, but we do know that Syria had objected to the prices offered by Lebanon and that the Syrians were adamant to retain the old prices. This makes us doubt the authenticity of the Syrian claim that the harvest was bad.'[26] Even a British consular report described Syrian fears of a bad harvest as exaggerated.[27]

Lebanese Arab nationalists explained Damascus' intransigence as being due to upcoming parliamentary elections. They maintained that a large number of the Syrian electorate was made up of farmers and even future parliamentarians. Should the current government agree to a low price of grain, Syrian farmers would undoubtedly express their dissatisfaction during the upcoming elections. '[Hence],…there is no need to rush. Better wait for the elections to be concluded.'[28] However, Lebanese nationalists refused to take Syrian qualms on the harvest seriously. Michel Chiha reiterated that Syria could expect abundant grain supplies, even during its weakest of harvests.[29] In his eyes, the Lebanese authorities were being subjected to negative harvest predictions in order to push Beirut to pay for Syrian grain at its old high price, an act that would bring the Syrian government the sympathy and support of the large grain producers and landowners of Houran, Aleppo and Jazira on the eve of the Syrian elections. Chiha indicated that the Lebanese negotiators were being subject to a war of nerves the premises of which were clearly visible when the Syrian authorities recently decided to overvalue the price of grain for the Syrian consumer by one and a half piastres a kilo. In his view, this measure by Damascus, as symbolic as it may be, was to pre-empt any Lebanese demand for a grain price reduction.[30]

Also discussed at the Shtura summit of 10 April was the TAPLINE issue. The Syrians reduced their original demand – that the pipeline emerge at the port of Latakiya – to having the pipeline emerge somewhere on the Syro-Lebanese border, near the outlet of Naher al-Kabir, in the vicinity of Tripoli and the Alawite area. Beirut objected to this proposal, maintaining that there were ample ports in Lebanon, which were ready and equipped. The Lebanese found it illogical to construct new ports and to bring up new cities there. Discussion broke down at this point. By that time, Syrian government officials approached the Saudi King to intercede with Aramco in order to ensure that the TAPLINE emerge on the Syro-Lebanese border.[31]

Despite the fact that the beginning of April witnessed the start of parliamentary electoral campaigns in Lebanon, between 16 April and 14 May 1947 alone, there were five prime ministerial summits in Beirut, Shtura and Damascus. No concrete measures or agreement emerged concerning grain or the TAPLINE. During these meetings, the Lebanese finally agreed to the Syrian proposal that the pipeline emerge at a point on the Syro-Lebanese border. However, this compromise had to be abandoned for technical reasons put forward by American engineers. After additional deliberations, the Syrians were persuaded that the TAPLINE emerge on the Lebanese coast. The question of Syrian fees remained. As there was progress on the Syro-Lebanese TAPLINE negotiations, Damascus suddenly decided to deliver 15,000 tons of grain to Lebanon.[32] It should be noted that it took excruciating negotiations – lasting throughout May and most of June – to decide on the price, which was set at 47 piastres per kilo. As shall be seen, the manner of payment as well as the subsequent grain supplies remained subject to controversy until the end of the year.[33]

Only three days after his last meeting with Riad el-Solh in Shtura on 14 May 1947, Prime Minister Mardam Bey sent a bill to the Syrian parliament in which his government formally requested that the *Mira*'s grain monopoly be prolonged until June 1948. Parliament convened on 20 May. The majority of deputies criticised the corruption of the *Mira*'s civil servants and inquired as to the government's intentions regarding the *Mira*'s profits. Minister of Economy Hikmat al-Hakim responded that all the *Mira*'s corrupt officials were being prosecuted. He estimated the *Mira*'s profits at 6 million liras, most of which was being funnelled into agricultural development. It was decided to extend the *Mira*'s mandate until 25 June 1948 and to annex it to the Ministry of Finance. It was noteworthy that Quwwatly had sent for Hakim to explain the latter's signature authorising forbidden shipments of grain to Palestine. Hakim's position as a large landowner and grain producer gave him a vested interest in *Mira* operations. This was one reason why the *Mira* was transferred to the Ministry of Finance. The *Mira* was delegated to purchase 80 per cent of the 1947 harvest. The trade and transportation of grain shipments exceeding 100 kg was subject to *Mira* licensing. The extension of the *Mira* was not well received by Syrian grain merchants, who sent a delegation to President Quwwatly expressing their surprise and regret. They informed the Syrian President that the *Mira* would continue to limit their income as well as their ability to export grain for hard currency.[34]

For a brief period, Lebanese and Syrian attention shifted from grain to the Lebanese parliamentary elections that took place on 25 May 1947. Damascus was following the elections very closely, to the extent that the Syrian Prime Minister kept calling Beirut every hour to be informed of the latest developments. Mardam Bey was also among the first to comment on the election results – the defeat of Emile Eddé's coalition. He described the poll as a hard lesson for the 'pro-colonialists' and a triumph for the 'nationalist conscience'. He added that the election results were further proof that Lebanon was not fertile ground for colonialism regardless of how much money colonial powers spent and whatever means they were utilising. The Syrian Premier indicated that colonial funds were unable to influence the mature conscience of Lebanese public opinion.[35]

Indeed, the radical Lebanese nationalist defeat, coupled with fraud allegations in the electoral district of Mount Lebanon, led to the resignation of a number of ministers and the outbreak of demonstrations and strikes.[36] At the house of Alfred Naccache, a meeting of unsuccessful Beiruti candidates demanded that the elections be repeated and cabled the Syrian Prime Minister, protesting his statements. Radical Lebanese nationalist indignation was further expressed through Maronite Patriarch Moubarak, who issued a strongly worded memorandum to Lebanese President Khuri:

> The Maronite Patriarch is today in a state of despair, for under your presidency he did not see justice, security and happiness for the Lebanese people. He saw only anarchy, the corruption of your ministers and members of parliament and injustice in the courts… We urge you to resign from the presidency because you failed in bringing security and justice to Lebanon. You were unable to guard Lebanon's freedom and honour, especially the freedom of the elections.[37]

On 30 May 1947, demonstrations took place in support of President Khuri and against the patriarch's letter. In Syria, opinion-makers reacted angrily to the radical Lebanese nationalist answer to their and Mardam's statements on the elections. The Syrians rejected allegations that they were interfering in Lebanon's internal affairs and highlighted the Judiciary Committee's findings that there was no fraud in Mount Lebanon. They wondered if the Lebanese nationalists' reactions would have been different had the election results favoured those candidates representing French *raj'iyah* – those set against an independent Lebanese regime, Lebanese Arabism and the charter of the League of Arab States. Syrian opinion-makers warned that if the elections had favoured Eddé, the Phalangists or the Jesuits, it would have been within Syria's prerogative to change its relations with Lebanon. It was emphasised that, should Lebanon witness a change in policy that removed Lebanon 'a hair's width' from its current principles and fraternity with the Arab nations, Syrian security would be threatened.[38]

> The [radical Lebanese nationalists] do their utmost to separate Lebanon from its Arab nationhood. They advocate that Lebanon seclude itself within its Phoenician-Christian identity – facing the sea, looking west towards France. They do not wish us to be happy about the victory of the Constitutionalists in Mount Lebanon. It is our duty to welcome the success of patriotic Arab candidates, because their victory, as our prime minister and we have said, is a victory of the common policy between us and Lebanon and the annihilation of the foreigner and his agents.[39]

By the time President Khuri called upon Solh to form a new cabinet,[40] the Syrian parliamentary elections were well under way.[41] Lebanese political circles followed the Syrian elections closely. They observed how most of the National Bloc's old guard, such as Jamil Mardam Bey, Sa'id Ghazzi and Faris al-Khuri, defeated the Syrian National Party and retained the majority in parliament. At the time, Syrian elections were occurring amidst rumours – propagated by King 'Abdallah and his followers – that internal and external forces were at work to achieve a Greater Syria. Consequently, the Lebanese, and the nationalists in particular, were content with the victory of Jamil Mardam Bey: 'For our part we are convinced that the wisdom of President Quwwatly and the competence of Jamil Mardam Bey will nail closed all the traps and false rumours… It is the duty of our government to carefully follow [the events in Syria] and to take every opportunity to firmly remind the [Syrian leadership] of the pact of the League of Arab states.'[42] In his usual eloquent manner, Michel Chiha reflected on the Syrian elections through the eyes of the Lebanese nationalists.

> Jamil Maram Bey saw in the elections a plebiscite for Syria as it is and the decisive lesson that the noble pretext of enlarging Syria presages its enslavement.
>
> There is, by the way, no Syrian who has not understood that a Greater Syria under the King of Trans-Jordan can only mean the end of independence, suppression, the beginning of political dissemblance, the withdrawal of a reasonable democracy and the destruction of equilibrium. The orientation that has just been given to Syrian policy by President Shukri al-Quwwatly and his government is full of promise and it can, with the imagination of the governmental team, provide results that would be most favourable.[43]

It is noteworthy that most government leaders in Lebanon were convinced that the elections in Syria would be dominated by fraud and the devious manipulation of ballot boxes to ensure the re-election of deputies from the previous chamber. In general, all observers had unqualified praise for the manner in which the elections were conducted and even hailed the Syrian example as the first free expression of public will in any Middle Eastern country. There was even universal displeasure at Lebanon's own unsavoury elections. The fact that opposition candidates could be elected in Syria was further proof of the need for electoral reform in Lebanon. However, if measured in terms of political evolution and progress, the Syrian election results were regarded in Lebanon as a definite regression. The prevailing opinion in nearly all circles was that the Syrian public had displayed a lack of maturity, and had revealed a tendency to revert to the age-old interdictions and taboos of Islam. According to Christian protagonists, the propaganda of the *ulama* and the Muslim Brotherhood was all too effective during the election campaign. In Lebanon it was felt that Syria had reverted to the traditional Islamic conception of a state based upon religious precepts and fanaticism.[44]

It should be remembered that before the Syrian elections, the Syrian Prime Minister had in principle agreed to sign an agreement with Aramco. However, Mardam Bey then decided to postpone the signing until after the Syrian elections, which not only irritated Aramco but was the cause of great concern in Beirut. Lebanese fears were justified. Lenahan had patiently sat out the Syrian elections and after their conclusion came to Damascus on 29 July to sign the pipeline agreement. Assured that the Syrian government was favourably predisposed, Lenahan learned that Sharabati had re-opened the question in cabinet and that until the breach between Sharabati and Mardam Bey was healed, negotiations would have to continue. Lenahan returned to Beirut to wait for the Syrian ministers to make up their minds.[45] To make matters worse for Aramco, during the early days of August, Damascus put forward new conditions. Syria's delays greatly annoyed Beirut.

The Syrians demanded that they receive the same conditions that King 'Abdel al-'Aziz Ibn Saud received when he granted the American company the right to invest in Saudi oil. The Syrian government demanded to receive 400,000 tons of oil at low rates similar to the Saudis. The Syrian government also demanded that – like the American–Saudi agreement – its revenues be paid in gold dollars. Aramco argued that there was a certain difference between Saudi and the Syrian concessions. It categorised the former as an investment concession while the latter as a transit concession.[46]

Some of the new Syrian demands were also directed towards Lebanon. Among these were that the executive director of the TAPLINE in Syria and Lebanon be a Syrian national, that the number of Syrian and Lebanese consultants, employees and labourers should be equal and that the profits should be divided equally between the two states. Aramco refused the Syrian demands and insisted that the executive director be an American national. Concerning the recruitment of Syrian and Lebanese staff, Aramco representatives insisted that their selection be based on merit and qualifications.[47] Among the other points of difference with Aramco, aside from the quantities of crude oil and transit fees, was the oil company's insistence that Syrian security officials should not have access to the desert pumping stations.[48]

Aramco agreed to grant Syria its needs in Saudi oil at the price of delivery (which it sold to Syrian and Lebanese oil companies). Aramco also conceded to pay a portion of the revenues (transit fees) in gold dollars. But the company pressed the Syrian government to hasten the ratification of the agreement, in order that it could commence work immediately. American engineers were already in Lebanon and Syria, and equipment and machinery were on their way from the United States. The Syrian government replied that it was unable to grant its final approval before October (1947) since it had to wait for the newly elected parliament to convene and for the formation of a new government. Syria's incumbent government claimed that it did not have the legal status to finalise the matter. The new government would submit the agreement to the newly elected body for ratification. Aramco therefore had to wait until autumn.

At this juncture tension rose between Damascus and Aramco. The company sent a memorandum to the Syrian government indicating that it would be impossible to wait and that its work should commence immediately. Aramco also ceased to hire workers in Beirut. Large posters were placed at the doors of its offices, explaining why hiring had ceased. Lebanese public opinion, regardless of political orientation, was outraged. Significantly, Lebanese Arab nationalist opinion-makers voiced strong criticism of Damascus. Lebanese deputies arose, a number of whom even threatened to withdraw their vote of confidence from the Solh government if this matter was not resolved.[49] Obviously, Lebanese deputies were eager to win political capital by ensuring that a certain number of their constituents would find employment with the TAPLINE.

Aramco's representative again began to lose patience with the Syrians. Lenahan referred to the already ratified agreement with the government of Palestine according to which the pipeline would emerge from the port of Gaza. He hired a well-known Palestinian lawyer, Henry Qatan, to begin investigating the prospects of laying the TAPLINE through British Mandate Palestine. Then, during negotiations between Aramco and the Lebanese and Syrians in Soufar, a British official unexpectedly appeared. The Lebanese got anxious, in spite of assurances from Saudi Arabia that King Saud insisted that the TAPLINE terminus would not be in Palestine. The Syrians claimed that they were working for Syrian and Lebanese interests. Complicating matters further for the Americans was a Lebanese notification that any concessions gained by the Syrians should also be reflected in their agreement with the oil company.[50] There were also reports in Beirut that, due to the Common Interests agreement, the Syrian government was demanding 56 per cent of the customs rights over the equipment that the TAPLINE would introduce in Lebanon. However, the Lebanese government had agreed with Aramco that its equipment and machinery would be free of customs. Under such circumstances, Lebanon was obliged to compensate Syria. The funds would be deducted from the revenues of the TAPLINE to the Lebanese Treasury.[51]

As political and economic circles in Beirut feared for the fate of the TAPLINE project, Premier Solh came under strong pressure from Lebanese public opinion: 'Solh should not forget that before worrying about the Syrians and safeguarding Syro-Lebanese fraternity and solidarity, he has the duty to defend the political and economic interests of Lebanon... Today the Lebanese government has the obligation to ensure by all means – and all means are good – that the petroleum of Saudi Arabia does not emerge anywhere but Lebanon.'[52]

Chiha attributed the sudden Syrian volte-face vis-à-vis the TAPLINE to the political leadership. He wondered if the indecisiveness of the Syrian political elite was due to internal politics, in particular divergences among the parties that came to power in the new elections. He asserted that political instability did not permit

Syria to make firm commitments in matters of policy or in international accords. According to Chiha, another reason behind the Syrian volte-face could be a well-studied manoeuvre by Damascus, 'a war of nerves and a [light attempt of merchandising]' to gain additional concessions. But

> even if the accord is concluded immediately, [the affair] risks introducing into Syro-Lebanese relations a factor of rigidity and discord that has been camouflaged or at least attenuated up to this day. It would be sad, even imprudent – so soon after the first parliamentary elections, just after their mutual and simultaneous ascension to independence – for their governments to show such flagrant inability to be in agreement on issues as vital as those with which they find themselves confronted today.[53]

Throughout July and August, Solh was shuttling between the different parties in order to align Syrian demands with Aramco's interests. In a particularly heated meeting in Damascus, between Syrian officials and Aramco's senior management, the Americans were ready to abandon the whole project. The Syrian government sent Foreign Minister Mohsen Barazi to Saudi Arabia to persuade the Saudi King to intercede with Aramco. At the King's court, Barazi ran into a high-ranking Aramco delegation, which had already met with Ibn Saud. The Syrian Foreign Minister learned that Aramco had informed the Saudi King that unless Damascus agreed to the American oil company's proposal by 30 August, it would alter the route of the pipelines.[54] Prime Minister Solh intervened. So extensive was Solh's involvement in the negotiations between Aramco and Syria that he requested of his Syrian counterpart that their negotiations with the oil company take place in the Lebanese mountain resort town of Soufar instead of Damascus – so that the Lebanese Premier would be able to follow developments closely. By the end of August, Solh's efforts bore fruit. The Syrians and Aramco signed an agreement. The following month, the Lebanese agreement with Aramco was amended in light of the concessions gained by Syria.[55]

In spite of the conclusion of the Aramco agreement, there was irritation among political and economic circles in Syria of Lebanese conduct during their negotiations with the oil company. Expressing Syrian dismay, Raiyyes commented on the position of some Lebanese dailies, which attacked and insulted Syria. Significantly, Raiyyes' criticism was not only directed against the radical Lebanese nationalist mouthpieces but also what he described as the patriotic papers (Lebanese Arab nationalist dailies such as the *al-Nahar* or *Beirut al-Masa'*).

> The dailies of the Phalange, Eddé and others, even the patriotic papers in Beirut, instead of attacking the Lebanese government for signing the agreement, and the Lebanese parliament for passing it, attacked the Syrian government that was safeguarding Lebanese interests. God willing, Syria will serve Lebanese interests, in spite of the disgust of some Lebanese dailies, in the greatest economic transaction,

as Syria has served Lebanese political interest in spite of them, in the greatest political transaction, the transaction of independence and withdrawal. [In any case,] the Lebanese government, headed by a man such as a Riad el-Solh, should have stopped the campaign against Syria.[56]

At a press conference of 1 September 1947, Prime Minister Solh announced the signing of the agreement between Syria and Aramco. He revealed how the campaign against Syria in Lebanon had created difficulties on the road towards an agreement. Solh indicated how certain political parties attempted to profit from the situation to call for a boycott of Syria. He stressed the fact that, throughout the negotiations, Syria had always looked after Lebanese interests, pointing out that Damascus was able to gain concessions for both states.[57]

Solh's Syrian counterpart also announced his government's agreement with Aramco. Mardam Bey indicated that the delay came as a result of Syria's insistence on certain conditions that were not part of the Lebanese agreement with the American company. Aramco accepted to bear the expenses of keeping the pipeline secure, agreeing to provide Damascus with funds (that were not to exceed £40,000 annually). Mardam Bey emphasised that the most important concession gained was the annual supply of 200,000 tons of crude oil at stock market rates. He estimated that this would save the Syrian government 15 million liras annually.[58]

A comparison of the Lebanese–TAPLINE agreement and the Syrian–TAPLINE agreement, made by Lebanese Arab nationalist commentators, revealed that the agreements were identical except for three different points. Revenues received by the Syrian government from the TAPLINE were one and a half English pence for every ton of oil going through the pipeline within Syrian territory. Aramco undertook to deliver to the Syrian government 200,000 tons of crude oil annually, at production costs. Syrian technicians would be given employment preference over American technicians, provided they were of equal competence and qualifications. Syrian and American staff would be treated equally in pay and benefits. Interestingly, *Beirut al-Masa'* asserted that the Syrian agreement was a disappointment for those who were optimistically expecting great profit from the agreement.[59]

In any event, by December 1947, Hull declared that the only obstacle to the company's operations was the fact that the Syrian parliament had not ratified the agreement and that in the event that Syria refused ratification, the TAPLINE would go through Palestine. Syrian delays were starting to irritate the Saudis. The Saudi King expressed his displeasure to Quwwatly, the former demanding that the agreement be ratified. By that time, demonstrations were taking place in Arab capitals against the news of the United Nations' decision to partition Palestine into Arab and Jewish entities. Anti-American feeling was running high in the Arab streets. Fearful of public opinion, the Syrian ruling elite preferred to delay the ratification of the agreement until more favourable conditions arose. Quwwatly responded to the Saudi King's persistence by pointing out that 'Arab national interests were above economic considerations'. The Syrian President's response irritated the Saudi King further, the latter feeling insulted and his prestige undermined.[60] For the time being, the issue was shelved.

As the TAPLINE affair simmered down, the concern of Lebanese public opinion shifted back to their country's grain supplies. Consequently, from the middle of September until November 1947, Lebanese dailies were mainly preoccupied with this matter, while the issue of supplying Lebanon with grain was conspicuously absent from the headlines and editorials of the Syrian press. During that time, in spite of numerous meetings, agreements and promises, Syria was reluctant to supply Lebanon, claiming that it was suffering a shortage.[61] With great vexation, Lebanese political and economic circles were witnessing how Damascus agreed to supply very minimal quantities of grain, and that at exorbitant prices. The Lebanese public also criticised its government for having failed to secure the necessary supplies from sources other than Syria. Demonstrations in Lebanese towns such as Marj'youn and Zahle often led to clashes between the population and Lebanese security forces. People were demonstrating against the poor quality of grain and the inadequate rationing system. The incidents were taken up by opposition leaders, such as Kamal Jumblatt, who was not only critical of the administrative chaos existing in numerous ministries but accused officials as well as politicians of irregularities. Consequently, the Lebanese government's grain difficulties with its Syrian counterpart not only strained bilateral relations but created difficulties for the Solh government vis-à-vis the opposition.[62]

It was noteworthy that it was the Lebanese Arab nationalists who took the lead in criticising Syria for its unenthusiastic assistance in alleviating the grain shortage in Lebanon. 'They said that the harvest was poor and that there is no surplus. If they sense our desperate need for grain, they raise the price and, after we agree to their charge, grain is easily found.' Lebanese Arab nationalists also criticised how – in spite of the bilateral grain agreement and the pre-fixed price, which was already 50 per cent higher than the world market value – the Syrians unjustifiably increased the price by an additional 10 per cent. Displeased, Lebanese Arab nationalist commentators reported that a kilo of grain cost Lebanon 43.5 piastres, while in Palestine, East Jordan, Egypt and Iraq, a similar amount and quality of grain was sold at 25 piastres. 'We do not blame our prime minister who concluded a deal under such preposterous and deceitful conditions, because of the urgent need that drove him to do so. It was Hajj Wehbe Hariri, the minister of finance in Syria, who disregarded political considerations, neighbourly and brotherly relations for profit.'[63] Strict Lebanese government measures and continuous smuggling of grain and other supplies from Syria prevented serious shortages in Lebanon.[64]

To the regret of the Lebanese, a cabinet shuffle of 6 October retained Wehbe Hariri as Minister of Finance. The new cabinet ordered the Syrian army to the Palestine frontier.[65] After the month of October, the issue of grain disappeared from Lebanese headlines and editorials. National governments faced widening resentment against mounting budget figures. Opinion-makers were bitter about the subject of entertainment charges, the high cost of diplomatic representation abroad, the extraordinary expenses arising from conferences and meetings which had been held on Lebanese and Syrian soil, and for which both governments had been host, the countless incursions into public funds by venal and unscrupulous functionaries who used political influence to obtain special favours. An increasing number of parliamentarians were voicing their demands for a general overhaul of the executive and the heavy administrative apparatus.[66]

However, the precarious state of affairs between the two governments and the increasing economic strain did not improve Syro-Lebanese bilateral relations. In a meeting between Wehbe Hariri and Musa Moubarak, held in Damascus on 7 November, a serious difference of opinion arose in connection with the exemption of certain raw materials – required for the Lebanese and Syrian industries – from taxation. Among the items considered were molasses for the Syrian alcohol industry and cacao for the Lebanese chocolate industry, in addition to reclaimed rubber for shoe soles, plastic raw materials for handbags, and powdered milk. Moubarak, heading the Lebanese delegation, objected to the proposed free entry of molasses for the Syrian alcohol industry, on the grounds that it would give it a special advantage over its Lebanese rival. On the other hand, it was felt in Syrian circles that tariff concessions to the Lebanese chocolate industry were greater than needed. Recriminations ensued, the upshot of which was that the Lebanese delegation abruptly walked out of the meeting and returned to Beirut. Presidential mediation saw a compromise reached. Despite the months of constant negotiations, the incident clearly demonstrated that Beirut and Damascus had been unable to reach an agreement.[67] Agreement would have to wait. The situation in Palestine was increasingly commanding the attention of the public and officials in Lebanon and Syria.

As demonstrations against the United Nations' partition plan for Palestine were taking place in Arab capitals, and with fighting in Palestine increasing in severity,[68] the convention of the Common Interests between Syria and Lebanon was set to expire on 31 December 1947. Consequently, Syrian and Lebanese leaders were preparing to discuss the future of this apparatus. These discussions, coupled with an emerging discord over the future of Syrian-Lebanese monetary relations with France, were to become sources of additional strain on 'brotherly relations'.

5 *Functional Separation*

In the first months of 1948 the great majority of the Lebanese political and economic elite were uneasy about the dwindling financial resources of the state. Consequently, the Lebanese Premier called for the reduction of expenditures in certain ministries, particularly Foreign Affairs, Public Works and National Economy. However, it remained necessary to overhaul the entire tax structure, since too much of a burden was carried by low-income groups in indirect taxes, many of which were imposed on food, services and necessities in general.[1]

Aside from financial and economic considerations, the month of January witnessed one of Beirut's most heated parliamentary debates. In an effort to prevent Zionists from acquiring land in Lebanon, a law had been passed towards the end of the French Mandate prohibiting non-Lebanese from purchasing land except by presidential decree. A new bill, sponsored by the government, would permit persons born in Lebanon who had acquired foreign citizenship to purchase land for their own use. The bill would address those expatriate Lebanese who had built up considerable fortunes, particularly in the West, to return home and invest their capital in Lebanon, to own property and ultimately to resume their status as Lebanese nationals. Fervent opposition to the bill was voiced by former Prime Minister Sami el-Solh. Solh had long laboured to obtain the support of his Muslim co-religionists to conduct a census, which he believed would reveal Lebanon to have a Muslim majority. Solh was bitterly attacked by Henri Phar'oun, who pointed out that the former Premier had frequently worked to enfranchise Lebanon's Kurdish population. Phar'oun argued that the native-born Lebanese were more entitled to consideration than a refugee minority that had no ties with the country at all. Riad el-Solh intervened, condemning the talk on majorities and minorities in the House. He declared that now that the state had been built and independence achieved, it was necessary to build the nation. Solh deplored his cousin Sami's efforts to conduct a new census, which he said could serve no useful purpose in the country's present state of development.[2]

The debate in parliament revealed the evolution of the Lebanese Arab nationalist faction, led by Riad el-Solh, and its thinking regarding the subject of confessionalism and the census. They had given lukewarm support to calls for a population census, which would establish the Muslims as the majority. Riad el-Solh came to believe that the status quo was the only possible solution for a government in Lebanon. He became determined to stop any debate on the subject, in order to avoid arousing Christian sensitivities.[3]

Like its Lebanese neighbour, Syria was plagued with internal problems. Aside from the economic crisis facing the government, which was identical to Lebanon's, the Syrian leadership had its own troubles with its minority communities. There were separatist sentiments among the Druze and Alawites. Moreover, at a national level, the socio-economic gap between the old landlords, merchants, and industrialists and the lower classes of peasants and workers was widening. In addition, the modern middle class's persistent drive to upward mobility represented a major threat to the old socio-political status quo – which had been maintained by Syrian rulers like Quwwatly, Mardam Bey and their associates.[4] For the last nine months of the year the Palestine question almost completely dominated the Lebanese and Syrian scene, and its developments profoundly affected nearly every important issue, from the re-election of Presidents and opposition tactics to the fate of the Monetary Agreement with France.[5]

Moshe Ma'oz argues that, while announcing their intention to destroy Zionism and rescue Palestine, Syria's ruling elite – and President Quwwatly in particular – utilised the Palestinian–Zionist issue as an outlet for domestic pressures and as an instrument for strengthening its own political position.[6] Syria's ruling establishment also used its differences with the Lebanese to divert the Syrian public from domestic challenges. This argument is easily substantiated from a look at the disputes between Beirut and Damascus. In 1948, at the height of Arab–Zionist confrontations in Palestine, Damascus was prompted to cut vital food supplies, including grain, from Lebanon. Moreover, while the conflict raged in Palestine, the Syrian authorities exerted no serious efforts to restrict public opinion-makers, merchants and industrialists from voicing their strong criticisms of Lebanon. Press campaigns against Lebanese 'misdeeds' were conducted openly, prompting such strong responses from Beirut that at times the conflict south of the Syrian and Lebanese borders was forgotten.

Damascus was the first Arab state to mobilise troops along the Palestine border, in October 1947. During the last months of 1947, Syrian authorities deployed troops along the Golan and began to smuggle arms into Palestine. An irregular volunteer force – 'the Liberation Army' – was organised and led by Fawzi al-Qawuqji, a veteran of Palestine's 1936–1939 Arab revolt. Trained and supplied by the Syrian army and commanded by Syrian officers, the Liberation Army was composed of Syrians, Palestinians, Lebanese and Iraqis. Armed with an Arab League mandate, the force moved into Palestine towards the end of 1947 with the intention of securing Palestine from the Zionists. The Liberation Army failed in its mission and on 15 May 1948, five Arab states dispatched their armies. Syria sent 3000 troops, which attacked south and north of Lake Tiberias. It was able to hold on to the area north and east of the lake. Aside from these two operations, the Syrian army remained inactive during the 1948 war and delegated the task of attacking Zionist targets in the Galilee to the Liberation Army. By the end of 1948, however, the Israelis managed to destroy the Liberation Army. The Syrian army's poor performance may be attributed to a lack of arms and ammunition, nor could they count on any support from other Arab armies. Lebanon was too weak, Egypt was too far away and Hashemite Iraq and Transjordan – known for their ambitions in Syria – were not trusted by Damascus. Despite its poor military performance, the Syrian government assumed a tough diplomatic position against Israel, objecting to the arrangement of a truce and long refusing to sign an armistice agreement. Syria refused to recognise the United Nations partition resolution of Palestine. Still, the Syrian public was furious with the regime.[7]

There is no novelty in governments' efforts to divert public attention from domestic to foreign issues nor was Arab, particularly Syrian, animosity towards twentieth-century Zionism particularly new. What was surprising was the fact that the 1948 Arab–Israeli war for Palestine did not drive the Lebanese and Syrian political and economic elites to look beyond their divergent interests. On the contrary, 1948 witnessed the most vocal confrontations between Beirut and Damascus over such issues as monetary policy and the restriction of imports.

On May 1947, the Syrian government had addressed its Lebanese counterpart with a memorandum signalling that it would look favourably upon the maintenance of its economic partnership with Lebanon, under the condition that certain clauses of the January 1944 convention be reconsidered. The Syrian government confirmed its memorandum on November 1947 and assigned a commission to draw up the articles of litigation, which were to be the subject of the upcoming amendment talks. In general terms the commission's recommendations were inspired by one essential idea: establishing one economic policy in Syria and Lebanon that would bring greater coordination and reinforce economic union. The commission noted that close coordination among Syro-Lebanese institutions was not supported by the existing convention.

The commission also recommended that the HCCI be strengthened. In fact the Syrian cabinet had adopted a proposal by Minister Sa'id Ghazzi, Syria's former Minister of Finance, who had suggested that the authority to issue export/import licences reside not with the Ministers of Economy but the HCCI, which would examine licence applications on the basis of Syria and Lebanon's mutual interests. The Lebanese government did not concede to Syrian demands, arguing that any measure that saw vital prerogatives entrusted to a body that was not accountable to the Lebanese parliament flew in the face of the Lebanese constitution.[8]

By that time, matters were complicated by Syrian public dissent, specifically among the merchant class. Syria's business community was increasingly under the impression that, in addition to political concessions, Syria was sacrificing its vital economic interests in order to maintain the economic union with Lebanon. Echoing these concerns, the secretary general of the Syrian chamber of commerce, 'Aref al-Laham, wrote that the Lebanese were challenging the Syrian economy and undermining Syrian trade. Laham pointed out that if Syria proposed a policy to limit imports, Lebanon stubbornly claimed that Lebanon lived on tourism and that it was impossible for the Lebanese to limit imports. Laham argued that this was diverting Syrian trade to Lebanon and depriving Syria of all progress and activity. He underlined the fact that Beirut's big merchants were dictating all Lebanese government positions during their negotiations with Syria. He concluded by warning that

> Lebanon sees itself as a country of trade, transit, tourism and entertainment, whereas Syria sees itself as a country of industry, agriculture and trade. The latter is obliged to protect its nascent agriculture and industry and strives to find markets for its products. If we take a look on these two opposing trends, we realise that there can be no reconciling them, that there can be no common economic policy between them, unless Syria agrees to sacrifice its economy to satisfy Lebanese policies.[9]

Strong reservations about the Syro-Lebanese economic relations were also voiced in the Syrian parliament, where 15 Syrian deputies demanded the termination of the customs union and the safeguarding of Syria's vital interests, which Lebanon was 'determined to step upon'. For two consecutive hours Syrian deputies attacked the Syro-Lebanese economic edifice, insisting upon the repudiation of a sad marriage that has lasted for over a quarter of a century.[10]

Laham's article resonated in Beirut, especially among economic and financial circles. It was maintained that the difficulties in bilateral economic relations derived from disputes in the administration of the customs services, the TAPLINE affair and the Common Interests. They held that the dispute over the Customs Directorate was purely administrative in nature and that the Syrians had to abandon their claim to the customs directorship, since that post was already occupied by Jamil Shehab: 'Shehab's incumbency constitutes a safety bolt for the normal and systematic functioning of the two states' customs administration.' As to the TAPLINE affair, Lebanon's ruling elite was extremely critical that, although Syrian Prime Minister Mardam Bey signed the agreement with Aramco on 1 September 1947, four months later the agreement had not been submitted to parliament for ratification. Rumours were rife that the American company was considering altering the pipeline's route and had in fact suspended preliminary work on the pipeline terminus in south Lebanon. Aramco had also ceased hiring workers. By that time, the majority of Lebanese policy-makers believed that Syria was striving to deviate its foreign commerce towards Latakiya and thereby escape the tutelage of Beirut.[11]

The aforementioned issues of contention between Syria and Lebanon remained unresolved, in spite of the continuous and well-established practice of Syro-Lebanese summitry. In January alone there were three meetings headed by the Syrian and Lebanese Presidents and their Prime Ministers, in addition to frequent telephone conferences and correspondences.[12] The general public, particularly in Syria, was starting to lose patience with what opinion-makers described as sterile meetings. Calls were reiterated that the two governments should separate issues of trade and finance from those of politics and nationalism. It was generally maintained that the Syrian people had sacrificed enough and should not sacrifice any more.[13]

Numerous disputes between Syria and Lebanon remained unresolved and the two states were being confronted by new difficulties that in turn exacerbated the unresolved ones. The year 1948 brought with it the dispute over Syrian and Lebanese monetary policy.

A. THE MONETARY ISSUE

'Traditional meetings' between Lebanon and Syria in January 1948 were dominated by negotiations with France on the future of the Syrian-Lebanese currency. Franco-Syrian-Lebanese monetary negotiations had in fact started in October 1947 in Paris. They were deadlocked over France's recognition of its debts to Lebanon and Syria. They resumed only after direct intervention from French Foreign Minister George Bidault, when the French delegation recognised the debt, which formed in fact the coverage of the lira. After strenuous deliberations, France's debt was set at 23 billion French francs.[14]

These talks were never the focus of opinion-makers in Beirut and Damascus. This changed at the end of the year, when fundamental differences emerged between Lebanon and Syria over future monetary relations with France. From January 1948 until well into 1949, political and economic circles in Lebanese and Syrian capitals were preoccupied with the monetary issue – one that was to have profound repercussions on Syrian and Lebanese bilateral relations.

Prior to the formalisation of the French Mandate over Syria and Lebanon, the French had introduced a new financial system to the region. In 1919 the mandatory authority bestowed on the *Banque de Syrie et du Liban* (BSL) the right to issue notes – in a manner seen in other French-administered areas. The BSL enjoyed extensive influence over monetary policy and credit allocation. Syro-Lebanese paper currency was pegged to the French franc and, consequently, the local currency suffered from the extreme fluctuations and devaluations of the franc. From 1920 to 1939, the lira was devalued more than 64 per cent against the US dollar.[15]

In December 1939, the French authorities created the *Office des changes*, which was attached to the French-owned BSL. The *Office des changes* allocated foreign currency for licensed imports, controlled the flow of foreign capital and currency, and regulated other financial transactions. These regulations were designed to improve France's foreign exchange position in order to fight what was expected to be a long war. The numerous intertwined regulations made it possible for France in 1939 to borrow 50 million liras from the Levant states for the purchase of military and civilian supplies needed for the war effort.[16]

By 1940, when the Vichy regime was installed in the Levant, foreign exchange was in great demand and had largely been exhausted. Official gold reserves, a large share of which had been appropriated by the mandatory authority, were completely wiped out by a transfer of six million liras in gold to France in June 1941. With strict restrictions on the official exchange market and growing demand for hard currency, a parallel exchange market developed. Vichy authorities had tolerated a growing black market in sterling-backed Palestinian lira. With Vichy's defeat in the Levant, the Allies made sterling available on the open market. In 1944, the Levant states were forced to return to the franc bloc, freeing Britain from its sterling obligations to the economies. The 1944 Catroux Accord, which forced the Levant states to re-enter the franc bloc, returned the *status quo ante*: local economies no longer had secure access to the highly valued sterling and were again financially dependent on France. French authorities were keen to exercise exclusive financial control over Lebanon and Syria, since a financial monopoly over the Levant states enhanced their political influence over Beirut and Damascus.[17]

The franc was devalued in late 1947 and early 1948, just as it had been between 1920 and 1939. During that time, the French economy was in crisis, suffering from an enormous budget deficit. Inflation was increasing unchecked. So desperate was the economic situation that Paris was compelled to issue bonds from the United States to be able to pay for its fuel, food and raw material supplies. Consequently, the French government was unable to fully honour the commitments it had made in the Catroux Accord. According to the agreement, in the event of devaluation the French government undertook to cover any discrepancy between the franc and its mandates' currency.[18] As mentioned above, negotiations in Paris ensued during the second half of 1947, and by the end of that year the Lebanese and French were able to reach an accommodation, while the Syrians suddenly withdrew from the talks.[19]

In a series of meetings held in January 1948, attended by the Lebanese and Syrian Presidents, Prime Ministers and Ministers of Finance and Economy, the Syrian leadership informed the Lebanese that they had to consult Syrian merchants before committing to the Paris agreement. Meanwhile, even during the Paris deliberations, in fact, some among the Syrian public called for Damascus' monetary separation from France and for Syria and Lebanon to establish their own bank to issue and circulate a new currency, one independent of the franc and tied to the US dollar or British sterling. Such sentiments were not restricted to the predominantly nationalist political circles in Syria, but were widespread among the Syrian merchants. The latter called upon their government to separate from the franc as soon as possible by securing (through the Paris negotiations) the maximum amount of hard currency from France, even if Syria and Lebanon had to sacrifice some of their legitimate rights. The merchants warned that if Syria and Lebanon remained bound to the franc after the Paris negotiations, their economies were threatened with collapse.

> It is a crime that the Lebanese and Syrian currency should be bound to France with such conditions there. The economic situation in Lebanon and Syria is strong since both states do not have any external debt. And if they are able to agree on a common economic policy, mainly to increase exports, they will have large deposits of hard currency.[20]

Similarly, public opinion-makers vigorously argued that separating the common currency from the franc was in line with the French withdrawal from Syria. There was a consensus among the country's leadership to liberate Syria's economy, for 'there is no life to a country whose livelihood is bound to another, especially if that other is threatened by bankruptcy'. Monetary separation was 'a new test of Syrian patriotism and sacrifice'.[21]

At a Syro-Lebanese summit at Shtura on 30 January 1948, the Syrians explained the reasons behind their rejection of French proposals. The Syrians held that they could not accept the French contention that no further compensation was possible for the devaluation of the franc. They also rejected French terms for the liquidation of Syrian franc holdings. The Lebanese attempted to find a middle ground between the Syrian and the French views, but failed. The meeting ended with the Syrians officially informing their Lebanese counterparts of their rejection of the French proposals and their separation from the franc bloc. In addition, the Syrian delegation demanded that, like Syria, Lebanon adopt a united economic programme. The Syrian delegation was frank with their Lebanese counterparts, pointing out the dangers to Lebanese food supplies – as well as Lebanon's future trade with Syria – if Beirut continued to insist on remaining bound to the franc. The Syrians also warned that should Lebanon unilaterally decide to remain bound to the franc, Syria would establish trade barriers that would eventually terminate the economic union. Such circumstances, the Syrians stressed, would entail enormous losses to Lebanon but would invigorate the Syrian economy. They pointed out that Syria would be able to export its grain that the Lebanese consumed and for which the latter paid in local currency. Damascus could export its grain to earn hard currency. Aside from grain, the Syrians were also counting on their ability to export 10,000 tons of olive oil to the United States, which could earn them up to $15 million. Damascus was well aware that Beirut must insist on remaining within the franc bloc because Lebanon did not have any other means to cover its currency. However, policy-makers in Damascus were confident that, if Syria should insist on monetary separation, then the Lebanese would be compelled to follow since the latter's economic interests lay with those of Syria.[22] The Syrians followed their warnings by closing their border with Lebanon.[23]

Shortly after the Shtura meeting, on 2 February 1948, Syrian Prime Minister Mardam Bey met with a large delegation of merchants, heads of the chamber of commerce and industry, financiers and newspaper owners. In the presence of the Syrian Ministers of Finance and National Economy, Mardam Bey attributed the Syrian refusal to conclude the agreement to French demands concerning the costs of occupation, as well as French insistence that Syria continue to recognise the economic privileges of French-owned concessionary companies. Mardam Bey indicated that the French government imposed 31 January 1948 as a deadline for Syria's final decision. He pointed out that from the Paris negotiations until the deadline, the French franc had been further devalued. Mardam Bey maintained that the Lebanese were proposing a compromise while the Syrians were bound for the liquidation of their financial relations with France. The Syrian point of view was based on the fact that the Syrian economic situation was healthier than that of the country from which guarantees were being sought. He pointed out that expectations for the 1948 harvest were excellent and would allow the export of 100,000 tons of grain, which would bring Syria more than $20 million. Syria would also be able to export more than 4000 tons of olive oil, which were worth more than $4 million on the international market. He emphasised Syria's objective of economic independence. Mardam Bey reminded his audience that every political independence required economic independence and that the purpose of colonisation was to dominate the economy of a country.

The Syrian Premier stressed that his government had tried to convince the Lebanese to adopt the Syrian position and that Damascus had offered to share all of Syria's resources with Lebanon. According to Mardam Bey, the Syrian offer was made while safeguarding the dignity and sovereignty of Lebanon. However, 'the men in Lebanon, opted to take a different course of action which will eventually threaten their interests as well as our own. We are adamant to maintain and develop the best of relations with Lebanon, however their decision will create difficulties.' The Syrian Prime Minister assured his audience that parity was maintained with respect to foreign currencies but no decision had been taken concerning the Syrian currency's parity with that of Lebanon. He stated that the basis of the coverage of the Syrian lira (S£) was being studied and would be announced in the proper time. Speaking on behalf of the merchants present at the press conference, Michel Ilyan demanded economic and customs separation with Lebanon.[24]

Like his Syrian counterpart, Prime Minister Riad el-Solh held consultations with Lebanon's leading economic and financial figures. Solh briefed the meeting on the Shtura discussions, then he asked them to present their views. Some warned that Syria might separate from the customs union, others maintained that the presence of two different currencies would not necessarily lead to separation – the Benelux countries, which had one customs union with different currencies, were highlighted as a model for the future of Syro-Lebanese economic relations. In a press conference, Solh characterised the monetary issue between Syria and Lebanon as representing a fraction of the problems resulting from independence.[25]

Regarding the Syrian position, the Lebanese Premier maintained that Syria opted to resort to the International Court of Justice. He characterised the Syrian position as originating from a certain spirit of initiative from which Lebanon could benefit greatly. He pointed out that this would not be the first time that Lebanon profited from Syrian boldness.

> Lebanese and Syrian bonds and interests will not be troubled by this monetary separation, which is of a temporary and provisional aspect, due to the fact that Syria has more economic potential than we do. [In any event,] public opinion should know that the interests of the country have been safeguarded and will not be threatened.[26]

Opinion-makers in Damascus viewed the Lebanese Prime Minister's acceptance of the Monetary Agreement with France as a betrayal of the Arab nationalist cause. 'They ally themselves with France against Syria, then they say that between Syria and Lebanon are common interests' read the headlines in Syria. Solh was seen as backtracking on his famous pledge that Lebanon would not be a centre or path for the foreigner. He was called upon to retract his pledges after he confessed that he could not 'abandon' France financially and economically. The Lebanese were also depicted as having less confidence in Syria's trade, agricultural and industrial potential or its wealth of natural resources – which were offered to the Lebanese on an equal basis – than the influence of Paris. Consequently, according to Damascene opinion-makers, Solh's claim that there were eternal common interests between Syria and Lebanon was no longer factual. 'The Syrians regard Solh's statements as an insult to their intelligence.'[27]

In Lebanon, while most Arab nationalist opinion-makers restrained themselves from criticising the cabinet's decision to endorse the Monetary Agreement with France, there was nevertheless lively controversy among the Muslim population, which, but for Solh's advocacy of the agreement, would have undoubtedly resisted it en masse. This was not the case among Lebanese nationalists, who vigorously defended the Premier against Syrian condemnations. *L'Orient*'s headline read 'we owe our homage to Prime Minister Solh'. Similarly, *Le Jour* paid its respects to the Lebanese Premier and underscored that, by safeguarding the value and stability of the currency, the government had rendered Lebanon a priceless deed. *Le Jour* called for the continuation of intimate relations with Syria, even if the Syrian and Lebanese liras were valued differently, for a constant parity could emerge and make both currencies automatically interchangeable, as was the practice within the Benelux states.[28]

Lebanese leading financiers and economic experts unanimously regarded their government's measures as sound and serving the interests of the country. Gabriel Menassa stressed that the differences between the two states' economies imposed two different economic approaches, as was witnessed in the monetary issue. Menassa also stressed that Lebanon could not rely on Syria for its needs since Syrian goods were more expensive than those found on the international market. The Lebanese economist indicated that Lebanon signed the Monetary Agreement to ensure monetary stability and the lira's exchangeability with both the sterling and other Arab currencies. Menassa concluded by indicating that the Lebanese balance of payments was suffering from a deficit and that a Lebanese currency independent of the franc would undoubtedly lead to inflation. He emphasised that while Syria could safeguard its currency through its products and exports, Lebanon on the other hand had no such basis for its currency. Menassa hoped that the Monetary Agreement would not cause a rift in Syro-Lebanese economic relations.[29]

Also defending the Lebanese government's decision, Michel Chiha wrote that there was an almost equal quantity of banknotes in circulation in Lebanon and Syria. He pointed out, however, that the banknotes in circulation averaged 160 liras per head in Lebanon while in Syria there were only 60 liras. Chiha argued that this was one of the factors that gave the Lebanese monetary problem a very different aspect from the Syrian one. Aside from numerous other technical considerations, this protected Lebanon, monetarily, from risk. The effects of devaluation in Lebanon would be four times greater than in Syria and the disorder that would emerge, as a result of the disappearance of monetary stability, would be proportionally larger. He attributed this to the modest circulation of banknotes in Syria, which were spread over a large territory. In Lebanon, banknotes had a more restricted space, which made it more sensitive. Chiha concluded it was always evident that Lebanon was, and had always been, a country of trade and transit, and that if its currency was devalued then the country would suffocate and die.[30]

In a number of other editorials Chiha expressed his scepticism of Syria's decision to resolve its dispute with France at the International Court of Justice at The Hague. According to Chiha, Syria, like Lebanon, had French francs to cover its currency but that after the franc's devaluation, they had become quantitatively insufficient and became bound to the outcome of the court's ruling. The Lebanese economist revealed that Syria had thereby made half of its currency hostage to legal action whose settlement could take a long time. The Lebanese banker pointed out that Syrian economic designs, as drawn by its ministers, 'will ruin its institutions and elites... The formulas as conceived in Damascus are dangerous where they are exclusive, [and] they are founded on an unstable future of projects.'[31] As if predicting the coming coups d'état in Syria, Chiha voiced his concern for the future of the Syrian political elite if it continued adopting radical protectionist economic policies. Chiha held that the demographic situation in

Syria clearly showed that Damascus' economic policy could not ignore the country's human element and that Syrian economic necessities could be very different from what Syrian policy-makers believed. He based his assumptions on Syria's relatively reduced rate of consumption.

Chiha pointed out that the best way to increase purchasing power was to develop the land, and with it the social condition of the peasant. Syrian industries, like the Lebanese, could not pretend to conquer foreign markets. The population in Syria should increase and the life of the peasant must be elevated. This necessitated another working plan. Syria had no hinterland capable of buying its industrial products. Lebanon evidently had every interest in seeing Syrian purchasing power reach another level, but it was also convenient for Lebanon that Syria became strong in social-structural terms. He concluded his editorial by warning that if the social aspects of Syrian policy were not well developed, the political side was always threatened and precarious.[32]

Syria's economic and political establishment was not convinced of the Lebanese perception of Lebanon's economic potential. They strongly believed that Lebanese economic potential alone was sufficient to cover its currency. They held that Lebanon was a tourist attraction that had no competition in the Middle East, and that the Lebanese earned sufficient hard currency from tourists to cover a large part of the country's needs, aside from what Lebanon received from expatriate remittances. It was estimated that, quite above and beyond exports, the sums repatriated from Lebanese abroad were approximately three million dollars annually. It was also maintained that Lebanon produced a number of goods that filled the region's market needs – such as textiles, cotton and silk. It was claimed that the sum of capital earned by the Lebanese textile industry, through exports to Syria alone, was several times greater than Syrian grain exports to Lebanon. This was in addition to what these factories sold to Iraq, Jordan and other countries. Other Lebanese products – like pasta, biscuits, soap, sweets, etc. – earned revenues comparable to those of some European states. In light of these observations, opinion-makers in Damascus posed the following questions: 'Aren't these economic capacities in agriculture, industry and trade – as well as Lebanese expatriate remittances and tourism revenues – sufficient to cover L£150 to L£200 million? Are Syrian capacities greater than the Lebanese, taking into consideration the land area and population of both countries? The truth is that Syria has confidence in itself while Lebanon does not...'[33]

Syrian resistance to the agreement was also inspired by a lack of confidence in France. Trust in the agreement and the goodwill of the French partner did not exist in the Syrian mind. This element of mistrust played the most important role in the minds of those who negotiated with France and those ultimately responsible for approving the agreement.[34]

On 6 February 1948, Lebanese Foreign Minister Hamid Franjieh and his French counterpart George Bidault signed the Monetary Agreement, thereby concluding five months of tedious negotiations.[35] Some days before the conclusion of the Paris Accord, and the Syro-Lebanese 'monetary' parting of ways, a new financial situation was beginning to have an impact on the Syrian and Lebanese populations. A number of Beirut's local and international companies, as well as banks, put up notices that they would not accept Syrian lira. Syrians streamed into Beirut to purchase whatever they could and to convert their Syrian currency into Lebanese. Although stagnant markets made Lebanese merchants eager to sell, they refused to accept Syrian banknotes at any exchange rate. The Sursuk market in the central district of Beirut, where gold and hard currencies were sold, was unusually calm. There was no selling or buying. Syrian merchants, it was reported, were going through the markets with puzzled faces.[36]

This state of affairs was not restricted to large companies and financial establishments. In a leading article, a reporter of *al-Qabass* related how he had tried to purchase a pack of cigarettes using Syrian lira. The shopkeeper refused to accept the currency. He pointed out to his Syrian customer that he was unwilling to go to Syria to exchange the Syrian currency he had received. In vain the Syrian reporter tried to persuade the Lebanese shop-owner that the two currencies' fate was one and that they were issued from the same central bank. The Lebanese shopkeeper explained the reasons for his reluctance, describing how on Saturday 31 January 1948, a large number of Syrians came to Beirut and bought large amounts of gold. Consequently, the Lebanese government issued directions for the BSL to cease accepting Syrian currency for gold. The government's measure affected the people's confidence in the Syrian currency. Even a tramway conductor refused the *al-Qabass* reporter's money.[37]

Due to the Franco-Lebanese Monetary Agreement, the Lebanese authorities were not compelled to take any special measures in the financial markets and banks. However, the Syrian government had to take action to boost confidence. Syrian authorities requested the BSL administration to announce that the bank was ready to accept Syrian currency.[38] Damascus also ordered the closure of the BSL branches in Aleppo, Homs, Hama, Suweida, Deir al-Zor, Tadmour (Palmyra), Jazira and Latakia. The Syrian government asked private banks and financial companies to establish the quantities of banknotes they had. This disruption in banking had repercussions on the market. Merchants who had to settle their accounts were unable to obtain Syrian cash and were forced to resort to exchanging their gold reserves for banknotes. But the supply of banknotes in circulation was not sufficient to meet demand. Syrian merchants were forced to go to Beirut, where they sold their gold for banknotes, which compelled the Syrian authorities to reinforce security measures on the Syro-Lebanese border to prevent the smuggling of gold to the Lebanese capital. In addition, the Syrian government, in desperate need of hard currency, exerted great efforts to market its agricultural surplus, particularly grain and olive oil. But potential buyers regarded Syrian produce as overpriced.[39]

Beirut refused Damascus' instructions to the BSL to fix the exchange rates of foreign currencies. The Lebanese held that the Syrian lira had lost its value after Damascus refused to sign the Monetary Agreement with France. Hence, the Lebanese currency was covered, while the Syrian lira remained exposed. Still under strong French influence, the BSL froze Syrian funds in order to cover the difference in value resulting from the exposed Syrian lira. Opinion-makers in Damascus regarded this freezing of currencies on the Syrian account as a war of nerves against Syria. There were calls for the issuance of a new Syrian currency and the creation of a Syrian central bank – a 'National Bank of Syria' – independent from the BSL. The collusion of the Lebanese government, as well as private financial establishments, with the BSL measures was regarded as 'a vulgar Lebanese conspiracy'.

> We had expected that France do everything against our country, but we are very much surprised that Lebanon, a government headed by a man such as Riad el-Solh, takes part in this conspiracy.
>
> Lebanon has regrettably begun a campaign against Syria, first instructing the BSL in Beirut not to accept Syrian currency. Then it has announced, in agreement with the Bank, that the Syrian lira is not accepted in Lebanon anymore and must be replaced with the lira that carries the Lebanese name. Moreover, it has shortened the period in which the exchange can be made to the degree that only 10 to 25 per cent of the Lebanese who carry Syrian lira will be able to exchange their money.[40]

In fact, the Lebanese Ministry of Finance designated 4:00 pm Monday 2 February 1948 as the deadline for the exchange of Syrian banknotes into Lebanese. For its part, the BSL issued the following communiqué: 'The *Banque de Syrie et du Liban*, in its capacity as the issuing institution, announces to the public that starting 4:00 pm Monday 2 February 1948, no currency but the Lebanese lira will have purchasing power and that any facility enjoyed by other currencies will cease until further notice.'[41]

The 4:00 pm deadline caused large masses of Lebanese to converge upon BSL offices to exchange their Syrian banknotes. The Lebanese authorities had to prolong the deadline till 11:00 pm, in fact, then again to the following morning. All over Lebanon people complained of the short deadline and governmental and public institutions were flooded with cables beseeching officials to extend it. There were numerous reports of border closures between Syria and Lebanon as well as officials causing difficulties for the few travellers who managed to get through to either side. Gold in particular was being smuggled from Syria to Lebanon.[42] On 4 February 1948, the BSL ceased to exchange Syrian to Lebanese currency. Estimates indicated that around 40 million Syrian lira had been exchanged.[43]

The Lebanese daily *al-Nahar* made a tour of the main trading districts in Beirut, where most merchants declined to comment on the Monetary Agreement. Nevertheless, financial and political circles in Beirut were critical of Syria's sudden decision to withdraw from the negotiations without warning Beirut. They were also sceptical of Syria's capacity to cover its currency on its own. The Lebanese banking community held that it would not be easy for Syria to establish a central bank within a short period of time, even if it managed to cover all its currency 100 per cent in gold. It was believed that Syria's industrial and agricultural potential was financially insufficient to gain the international community's faith in the Syrian currency.[44]

Lebanese nationalist circles attempted to paint a more positive picture of the monetary crisis between Lebanon and Syria. It was believed that the economic state of the two countries was healthy – basing their assessment on the fact that Syria and Lebanon had no internal nor external debt and that their means of production, far from being destroyed, had developed due to the war. It was also believed that the situation could only worsen if monetary rupture were followed by economic or customs separation. Lebanon depended heavily upon Syria for agricultural supplies, especially grain. To pay for those products the Lebanese possessed nothing but their cotton lines as well as their intermediary and transit services with Syria. They reasoned if those declined, Lebanon's balance of payments with Syria would always be in deficit. This would have two consequences: Lebanon would see all its currency drain into Syria; the more probable scenario would see Lebanon buy from abroad for the Syrians, thereby converting Syrian liras into foreign currencies. In other words, Lebanese merchants would use their commercial contacts to satisfy Syrian market demand for imports, paying in hard currencies and then selling the imported products on the Syrian market against Syrian liras, thus indirectly converting Syrian liras into hard currencies. For these services, Lebanese merchants would impose a premium on the value of the Syrian lira that would widen the gap between the two countries' currencies. Syria's trade with Lebanon would become a loss-maker. Lebanese nationalists were hopeful that the two governments would soon realise that it was of vital necessity to maintain the customs union, for a customs union implied a fixed parity for the two currencies.[45] Even the Phalangist daily al-'Amal maintained that, regardless of the Syrian government's position towards Lebanon, and the insults of the Syrian press, 'we in Lebanon still maintain that the partnership with the Syrians must remain'.[46]

These sentiments were quickly addressed by al-Qabass, which wrote:

Lebanese dailies, which have been known for their loyalty to France, are now pleading with Syria not to forsake Lebanon. Independence has exhausted Lebanon… Their spirits that have gotten used to slavery and are repulsed by freedom and sickened by liberty. They are always in search of a master…who will suck their blood because the responsibilities that come with independence are great and tiresome… Syria, which has paid heavily for its independence, will know how to pay for its monetary independence.[47]

By that time, the Syrian political and economic elite believed that the dispute had long gone beyond monetary issues and that almost every aspect of the

Syro-Lebanese partnership had been characterised by discord. This state of affairs was attributed to doctrinal conflicts among the economic elites of the two countries and the increasingly poisoned atmosphere between Beirut and Damascus. It was held that, despite the weekly meetings in Shtura, economic divisions between Syria and Lebanon were becoming deeper and more numerous by the week. Established under special political contingencies, the October 1943 HCCI convention was becoming more and more unpopular in Damascus. It ceased to be a modus vivendi for responding to the needs of the two states. The monetary dispute widely came to be viewed as a blow of mercy, precipitating a separation that had become inevitable.[48]

By the time Arab irregular forces began arriving in Syria en route to Palestine, the mood in Damascus was increasingly tilting towards economic separation from Lebanon. A communiqué from the Damascus trade association declared its full support for its government's position, emphasising that separation from the franc bloc and Lebanon would strengthen the Syrian economy.[49] In a statement justifying Lebanon's signature of the Monetary Agreement, Lebanese Minister of Justice Ahmad Husseini declared that Lebanon was forced into signing the agreement with France due to the fact that Lebanon had many expatriates residing in French colonies. Husseini cautioned that a disagreement with France would have threatened the livelihood of the expatriates. The Lebanese Minister of Justice reiterated that the Lebanese and Syrian economic partnership would continue without any changes. Shortly after Husseini's statement, al-Qabass wrote a commentary entitled 'Lebanese Minister justifies forsaking Syria'. The commentary stressed that the Syro-Lebanese partnership was not based on figures or profit but on national sentiment due to the stance Lebanon had taken against France. 'However, since Lebanese affection has returned to France, the partnership between Syria and Lebanon should be reconsidered... The Lebanese government preferred a state that had for 30 years been exploiting us to the point of poverty.'[50]

On 4 February 1948, amid the squabbling of the Syrian and Lebanese political and economic elites, the Lebanese parliament convened to discuss the Monetary Agreement with France. Prime Minister Solh presented a detailed account of the Paris negotiations as well as the Monetary Agreement. He concluded his presentation by strongly rejecting the popular description of the agreement as an economic agreement that gave concessions to French companies. Instead he emphasised that the agreement was mainly concerned with liquidating French debt to Lebanon and facilitating Lebanese affairs, and those of its expatriates, with France.[51]

Parliamentary opposition was led by Sami el-Solh, who held that the Monetary Agreement with France was a victory for French colonialism. He maintained that, in concluding the agreement, 'we have written with our own hands the contract of our serfdom', criticising the agreement for weakening the middle class, draining the country of its economic liveliness (hayawiya) and leading the country's youth to emigrate. The deputy warned that the agreement would establish two clashing social groups: the capitalists and the poor. He indicated that Lebanon's financial and economic situation was better than that of France and that it was well within Lebanon's ability to cover its currency. Philip Takla expressed his annoyance with the clamour raised about the government's signing of the agreement, maintaining that any such decision should be based on the national interests, not sentiment. He cautioned the government of the agreement's repercussions on brotherly relations with Syria. 'Abdallah al-Yafi stated that he blamed the Syrian and Lebanese governments for not cooperating more closely during negotiations with France and for not taking necessary measures to face the situation when Lebanon decided to sign the agreement unilaterally. In response, Prime Minister Solh made the following strong statement:

> May my tongue be cut [out] if I say anything that is not in friendship to the Syrians and may my hands be cut off if I sign any agreement that infringes upon the sovereignty of Lebanon and Syria… We did not sign an agreement that is a means to colonialism… If it is not possible to retain our common interests with these monetary differences I will, if I must, resign the premiership and go to the ranks of parliamentarians to work for the conclusion of this agreement.[52]

Reflecting the sentiments of Arab nationalists the daily *al-Nahar* maintained that Lebanese interests should be placed above all considerations. The paper advocated that the government should not be asked to turn a blind eye to Lebanese national interests for the purpose of certain ties. It rejected the notion that every time the Lebanese decide to do something on their own, they are accused of being agents of colonialism.[53]

Rather than concentrating on that part of the Lebanese Premier's speech that addressed the Monetary Agreement, opinion-makers in Damascus interpreted his address as a reaction to Jamil Mardam Bey's declaration of 2 February 1948. They focused on Solh's announcement that Syria was with Lebanon at all stages of negotiations with France and was leaning towards accepting and signing the agreement. According with the Lebanese Premier, his government had always acted in compliance with the views of the Syrian government so as to maintain unity of policy between the two states. Solh pointed out that the Syrian government preferred to take a last-minute legal action against the French government at the International Court of Justice, while the Lebanese government opted to sign the agreement in order to prevent a Lebanese currency loss and to spare the country a monetary collapse. Opinion-makers then highlighted the Lebanese Prime Minister's anger at the Syrian government that, as he saw it, attempted to mingle patriotism and economics. Solh stated that he did not accept decrees issued in the name of patriotism from any government or personality. He said that he preferred that the League of Arab States (LAS) arbitrate Lebanon's monetary differences with Syria, saying he accepted its verdict, whatever it may be.

Syrian opinion-makers admitted that their government was with Lebanon in all the stages of negotiations but, after consultations with Syrian men of business, finance and economy, the leaders in Damascus became convinced that in the long term Syria would profit from the liberation of its currency. Exacerbating matters was an article in the 3 February 1948 issue of the French magazine *Le Figaro*, which observed that the Franco-Lebanese Monetary Agreement was a political victory for France and its allies in Lebanon. The piece was widely publicised in Syria and used against the Lebanese Prime Minister. Referring to the article, Arab nationalist circles in Syria maintained that Syria was compelled to refuse the agreement out of patriotic and nationalist conviction. The same circles criticised Solh for only consulting politicians and shareholders of the BSL – like Henri Phar'oun and other businessmen – who benefited from France on the account of their country. They maintained that France's clients in Lebanon planted fears in the Prime Minister's head that a monetary catastrophe would befall the Lebanese if he did not sign the agreement with France. It was also thought that these clients drove Solh to attack Syria by ordering the BSL to announce that Syrian banknotes would not be accepted in Lebanon within 24 hours – thereby attempting to weaken confidence in the Syrian currency.[54] Prime Minister Solh's announcement that the Syro-Lebanese partnership would remain was not taken seriously in Syria. On the contrary, the Syrians were calling on the Lebanese to reject the agreement with France and to walk with Syria; otherwise there would be economic separation.[55]

A statement by Syrian Finance Minister Wehbe al-Hariri, and the subsequent commentaries on it, was instructive of the 'post Franco-Lebanese Monetary Agreement' thinking in Damascus. The minister maintained that Syria's priority would be to export its goods in return for hard currency. Hariri indicated that Lebanon would be given priority in purchasing Syrian goods but only with hard currency. The Syrian minister's statements were widely endorsed by Syrian commentators, particularly Najib al-Raiyyes. Raiyyes wrote that there were a number of Lebanese ill-wishers who favoured total economic separation from Syria. Raiyyes pointed out that the Monetary Agreement with France had realised their dream and

> here is Riad el-Solh who did not disappoint them, he worked for the 'Lebanist interests of Lebanon' (*faqad 'amila li maslahat lubnan al-lubnaniya*), sacrificing his Arab popularity outside Lebanon, as a true Lebanese. We are justified in establishing strong barriers and strict surveillance between ourselves and the Lebanese so that the wealth (*khairat*), which the French shall throw at the Lebanese, does not infiltrate our borders... we are not ready for our country to become a market for this hidden colonialism. This is why the minister of economy stated that Syrian measures are not directed against the Lebanese but to protect the Syrian economy.[56]

It is important to mention that throughout February manoeuvres by the Syrian President to alter the constitution to enable him to hold a second consecutive term in office increased in intensity. Quwwatly utilised Syria's refusal to sign the

Monetary Agreement to publicise his determination to maintain Syria's complete independence and sovereignty.[57]

Both states were well on their way towards separation. Jamil Shehab, head of the Customs Directorate, had issued a directive to all customs stations not to accept Syrian currency in the payment of fees on imported goods, even if such goods were imported on the basis of licences from the Syrian Ministry of Economy. The Syrian government retaliated by not permitting the export of agricultural and industrial goods to Lebanon and intensifying controls at its border.[58] Significantly, Michel Chiha attributed Lebanese mistrust of any form of economic reliance on Syria to Damascus' restrictive measures on the circulation of food supplies, which was in force well before the Paris Monetary Agreement. In a strongly worded editorial, Chiha wrote that the Lebanese were not afraid of being without meat for a couple of days per week. 'Shall our neighbours persist to put us in penitence.' Chiha was reacting to a directive by the Syrian Ministry of Economy prohibiting the export of livestock to Lebanon. The Syrian directive came exactly 24 hours after Lebanon signed the Monetary Agreement.[59] Much ink was spilled in Lebanon about Damascus' 'petty policy' that was revealing itself daily at the Syro-Lebanese border – customs duties having gone as far as confiscating three eggs.[60]

Henri Phar'oun, a renowned Lebanese businessman and politician, declared that the Syrians who believed that they could suffocate the Lebanese by closing their borders were completely losing sight of the fact that when a producer loses a client, it was he who suffered the greatest loss. Phar'oun dismissed any notion that Lebanon could not survive on its own. He believed that the continuous threat of the closure of borders, although a discomfort to many Lebanese, was useful for the country since Lebanon would be forced to develop its own agricultural sector more rapidly. Regarding the Paris Accord, he maintained that he did not understand the reasons behind Syrian attacks against the Lebanese, especially since the agreement did not harm them, 'unless they are bothered by our existence as an independent state'.[61]

Syrian Unionist Ghassan Tweini commented on the consequences of Syrian economic measures against Lebanon and warned Damascus of their political ramifications.

> We, who have frequently conducted campaigns against stubborn isolationists in Lebanon … find ourselves obliged to take the same position against our stubborn neighbours. The policy of separation, which Syria is waving at us, only agrees with the [radical nationalist] isolationists in Lebanon.
>
> We have frequently called upon the Syrians to put an end to press campaigns that poison the atmosphere … We would like to point out to the Syrian government that its economic interests lie in cooperating with Lebanon. Regardless of the extent of necessary economic separation between the two states, this does not justify the barriers it establishes and the restrictions it is imposing. We repeat that economics and politics are inseparable, and this is why we are concerned that the barriers that

Syria is establishing will have political ramifications that neither the Syrians nor the Lebanese wish.[62]

Lebanese financial and business circles were in agreement with Tweini. They predicted that the decision to pursue monetary separation between Lebanon and Syria was expected to have repercussions not only on bilateral relations but also on individual relations between Lebanese and Syrians. They blamed the poor manner in which the monetary relations were negotiated and conducted. The majority of Lebanese businessmen had particular reservations about the selection of the official delegations to Paris, and the failure of both governments to inform their respective business communities on the progress of negotiations and to alert them about what future course Beirut and Damascus were planning. They strongly objected to the policies of both governments, which lacked planning. There was consensus on Lebanon's signature of the Paris Accord. It was believed that, had Lebanon followed Syria, the next day the Lebanese currency would have dropped to a tenth of its value. Lebanon alleviated itself of this prospect and gave Syria an invaluable opportunity to benefit from the retained confidence in the Lebanese currency until such time as she was able to manage her financial affairs.[63]

Giving credence to the predictions of Lebanese opinion-makers and business-men, reports from Damascus indicated that Syrian merchants refrained from exporting their merchandise to Beirut on their own initiative,[64] preferring destinations that would surely earn them hard currencies. Indeed, monetary separation was beginning to affect Lebanese and Syrian economic behaviour. The Syrian government was applying its 'grain for dollars' policy to Lebanon. At a meeting between the Economy Ministers of both countries in Shtura on 12 February – two days after Syria closed its border with Lebanon – the Syrian minister stated that his government would not prohibit the export of grain as long as the grain was paid for in dollars or sterling. Syria's grain embargo generated hostility on the part of the Lebanese public and increased the Syro-Lebanese trade imbalance in favour of Lebanon, thus weakening the newly 'independent' Syrian lira.[65]

Syrian measures against Lebanon were also starting to make themselves felt at the popular level. After signing the Monetary Agreement in Paris, several staples increased in price. Lebanese bakeries were facing increased difficulties in maintaining their flour supplies so the price of bread and other flour-based goods rose by 25 per cent. The price of meat went up by 30 per cent. Vegetables and beans had seen a 24 per cent price increase. Fat (*samneh*) had a 10 per cent price increase. The fabrics and textiles market faced almost complete paralysis. On the other hand, while prices were rising in Lebanon, the same goods were stockpiling in Syria, causing prices there to drop. Since most of the goods produced in Syria were consumed in Lebanon, the Syrian market came to a virtual standstill.[66]

As Syrian economic pressure mounted, the Lebanese cabinet convened on 13 February 1948, after which Finance Minister Muhammad 'Aboud stated that hopes of reaching an understanding with Syria had not perished. 'Aboud revealed that the cancellation of the Monetary Agreement had been suggested during the cabinet session, as a means of lifting Syria's economic measures against Lebanon. The majority of ministers saw that this was currently not possible because of the absence of the Prime Minister, who was in Cairo attending an Arab League summit conference.[67]

B. ARAB LEAGUE ARBITRATION

On 12 February 1948, the Arab League (LAS) summit was hosted in Cairo and attended by the Lebanese Prime Minister. Syro-Lebanese differences were informally discussed in a closed meeting between Solh, Mardam Bey and LAS Secretary General 'Azzam Pasha. The summit was an opportunity for the Lebanese Premier to promote the position of his government and defend its signing of the Paris Accord. Mardam Bey made also use of the summit to champion the Syrian stance.[68]

Solh had first raised the option of LAS arbitration in an address to the Lebanese parliament. He hoped that by inviting LAS to arbitrate, the Arab regional organisation would decide favourably for Lebanon.[69] The LAS had to decide whether, by unilaterally signing the Monetary Agreement, Lebanon was responsible for the deterioration of its relations with Syria or whether Syria had intentionally surprised Lebanon by suddenly withdrawing from the negotiations. Although LAS arbitration was not binding to either party, a favourable decision would grant the veteran Arab nationalist a legitimacy that would be to his political advantage. Should the LAS decide against the Lebanese case, Solh had declared that he would resign – thereby rendering the Lebanese government unable to implement any LAS recommendation. The Lebanese Premier thus skilfully made Syro-Lebanese relations the subject of arbitration, not Lebanese interests – a move widely appreciated by Lebanon's ruling and economic elites.

After eight days of intense meetings, an agreement was reached. The 'Gentlemen's Agreement', as it came to be known, was to last until 15 March 1948. In the Syrian view, the Gentlemen's Agreement was an opportunity for the Lebanese to reconsider their monetary ties with France before the Franco-Lebanese Monetary Agreement was ratified by the Lebanese parliament. Moreover, Damascus was under the impression that the Paris Accord would lead most of the Lebanese House to pass a non-confidence motion against the Solh government, but with the Gentlemen's Agreement this became less of a threat. The Syrian leadership intended to appease Riad el-Solh. Damascus was concerned about the political repercussions if their ally should turn up in Beirut empty-handed. Moreover, the Syrian ruling elite was growing increasingly apprehensive of their principal ally's turn to the Lebanese nationalist camp.[70] In fact, upon his return from Cairo, Riad el-Solh confided to the British ambassador in Beirut that for the first time since

1943, Lebanese Christians had regrouped and that communal feeling, which had been dormant since then, was again on the rise. Not only was the regime – which was based on cooperation between Muslims and an important section of the Christians – in danger but the territorial status quo might be threatened should the Muslim parts of Lebanon agitate for incorporation in Syria. If the movement was successful, this would leave what Solh called the 'cancer' of a little Lebanon in which French influence would be predominant. Solh expressed the hope that the British ambassador in Damascus would counsel moderation, with a view to the prolongation of the 'Gentlemen's Agreement' so that tempers could cool. The Lebanese President, and later the Foreign Minister, made similar advances towards the British legation.[71]

Beirut and Damascus saw the agreement as a truce. The only cause of apprehension was its short duration. Syrian public opinion did not have much confidence in the Gentlemen's Agreement. Newspapers warned Syrian merchants to release their goods from Lebanese customs before the agreement's termination.[72] Syrian editorials called for the need to reconsider the agreement of the Common Interests, regardless of whether the Lebanese parliament ratified the Paris Accord or not. There was a consensus in Damascus that the Lebanese would ratify the Monetary Agreement and that consequently the economic partnership would come to an end by 15 March. Syrian opinion-makers called on their government to be prepared for such an eventuality. It was suggested that the Syrian authorities find specialised civil servants to manage the Customs Directorate and establish customs. These directorates should be run directly from Damascus. In Syria, the Ministries of Finance and Economy began the systematic liquidation of any joint Syrian and Lebanese administrative and governmental transactions.[73]

On the other hand, political and commercial elites in Lebanon viewed Damascus' signing the Gentlemen's Agreement as a sign of Syrian moderation. Commenting on what had transpired in February, Lebanese analysts confessed that although they were fully aware of Syria's favourable attitude to a radical command economy, they never expected it to go to such extreme lengths as to force its will on Lebanon. Almost gloating, Michel Chiha wrote that the Lebanese lira's purchasing power was safe, that 'our windows to the world remain open and here we are free to determine our future away from worry and constraints. Our Syrian friends should like us the way we are and should be very satisfied that we can afford to buy more from them.'[74] As a matter of fact, shortly after the Gentlemen's Agreement was signed, and the Syrian embargo lifted, Syrian merchants flooded the Lebanese market.[75]

With news of the deteriorating situation in Palestine and escalating fighting between Zionists and Palestinian Arabs,[76] high-level delegations headed by the Syrian and Lebanese Premiers met in Shtura on 1 March 1948. It was their first meeting after the boycott.[77] The Lebanese aim in the negotiations was to achieve freer and equitable trade and a minimum of Syrian protectionism. Lebanon's biggest challenge was to avert the Syrian tendency to stress politics at the expense of economic considerations. This was mainly due to the Syrian resentment of the Lebanese intention to sign the Franco-Lebanese Monetary Agreement. Lebanon's ruling elite wished to retain the economic union but not at the expense of sacrificing Lebanese political autonomy.[78] Hence, it was no surprise that neither this meeting, nor subsequent meetings, nor the numerous reciprocal visits of the Premiers, were unable to resolve any of the outstanding issues between Beirut and Damascus. Nevertheless, they managed to generate an atmosphere of calm among political and commercial circles in both states. More importantly, by the middle of March, Syro-Lebanese discussions resulted in extending the Gentlemen's Agreement until the end of that month.[79]

It was hoped that the modus vivendi between the two states, particularly the easing of tensions, would provide additional room for bilateral talks. In safeguarding the calm atmosphere, Prime Minister Solh indicated in a press conference that the Syrian government had given strict instructions to the press to abstain from 'sterile and dangerous polemics'. Similarly, he instructed Lebanon's Interior Ministry Director General Adib Nahas to restrain the Lebanese press.[80] News of the agreement's extension was received with 'disgust and revulsion' by the Syrian political and commercial elite, especially since it was coupled with rumours from Beirut that the Lebanese parliament was not due to convene to discuss the Paris Accord until October. This was regarded in Damascus as a manoeuvre by the Lebanese to force Syria into a Monetary Agreement with France. Opinion-makers in Damascus called on Beirut to submit the Paris Accord to the Lebanese parliament so that 'the Syrians will know the Lebanese position before the harvest and before this harvest goes to Lebanon in return for Lebanese banknotes covered by the French franc'.[81] It was obvious that pressure was increasing on the Mardam Bey government to finalise economic relations with Lebanon. As the exchange rates of the Syrian and Lebanese currencies grew ever wider, the Syrian Prime Minister was pressed by public opinion into declaring that, should Lebanon not refute the Paris Accord, there would be economic separation.[82]

On 21 March, Beirut hosted the Council of LAS, which was discussing the situation in Palestine. It was also an opportunity for 'Azzam Pasha to mediate between the Lebanese and Syrian leaderships.[83] Mediation proved very difficult. Opinion-makers in both capitals urged their governments to prepare for economic separation.[84] In any event, the Syrians were behaving as if separation was in force. The Syrian government had drafted a bill that would supervise the banks in Syria and had drawn a draft bill to protect the Syrian lira. The proposal included strict penalties for citizens who did not abide by the new regulations. Damascus was also working to encourage agricultural development and to ration its grain supplies so as to export the rest for hard currency. Damascus had also initiated negotiations to sell grain to Cairo (at a price of $130 a ton). The Syrians offered 200,000 tons to the Egyptians, which left some Lebanese wondering what their government had done to ensure bread for Lebanon.[85]

It took 'Azzam Pasha 12 days of intense negotiations, during which the Kings of Saudi Arabia and Egypt intervened, to broker an agreement between Beirut and Damascus. Again, Riad el-Solh called upon the British to intervene with the Syrians. The new agreement simply extended the Gentlemen's Agreement for an additional one and a half months. The driving factor that led to this temporary understanding was the deteriorating situation in Palestine. Arab leaders urged Beirut and Damascus to patch up their differences in light of Zionist threats.[86] In fact, after 6 April, the Palestine conflict overshadowed Syro-Lebanese differences and was to remain the priority in the deliberations of the Lebanese and Syrian leaderships.

In May 1948, the Deir Yassin massacre and the fall of Haifa, and the uprooting of 200,000 Palestinian refugees, stirred Arab public opinion. Scenes of popular demonstrations and strikes became common. At the government level the Damascus meeting of the Arab League Political Committee was quickly followed by the Lebanese and Syrian heads of government meeting in Riyadh and later in Jordan, while the Regent of Iraq travelled to Cairo. A state of emergency was declared on 14 May and the Arabs formally decided for armed intervention in Palestine. The period from 15 May (the day the Syrian army crossed into Palestine) to 1 June (when the first truce was accepted) was one of Arab success and great optimism. The truce did not last long, however, and reverses soon followed. By July the Arabs had accepted the Security Council's ceasefire order. With it, chances for immediate successes in Palestine came to an end.[87]

In light of the situation in Palestine the Gentlemen's Agreement was duly extended, without much controversy or need for foreign mediation, first on 26 May and again on 27 June. The Gentlemen's Agreement did not witness much amendment from the version brokered by 'Azzam Pasha, aside from an article concerning Syrian and Lebanese banknotes retained by each government. In the discussions that led to the extension of the agreement in June, the Syrian government even undertook to supply Lebanon with grain supplies to last until the end of 1948. The Lebanese government was to pay for its grain in Lebanese or Syrian lira.[88]

Studying the communiqués issued after each meeting, opinion-makers saw how the two governments were unable to decide on a lasting economic agreement. Hence, in the last meeting, the Gentlemen's Agreement was extended another three months. During that time the Syrian and Lebanese representatives in the HCCI were delegated with creating a formula for a lasting agreement. In any case, the extension of the agreement, and Syria's agreement to supply Lebanon with grain, were indicators that both states were adamant in retaining the customs union and economic partnership, at least for the time being.[89] This was coupled with a virtual paralysis on the Lebanese commodities market, which was becoming more acute because of the situation in Palestine. Syrian and Lebanese consumers, already saddled with exorbitant living costs that continued to mount, were showing great reluctance to part with their money to buy commodities other than essentials.

Money was no longer plentiful. Merchants were forced to borrow to meet their obligations. The rush to borrow caused banks to tighten discounts. This state of affairs was further aggravated by the BSL policy, whose primary concern was monetary deflation. In Lebanon over a period of two months, the BSL had withdrawn 7.3 per cent of the banknotes in circulation.[90] These measures were coupled with measures on the part of Riad el-Solh's government to cut public expenditures by reducing the number of civil servants in the public sector and abolishing unoccupied positions.[91]

At the beginning of August, the *Office des changes* issued a decree in which it modified the convertibility of the Lebanese lira with the French franc. The regulation provided that all franc transfers from Lebanon on or after 3 August must have prior authorisation of the *Office des changes*. This regulation previously applied to other foreign currencies only. It was extended to French francs because, despite its remaining aloof of the Franco-Lebanese Monetary Agreement, the Syrian lira continued to be almost on par with the Lebanese currency (one dollar equalling L£2.185 at the legal rate, but L£3.45 on the open market, which was used for most transactions). Syria had thus been able to change her currency into Lebanese and make purchases in the franc bloc almost as easily as Lebanon. This pauperised Lebanon to the benefit of Syria and it was hoped that this new regulation would put an end to the practice.[92]

The Franco-Lebanese Monetary Agreement returned to centre stage again at the end of August 1948. During that time, Damascus had reopened monetary negotiations with Paris. At the same time, the Lebanese parliament convened to ratify the Paris Accord.[93]

Earlier in June, amidst the heaviest fighting in Palestine, the French general assembly ratified the Franco-Lebanese Monetary Agreement. During the debate, the French Foreign Minister informed the assembly that Syria would eventually sign a similar agreement with France. The French minister's statement resonated in Damascus. Shortly afterwards, Prime Minister Mardam Bey held a press conference in which he categorically assured the public that Syria would not go back on its position. After the French general assembly's ratification of the agreement, it was expected that the Lebanese would follow suit. Syrian commentators asked what their government's position would be if the Lebanese parliament ratified the agreement with France. 'We wonder when this country will have an economic and financial position that is not influenced by sentiment or that does not change as circumstances dictate [the situation in Palestine].'[94]

While Damascus continued denying its attempts to come to terms with Paris,[95] on 28 and 29 August, the Lebanese parliament convened and ratified the agreement, with 35 deputies in favour and 6 against. In preparing the grounds for ratification, the parliamentary committee of the Ministry of Finance examined the text of the agreement and Deputy Bahij Takiddine reported its findings to the general assembly. Takiddine informed the assembly that there was a consensus if the agreement were to be rejected: Lebanon would have to suffer considerable losses since an independent country needed a sound currency to avoid the shocks that the market undergoes from time to time. He rejected the argument that the agreement would lead to the dissolution of the Syro-Lebanese customs union, pointing out that customs unions exist among countries with different currencies. At the close of his report, he requested that the assembly ratify the agreement by saying 'of the two evils, one must choose the lesser'.[96] Addressing the general assembly, Finance Minister Hussein Oweini admitted that the agreement was prejudicial to Lebanon and that seven months had elapsed without the government being able to find a better solution: 'In asking us to reject the agreement with France, you must offer a better one.'[97]

Hamid Franjieh broke his eight months' public silence on the matter and gave the Assembly a detailed account of what had transpired during the Paris negotiations. He related how Beirut and Damascus approached a number of governments, among them the United States, the United Kingdom and a number of Arab countries, in an attempt to convince them to cover the Syrian-Lebanese lira. All these efforts failed. The Lebanese Foreign Minister related how in the Shtura meeting on 30 January 1948, Mardam Bey suggested the establishment of a central bank and the issuing of a new Syrian-Lebanese currency. Solh welcomed this idea and requested details of such a plan. Mardam Bey asked to be given one week. After the week had passed, a meeting took place in Saufar, where Mardam Bey repeated his proposals but without giving any details of how they would be achieved. After a number of meetings, Franjieh indicated that both governments decided to negotiate with France, during which the Syrians suddenly withdrew. As regards the concessionary companies, Franjieh disclosed a conversation he had with Mardam Bey. The Syrian Premier had emphasised that concessionary companies were not legally constituted because they had been granted their concessions by the High Commission. Franjieh stated that, contrary to Mardam Bey's statements, all existing concessions had been ratified by the legislative branches of both governments. He concluded this point by declaring that the provisions relating to the concessionary companies were drawn up in Beirut by the Syrian government itself. Addressing the opposition, led by Sami el-Solh, the Minister of Foreign Affairs explained that 'I had to provide these bitter details in order to answer Mr Sami el-Solh, who pretends that the agreement was prepared in one night. It was not prepared in one night, but over 136 nights, with the Syrian government present in 135 of these nights. It was prepared by 100 telegrams and hundreds of letters sent from Damascus and Beirut.' Prime Minister Riad el-Solh concluded the parliamentary session by insisting that the agreement did not mean economic separation from Syria.[98]

Unlike the Lebanese Premier, official circles in Damascus remained pessimistic regarding the future of bilateral economic relations.[99] On 2 September, the Syrian and Lebanese Prime Ministers met in Shtura. After the meeting Solh reiterated his views that economic union between the two states was still possible although Lebanon had ratified the Monetary Agreement. Mardam Bey left Shtura without issuing any statement. Reports were circulating that Syria intended to take economic measures against Lebanon. Wehbe al-Hariri indicated that Syria was in the process of taking serious measures to protect its interests. Hariri was alluding to decrees he himself had signed, which aimed at prohibiting the circulation of the Lebanese lira in Syria and restricting exports to Lebanon.[100] The Syrian minister's statements came while Michel Ilyan, the Syrian Minister of Economy, was holding talks with his Lebanese counterpart on 4 September. Political circles in Beirut interpreted Hariri's threats as a means to pressure the Lebanese government.[101]

The majority of the Lebanese public was disenchanted with Damascus' policies as represented by the statements and measures of Wehbe al-Hariri. His threats only served to further radicalise the Lebanese nationalists. *L'Orient* wrote that Hariri's February blockade was a big mistake on his part. It only served to prove Syria's ambitions in Lebanon. It concluded that the Syrian papers were the ones highlighting separation and that the Lebanese leadership and dailies wished to safeguard the customs union and develop the economic partnership, 'but not at any price and certainly not for the price of Lebanese vassalage'.[102] For his part, Michel Chiha asserted that the monetary convention had spared Lebanon from becoming 'a tributary to others'.[103] Hariri's acts even prompted the Lebanese Arab nationalist daily *al-Nahar* to write that the methods employed by Syrian officials were usually practised in negotiations between enemies and not between two brotherly states.[104] *Le Commerce du Levant*, commenting on how the atmosphere between the Lebanese and Syrian press was getting more poisonous, pointed out how the Lebanese Prime Minister was being called a 'clown' (*bahlawan*) in the Syrian papers. It maintained that the Syrian leadership's conduct would not bring a rapprochement with Lebanon. 'In fact, the Syrian leadership should rid itself of its superiority complex whenever they negotiate with our negotiators. We certainly need Syria, but with its excessive sales to Lebanon, Syria also needs Lebanon, which allows it to equilibrate its balance of payments.'[105]

It was not only in Beirut that Hariri's declarations were met with dismay. Syrian opinion-makers, as well as financial and economic circles, expressed their disappointment with their government's economic policies and empty threats that were supposed to bring Lebanon in line but had in fact harmed the Syrian economy. The manner in which the Syrian Finance Minister intended to prohibit the circulation of the Lebanese currency in Syria was questioned – especially since Lebanese banknotes were in very short supply.

> Does not the Minister of Finance see that the Syrian currency is offered in thousands and hundred of thousands by Syrians in Lebanon, which forced the Syrians, because of the sterile policy of the government, to become slaves to the Lebanese market. What has the Syrian government achieved during the nine months that have past

since the Syrian currency's separation from the franc? So far it only seems the inconvertibility of the lira.[106]

Echoing these concerns was 'Aref al-Laham, who maintained that since the separation of the Syrian lira from the franc bloc, the Syrian currency did not have a real exchange rate, only a fictitious one. Consequently, Syria was unable to purchase a single dollar. Moreover, the *Office des changes* had no hard currency, which caused the depreciation of the Syrian lira. Syrian factory owners could only import their raw materials through the black market, which in turn raised the prices of locally produced goods. The price of these goods was 70 per cent higher than that of the world market. Hence, Syrian goods were uncompetitive for export. Laham described the unstable monetary situation in Syria as the worst crisis in its history.

Syrian officials informally assured their business and manufacturing communities that the situation would improve as soon as the Lebanese followed Syria into an economic union. Laham criticised this policy since Lebanese decision-makers declared their intentions from the very beginning, making Syrian official optimism baseless. The secretary general of the Syrian Chamber of Commerce pointed out how monetary instability in Syria only served to increase Lebanese commercial activity, and consequently the demand on the Lebanese lira, which resulted in the rise in its value compared to the Syrian lira.

Laham underlined how Syria's inadequate export policies had allowed Lebanon to become the centre for the black market in hard currencies, which permitted the Lebanese to monopolise exports of Syrian agricultural and industrial goods. In fact, the acceptance of Syrian currency at Lebanese customs had only resulted in Syria's increased dependence on Beirut. Syrian merchants took Syrian banknotes to Lebanese banks, where they exchanged them for Lebanese currency in order to purchase hard currency.

> Syria is still waiting for Lebanon to return to its Syrian patron for the interest of good neighbourly relations and Arab brotherhood. The policy of Lebanon is a policy of pure opportunism. There are numerous examples of the Lebanese contradicting every decision or policy made by Syria. Therefore, the time has come for Syria to announce its independent economic policy and declare the liquidation of the Common Interests.[107]

Syria's economic blockade against Lebanon, which entailed the prohibition of exports and imports to and from it, was popular among the Syrian public. However, the conclusion of the Gentlemen's Agreement and its numerous extensions was met with dismay. Lebanon was accused of taking advantage of the situation in Palestine that called for Arab solidarity in the face of the Zionist onslaught. Unscrupulously, the Lebanese ratified the Paris Accord and presented Syria with a fait accompli. Syrian merchants and financiers were looking down upon their leadership, charging it with weakness and incompetence in guarding the interests of the country. It was also maintained that it was only a matter of time until the bad trade relations would spill over and poison political relations between the two states. Decision-makers in Damascus were being called upon to cease the signature of temporary agreements and liberate Syria from economic slavery to Lebanon.[108]

Although Syrian public opinion was calling on its leadership to terminate the economic partnership and customs union, official circles in Beirut seemed confident that their counterparts in Damascus were not seriously considering separation or another embargo. This could be concluded from the statement of the Lebanese Foreign Minister, who was asked to comment on Syro-Lebanese economic relations in light of the likely termination of the Gentlemen's Agreement at the end of September. Lebanese Foreign Minister Philip Takla declared that the Gentlemen's Agreement played a key role in the Syrian economy. According to the minister, the agreement protected the Syrian currency from an unstable position since it was not pegged to any currency and did not have any international exchange rate. Takla maintained that in the event that the agreement was prolonged at the end of September, the Lebanese lira would again be covering its Syrian counterpart, until such time as the Syrians found a way to keep their honour intact and serve Lebanese and Syrian interests. Takla concluded his statement by hinting that until Syria finalised its monetary policy, the country would continue with the Gentlemen's Agreement.[109]

However, the gulf between Beirut and Damascus was widening. In fact, ministerial-level Syro-Lebanese–Iraqi trade talks – planned for Syria during August and then postponed until September – did not materialise. Syro-Lebanese economic difficulties were blamed. These difficulties were further aggravated not only by the Lebanese chamber's ratification of the Monetary Agreement, but by the Syrian government decree of 12 August, which greatly tightened government control of foreign trade and foreign exchange transactions. The decree was promulgated without prior consultation with Lebanon. The Syrian action met with Lebanese disapproval and the Lebanese government contemplated how far it could go along with the latest Syrian measure.[110]

C. RESTRICTION OF IMPORTS

Towards the end of September and the following months, Syro-Lebanese negotiations intensified. The focus of the discussions was to replace the Gentlemen's Agreement with a more permanent accord. The debate concentrated on the limitation of imports; the encouragement and protection of local industries; the stabilisation of an equal exchange rate for the Lebanese and Syrian liras; Lebanon's grain supply. The beginning of negotiations was accompanied by optimistic declarations by Mardam Bey, who emphasised that the interests of the two states were one. He urged political circles and the members of the press to devote their efforts to bringing the two states together instead of calling for separation.

Although the Lebanese agreed to most of the Syrian demands with few amendments, including Damascus' demand to establish an equal exchange rate for the two countries' currencies, negotiations deadlocked on the limitation of imports. The extensive utilisation of experts by both states did not assist in bridging the views. Throughout the talks, the Syrians were careful to link any agreement on Lebanese grain supplies to the outcome of negotiations.[111]

After four long summits at the prime ministerial and ministerial levels during the third and fourth weeks of September, there was still no agreement in sight. In fact, 1 October 1948 was the first day to pass in which there was no written economic agreement between Syria and Lebanon. The public interpreted the number and intensity of meetings to be a sign that their leaders were adamant about reaching an agreement that would retain the economic partnership. Consequently, and in spite of the impasse, markets did not suffer. Market prices of vital foodstuffs remained unaffected in Syria and Lebanon; however, the gap between the two currencies grew from two to six per cent, putting more pressure on the Syrian negotiators. In addition, factory owners in Lebanon and Syria lowered their production to a minimum, awaiting the outcome of the negotiations on the restriction of imports.[112]

Negotiations between the two states had resulted in a draft agreement, which stipulated the maintenance of the economic and customs union; facilitated exports – provided that local prices remained unaffected; reorganised import regulations to end the anarchy on that front. The reorganisation of import regulations would take into consideration the two states' balance of trade. There was no consensus on the new import regulations. The Lebanese demanded that certain items be imported without restrictions, while the Syrians insisted on restrictions. The Syrians informed the Lebanese that if they agreed to their proposals, they would undertake to supply Lebanon with its grain needs and would accept payment in Syrian lira.[113]

Lebanese decision-makers preferred to consult the country's leading businessmen. On 3 October 1948, a delegation of 14 merchants, representing Lebanon's business community met with the Lebanese President. Also attending the meeting were the Ministers of Foreign Affairs, Finance and Economy. There was consensus that the customs union and the economic partnership should be maintained with Syria. However, the majority of merchants expressed their strong objection to the limitation of imports. Syrian demands would make imports subject to licences from the Ministry of Economy. The merchants argued that such a measure would hamper their business transactions. They pointed out that business offers were conducted through telegrams. Good business opportunities would be lost since the time needed to attain a licence would result in the loss of advantageous business deals. It was also argued that the application for a licence at the Ministry of Economy would force merchants to reveal their contacts and the source of their bargains. In addition, merchants with political clout would have the advantage of obtaining licences faster, if licences were in fact being granted. As a compromise, it was agreed to limit the import of luxury goods for a limited period of time. Accordingly, a list of such goods was drafted.[114]

Aside from the Ministers of Economy and Finance, the import-limitation discussions included the Lebanese and Syrian heads of the HCCI, Musa Moubarak and Hassan Joubara. Both civil servants were delegated to draw up a list of import goods to be restricted.[115] When the moment came to finalise that list, however, the Syrian negotiators proved too demanding, intending to restrict the entry of a great number of products vital to the Lebanese tourist industry.[116] Lebanese merchants stepped up their pressure. On 11 October another merchant delegation visited President Khuri, presenting him with a memorandum underscoring Lebanon's status as a consumer and mercantile nation and its interest in the adoption of a free-trade policy. It was claimed that any limitation on imports would threaten a great number of merchants with bankruptcy. The memorandum concluded by stressing that Lebanon had trade relations with other Middle and Far Eastern states, not only Syria.[117] On 14 October, Lebanese merchants convened a conference to present a report prepared by a previously established preparatory committee. The report concluded that trade had always been Lebanon's main source of livelihood, after which came agriculture. The conference condemned any notion of restricting trade. Should an accommodation with Syria prove difficult to reach, it recommended turning Lebanon into a free-trade zone.[118]

The efforts of the Lebanese merchants were not in vain. In a meeting between the Lebanese and Syrian Ministers of Economy and Finance, the Lebanese representatives demanded amendments in some of the articles of the agreement. The Syrian side maintained that the new economic policy was in the interests of Lebanon and Syria, that weakening the transit trade would affect 30,000 merchants while the reinvigoration of local industry would benefit hundreds of thousands. The Syrians even permitted the Lebanese to import any shortfall should local production fall short. The Syrians also pointed out that the transit and re-export trade would remain unrestricted. They declared their readiness to compensate Lebanon by providing 40 per cent of Syrian national production to Lebanese merchants for export. The Syrians even made concessions on the grain issue, declaring that they would not hinder Lebanese imports of grain from abroad. If it were decided to import from Syria, the Syrians reiterated their previous offer to accept payment in Lebanese or Syrian currency.[119]

Aside from the question of import restrictions, the economic and political elites in Lebanon feared that any state intervention in the economy would eventually lead to a command economy. In their view, a command economy would not work in Lebanon. The state itself, including its various directorates and departments, was weak and not obeyed – indeed any type of discipline was said to horrify the

Lebanese citizen. Moreover, any compromise on liberties would jeopardise national coexistence. A command economy was perceived as putting the country on the road to state socialism, and with it autocracy. In Lebanon, where different communities have to cooperate and live together, it was inconceivable that the state become omnipotent and start controlling the thoughts and movement of every citizen, particularly if that state retained a corrupt administration. Under these circumstances Lebanese commercial sense and initiative would be lost. Worse, in a multi-religious environment, which sect would control the state and its people?[120]

Lebanese advocates of laissez-faire saw through Syrian motives for a command economy. They believed that the considerable profits made by the Syrian industrialists and merchants during the war had raised their expectations to the degree that some ten large industrial projects had been laid down. These projects were begun without serious economic and technical studies. Most of them, such as the S£7–8 million glass factory and the S£7–8 million sugar refinery, had been overcapitalised. The private industrial projects that had been or were in the process of being established involved S£70 million, of which S£45–50 million had already been spent. Operation of these factories had yielded disappointing results. While a ton of imported sugar CIF Beirut, for example, went for 35 to 40 Syrian piastres per kilo, the production of a kilo of sugar by the refinery at Homs cost 90–110 Syrian piastres. Hence, the Syrian government envisaged granting maximum protection to its nascent industry in order to defend the capital spent on it.[121]

Although strong supporters of laissez-faire in Lebanon were calling on the Syrian and Lebanese leadership to reach common ground, there was strong criticism in Syria against the government's persistent negotiations with Lebanon. Some questioned the wisdom of negotiating with a state whose geographical location, economic policy and social nature did not permit the conclusion of an economic agreement with Syria. It was being advocated in Damascus to leave Lebanon to conduct its own state of affairs according to the desires of its commercial and ruling elite. 'Syria should not insist on Lebanon changing its nature. Why doesn't Syria leave them alone? Syria should organize its own economic affairs within its means.' Syrian analysts maintained that Syrian negotiators were giving the impression that Damascus needed to agree with the Lebanese and that the Syrian lira would collapse if it were not put on par with its Lebanese counterpart.[122]

Opinion-makers in Damascus regarded President Khuri's assurances to the Lebanese commercial elites as the most important indicator of Lebanese intentions. Upon receiving the memorandum outlining the merchants' recommendations, the Lebanese head of state declared that his mission was to safeguard the interests of Lebanon. He emphasised good relations with Syria but that such relations did not entail the sacrifice of Lebanese interests. He stressed the significant role Lebanese merchants were playing in the development of national and regional trade. 'Lebanese trade has managed to attain a good position [at the regional level], which we are not willing to give up. We will make every effort to retain the current economic system.'[123]

It became clear to the Syrian ruling elite that the Lebanese President was not willing to abandon Lebanon's economic system. He was seen to express what Lebanese negotiators were unable to reveal to their Syrian counterparts in their numerous meetings. Consequently, the sense of futility about negotiating with Lebanon had grown, not only in Syrian commercial and economic circles generally, but across the entire country. Aside from calls to suspend the Gentlemen's Agreement, and to terminate the Common Interests, Syrian demands that the currency be put on par with the Lebanese were found shameful and embarrassing.

> The most insulting aspect is the demand to equalize the value of the two currencies. This is unacceptable to a nation that is sovereign, wealthy and which had rejected a French offer to cover the Syrian lira. If we rejected having a country like France cover our currency, does this not insult our honour that a country like Lebanon is covering our currency? [...] The humiliation we are suffering in Lebanon, where our currency is being refused by Lebanese painters and is mocked by waiters, is enough.[124]

The leadership in Damascus was also questioned about how it expected the Lebanese to agree to limit imports while the Syrian lira was in dire straits.[125] The extent of Syrian public frustration was expressed by Najib al-Raiyyes, who wrote: 'We are sorry for this country where wealth and harvests are being stockpiled. We are sorry for this country, which has no foreign markets. We are sorry for this country which hasn't the brains and the know-how nor the people with good intentions [in its governmental institutions].'[126]

On 20 October, Syrian Minister of Finance Hariri arrived in Beirut and met with his Lebanese counterpart, Oweini. However, before his meeting with the Lebanese minister Hariri held two long meetings with the director of the BSL, René Busson.[127] It was generally known among Lebanese policy-makers that the focus of the discussion was Franco-Syrian monetary talks, which had resumed earlier. The Syrian cabinet was currently reviewing a draft agreement but had reservations on certain articles, which were the subject of discussions between Hariri and Busson. An official Lebanese government spokesman denied that Hariri's visit was aimed to resume Syro-Lebanese economic negotiations. Speculations in Beirut that the Syrians were on the verge of conducting a Monetary Agreement with France were increasing. Although these reports were being vehemently denied in the Syrian press.[128]

Nevertheless, Lebanon's ultra-Arab nationalist daily *Beirut al-Masa'* confirmed that the Syrian cabinet was on the verge of signing the Monetary Agreement that was negotiated in Paris by Busson, on one hand, and Joubara and 'Azem on the other. The daily maintained that after it consulted specialists to review the Franco-Syrian Monetary Agreement, it turned out that it was not much different from the Franco-Lebanese version, in spite of some minor alterations. The paper recalled how Mardam Bey accused Solh of taking the sovereignty of Lebanon lightly. The paper also recalled the statements of Mardam Bey and Hariri in the Syrian parliament, where both men declared that Lebanon had strayed from the Arab nationalist cause while Syria would not follow the same road and would not extend its hand to France another time. The daily concluded that, like Lebanon, Syria had conceded part of its financial sovereignty to France. 'Thus Syria became a path, headquarters and residence to colonialism.'[129]

Completely ignoring the reports of a Franco-Syrian Monetary Agreement, the Syrian financial and economic elite held a conference that focused on Syro-Lebanese economic relations. During deliberations in Damascus between 1 and 2 November 1948 it was opined that Lebanon's refusal to limit imports served the economic interests of a certain social class and discarded the national interests of Lebanon and Syria. The conference rejected Lebanese proposals to only limit certain imports. It called for the independent organisation of the Syrian economy, in such a manner that Syria would be free from the burden of an economic union with Lebanon that lacked equal benefits and hampered its development as a result.[130] Only two days after the conclusion of the Damascus conference, and in response to it, the executive body of the merchants' conference in Lebanon held a meeting. It was decided to establish an importers' association in order to promote cooperation between the merchants in the defence of free trade. The executive committee regarded the proceedings of the Damascus conference as falling under the influence of the large Syrian industrialists and their political associates, who were bound to damage the Lebanese economy and choke freedom of trade.[131]

Commenting on the polarisation of Lebanese and Syrian public opinion, Najib al-Raiyyes reiterated that maintaining the customs union would damage not only the economic relations but the political ties of the two peoples. Raiyyes related how the press in Lebanon had convinced the public that they were the ones being wronged in the economic partnership. Consequently, the Lebanese press conducted a campaign against the Syrian people as well as its government and managed to fill the Lebanese with hatred towards Syria. Raiyyes was convinced that sentiments in both states were so high that it would be difficult to return to the atmosphere that existed between the two peoples a year earlier. He added that both governments had become unable to convince public opinion of the advantages of retaining the union. Stressing the need to solidify Syro-Lebanese position against the struggle in Palestine, he asked, 'How can we fight a common enemy if we are fighting each other ... The dissolution of the union has become the only medication to treat the hatred that fills the Lebanese papers. It would treat the hatred of all the Lebanese people from the different social classes.'[132] Raiyyes' editorial is a clear indicator, if not admission, of the widespread dismay with Syria that had spread to all the Lebanese, regardless of political or economic affiliation.

As during the course of the Syro-Lebanese discussions of October 1943, political considerations had become inextricably interwoven into economic issues. They had prevented Syrian impatience from exploding into complete rupture and, according to some observers, this was believed to pave the path to a final accord.

The Syrian view, shared by President Quwwatly and the majority of the Syrian cabinet, was that Lebanon must not be estranged from the Arab camp and allowed to drift towards the West – with its attendant danger that she would become a base for the eventual economic conquest of the Middle East by European Powers. In addition, the Syrian and Lebanese leaderships strongly felt it desirable to preserve a semblance of Arab unity in the face of the Palestine situation. Tensions between Cairo on the one hand and Amman and Baghdad on the other threatened the disintegration of the Arab League, an eventuality Beirut and Damascus wished to avoid at all cost. Tensions surfaced when it became known that the Jordanian King wanted to annex the entire West Bank, which met with opposition from Cairo and Riyadh. In that regard, the Lebanese and Syrian governments dispatched Hussein Oweini to Cairo and Riyadh to mediate and prevent a total collapse of the Arab League. At the same time, Riad el-Solh was in Baghdad and Amman for the same purpose. The Syrian predicament was further exacerbated by the fact that, after June, the Zionists had completely reversed the military situation in their favour. From August onwards, the Syrian army took no active part in the fighting, confining its duties to the defence of Syrian soil.[133]

The basic dilemma confronting the Syrian government was one of how to maintain an economic union with Lebanon without at the same time compromising the economic programme upon which rested Syria's hopes for financial stability free of the franc. Syria's course consisted of prolonging negotiations, thereby avoiding either unsatisfactory alternative and keeping alive the hope that Lebanon would eventually agree to accept the major tenets of its position. However, the Syrian Minister of Economy had informed US diplomats that his country would not back down from her insistence on effective import and exchange control, adding that negotiations must be terminated in the near future in order to avoid serious economic and social dislocation in Syria. He reiterated the view of Syrian opinion-makers, who believed that the cause of Lebanese intransigence was the fact that its government was dominated by a relatively small clique of powerful merchants who preferred to pursue their personal financial ends at the expense of the economic interests of Lebanon as a whole.[134]

Nevertheless, the Lebanese government stood firmly behind the Lebanese merchants' demand for complete freedom of action in the commercial and financial domains. Moreover, towards the end of November, Beirut decided to lift all restrictions on imports and permitted the unrestricted exchange of currencies. Private banks, companies and citizens were allowed to deal in hard currencies freely. As soon as the news reached Damascus, representatives of the various commercial and economic sectors convened a meeting to study the ramifications. On 24 November a delegation met with Prime Minister Mardam Bey and urged him to liquidate the customs union with Lebanon. Through their new measure, the Lebanese authorities aimed to curb the activities of the black market and initiate a drop in value of the hard currencies. Although their value remained unaffected,

Syrian merchants took advantage of the new freedom to freely deal in hard currencies to conduct their transactions. This was facilitated by all the banks, which were able to accommodate demand. In addition, factories in Europe agreed to transport their products against bills of lading issued in Beirut, which drove a number of Syrians to conduct their business there. Moreover, the Lebanese government improved postal and telegram services, making it easier for merchants to communicate with their European suppliers. While Lebanon was witnessing a revival of business activity, Syrian markets were stagnant.[135]

The latest measures by the Lebanese government, the lifting of restrictions on imports and hard currencies, were met without response or countermeasure from Damascus. Syria was witnessing a cabinet crisis, in fact, which diverted the attention of the Syrian political and economic elite. The Lebanese move could be perceived as taking advantage of the Syrian political crisis, which was provoked by the sudden resignation of three National Bloc cabinet members. From the statements of the resigning ministers it became clear that they were in disagreement with the Prime Minister on the cabinet's foreign and economic policies. They objected to Syria's policy of isolation, in particular the refusal to sign the Monetary Agreement with France and the TAPLINE agreement. The resigning ministers voiced strong criticism of the government's economic policy, which, according to them, was non-existent. They also blamed the government for the economic difficulties with Lebanon.[136]

Political circles in Damascus attributed the resignations to differences on the Monetary Agreement, for by that time the informal monetary negotiations with Paris had resulted in an agreement.[137] However, Wehbe al-Hariri tried to dodge signing the agreement by requesting a month's leave of absence, which he intended to spend in Cairo. This caused the three ministers to object. They also expressed strong reservations against Prime Minister Mardam Bey for sanctioning Hariri's action. But when Hariri insisted on taking a leave of absence, and Mardam Bey approved it, the three ministers handed in their resignations.[138]

While negotiations on bilateral economic relations remained frozen, Beirut was following these developments with great interest, its analysts describing the resigning ministers' attitudes as positive. According to Lebanese opinion-makers, these ministers represented a departure from the nationalists' isolation policy.[139] Nevertheless, the resignation of the ministers led to a governmental crisis that lasted until 16 December 1948. This crisis was accompanied by violent demonstrations and strikes. The army had to be called in to maintain order. It enforced a curfew in Damascus and prohibited gatherings and carrying of arms. Disorder spread to most Syrian cities. A state of near-anarchy ruled the country. For 20 days a succession of politicians – Hashem Atasi, 'Adel Arslan, Khaled al-'Azem, then 'Adel Arslan again – tried in vain to form a cabinet. A government was finally formed after an agreement was reached between the two major parties, the National Bloc and the Republican Party (al-Hizb al-Jumhuri). There was a consensus among the political elites in both countries that both parties' marriage of convenience was neither an alliance nor a coalition. An agreement was formed for the sake of providing the country with a government. Khaled al-'Azem was again delegated by President Quwwatly to form a coalition cabinet. The two parties provided him with the needed parliamentary majority. Political circles in Lebanon had doubts that the 'Azem government would last. Some even feared for Syria's parliamentary system and noted that it was not only for the love of Palestine that the masses were mobilised, but their leadership's inability to improve the economic situation.[140]

D. THE 'AZEM GOVERNMENT: AN ATTEMPT TO CHANGE THE STATUS QUO

The immediate foreign policy issues confronting the 'Azem government, aside from the situation in Palestine and the negotiation of an armistice with Israel, were the conclusion of the Monetary Agreement with France and the ratification of the TAPLINE agreement. On 17 January 1949, the Syrian cabinet met and examined the TAPLINE agreement, which the Mardam Bey government had signed 16 months earlier but did not manage to have ratified by parliament. Eleven days later, an agreement was reached with Lebanon regarding the organisation of local labour, the distribution of revenues and taxation on TAPLINE's imported equipment and machinery. On the whole these arrangements had been made with little criticism from the Syrian public.[141]

Political observers in Lebanon saw that international and regional events were instrumental in driving the Syrian cabinet to finalise the TAPLINE issue. The establishment of Israel on Syrian borders, and the speed with which the communists were gaining ground in central Europe and China, were factors encouraging politicians in Damascus to consent to the TAPLINE agreement. In Beirut it was thought a strange coincidence that the Syrian cabinet met to study the agreement, and approved it, right after the US government recognised Israel and granted the Jewish state a huge loan. It was generally known that high-ranking officials at the company were expecting Syria to freeze negotiations because of US recognition of Israel. The Syrian leadership decided to do the contrary, based on Syria's economic and political interests.[142] According to foreign diplomatic circles in Beirut, President Quwwatly was advised that Syria's sovereignty would be better served when the interests of the big Powers were similar to those of Syria. Promptly the cabinet signed the TAPLINE agreement and sent it to the Syrian parliament, which began debating its ratification during the third week of February.[143] In parliament, the opposition voiced its criticism of the agreement, which centred mainly on the few job opportunities the construction of the pipeline presented. It was held that after construction was concluded, few posts would remain to be filled by the Syrian labour force. It was also held that the

Syrian Treasury's revenues and profits were insignificant compared to those of the oil company. The concessions given to the TAPLINE to construct railroads, telegraph and telephone lines, airports, power stations and the like wherever it deemed necessary aroused fierce objections.[144]

In follow-up to the former government's negotiations, 'Azem devoted much of his attention to reaching an agreement with France. Facilitating this task was the fact that he had led the Syrian delegation to Paris during 1947 and hence was very much familiar with the subject matter. He gave explicit instructions that the agreement be sent to parliament before its first session of 1949. 'Azem hoped that an immediate ratification of the Monetary Agreement would prompt public confidence in the Syrian markets to return and put an end to the monetary dispute with Lebanon. It was anticipated that the agreement with France would return the price of necessities to Lebanese levels, thus lower the cost of living.[145] Throughout their negotiations with France, the Syrian Ministers of Finance and Economy kept their Lebanese counterparts up to date on the progress being made. On 8 February 1949, the Syrian Minister of Finance and the French ambassador to Syria signed the Monetary Agreement on behalf of their governments in 'Azem's presence. Beirut was informed the same day. As soon as it became evident that a Franco-Syrian consensus had been reached, the difference in value between the Lebanese and Syrian lira shrunk to a record low of 0.5 per cent.[146] However, when it came to be known that there would be a delay in the presentation of the Monetary Agreement to the Syrian parliament, the difference between the two currencies again rose, fluctuating between 2 and 3 per cent.[147]

Like its predecessors, the 'Azem government was facing mounting pressure from public opinion to resolve its economic differences with Lebanon. Opinion-makers in Syria called upon their newly formed government to disregard political considerations when negotiating with the Lebanese. There was consensus that Syrians from all social classes had suffered from the economic partnership with Lebanon. It was generally maintained that by playing for time the Lebanese had managed to profit greatly from the partnership.[148] There were also calls for the newly appointed government to take steps to reduce red tape and simplify export regulations. The freeing of goods from Syrian customs should be facilitated, Syrian customs warehouses and free trading zones should be established to encourage transit trade.[149] These steps should be coupled with the parliamentary ratification of the TAPLINE and Monetary Agreements. Syrian political and economic elites held that it was only then that the government should approach Lebanon to address the precarious economic partnership. Syria should be armed with a strong currency, inexpensive oil and a government enjoying the support and confidence of its people. Otherwise, the Lebanese, with their strong currency, would retain the upper hand in any negotiations. There were also calls for the Syrian government to liberate Syria from remaining a slave to the Lebanese by establishing a port in Latakiya.[150] Echoing popular sentiments, Minister of Finance

Joubara declared that the two states' economies would either be united – and consequently succumb to the conditions of this union – or separated. Joubara warned that economic separation did not only entail customs separation but also had political ramifications.[151]

An oil agreement between Syria and Lebanon – concerning the distribution of foreign currency proceeds from, and taxes paid by, TAPLINE – was signed on 28 January 1949 and ratified by the Lebanese chamber on 3 February. In February, Beirut and Damascus were preoccupied with preparations for armistice negotiations with Israel. Coordination was very close. A Syro-Lebanese ministerial committee was established and met regularly. Premier Solh declared that Lebanon and Syria were in entire agreement on the armistice talks.[152]

Relations between Beirut and Damascus improved, both capitals wishing to avoid disputes for the time being. On 25 February a delegation headed by 'Azem visited Beirut and met with Solh. Although the discussions focused on the armistice talks, the Syrians raised economic concerns. They informed their Lebanese hosts that Syria had decided to lift restrictions on the grain trade. They also expressed strong reservations about the Lebanese director of the Customs Directorate, who, aside from being an official at the Lebanese Ministry of Economy, was also a director of the most important department of the Common Interests. Damascus found his dual role contradictory and against the interests of the Common Interests. Instead, 'Azem proposed that a Syrian national be appointed. The Lebanese requested that the issue of the customs directorship be postponed until an economic agreement between the two states was reached.[153] In spite of the differences, in a press conference after the meeting, the Syrian Prime Minister declared that separation of the present economic union undermined the interests of both states. He pointed out that the economic union had to be reinforced on a clear basis in order to avoid any future friction or contestation. The Syrian Premier concluded that in the current international situation Syria could no longer afford to remain in an ivory tower and that isolationist policies restricted the interest of the country.[154]

'Azem's statements were well received by opinion-makers in Beirut. Lebanese nationalists highlighted 'Azem's criticism of Syrian isolationism. The Syrian cabinet's hasty signing of the Monetary Agreement with Paris and the TAPLINE agreement were perceived in Beirut to be clear signs of Syria's rejection of autarky, isolationism and of the previous government's policies towards Lebanon. There was certainty in Beirut that economic relations with Damascus were bound to improve.[155] Similarly, Najib al-Raiyyes wrote that Syria was coming out of its isolation, his paper focusing on 'Azem's efforts to conduct trade agreements with a number of Arab states. However, on 30 March 1949 events took a new turn. That day Husni al-Za'im orchestrated a coup d'état in Syria and assumed power. With the tables turned on Syria's traditional ruling elite, their Lebanese counterparts could do nothing but await events.

6

Military Rule in Damascus and Relations with Beirut

Post-World War II inter-Arab relations, particularly since the withdrawal of the colonial Powers, were inward-looking, in search of a mechanism that would lead to unity. From the previous chapters it is clear that Syro-Lebanese relations were no exception to this trend. Although there was Syro-Lebanese debate on Arab unity, these states were not contenders for regional dominance as Egypt and Iraq were. Cairo and Baghdad were competing for the prestige of presiding over the Arab unity project and both powers vied for the control of Syria, with the aim of incorporating it. To this point, then, the struggle for Arab unity had been little more than one of rival bids to control Syria.[1] Aside from inter-Arab rivalry, Syria was also confronted with containing Israeli ambitions and Great Power rivalry. Military ascendancy in Syrian politics was to accentuate the regional and international struggle for Syria,[2] one which was to further complicate relations between Beirut and Damascus.

The defeat of the Arabs in Palestine in 1948 exposed the weaknesses of the colonial-era nationalists. Ill-prepared for the challenges of independence or Zionism – which it badly underestimated – they were brushed aside by younger and more radical groups, who allied themselves with the military. The Syrian army was regarded as the prize of the country's independence struggle. After the French departure in April 1946, the military academy in Homs transformed Syria's young officers into politically minded nationalists. Their predecessors, who had been enlisted into the *Troupes Spéciales* by the French, were drawn from the ranks of influential families. The mandate's aim was to secure the allegiance of the minority communities and after independence the majority of officer cadets were drawn from the lower middle class, who were eager and indoctrinated. They were to unseat the landed notables and urban merchants.[3]

A. THE INTERLUDE OF HUSNI AL-ZA'IM

Although the turbulence on the streets of the Syrian cities subsided with the appointment of 'Azem as Premier and Colonel Husni al-Za'im as army chief of staff, recriminations over who was responsible for the Palestine disaster continued between the politicians (or rather the traditional ruling elite) and the army. Tensions rose when it became known that the government of Mardam Bey had made no provisions for the war. The Syrian army was issued defective weapons and was insufficiently armed and equipped, supplies were not reaching the front lines and Captain Fu'ad Mardam – through fraud or negligence – failed to secure arms from Italy. Against this backdrop, the army's performance was under constant attack in parliament. Early in March 1949, 'the Cooking-Fat Scandal', in which a number of senior officers, among them Colonel Za'im, were implicated, drove the latter to seize power.[4]

At 2:30 am on 30 March Za'im issued the order to his associates to seize the Syrian capital. Vital public buildings were flawlessly secured. On 1 April, Za'im dissolved parliament by decree and established a committee to amend the constitution as well as the election laws. It was declared that until the re-establishment of the parliamentary system in Syria, legislative and executive powers would be assumed by Za'im.[5] The most pressing matter for Syria's new military ruler was the armistice talks with Israel, which were scheduled to recommence on 12 April. The colonel was desperate for a military alliance with a powerful Arab state to provide support in his talks with the Israelis and to lend recognition and legitimacy to his regime. He chose Iraq. On 9 April the Iraqis were informed of Syria's desire to conclude a military defence pact.[6]

Za'im was initially drawn to Baghdad because Iraq and Transjordan were the first Arab states to immediately recognise the new Syrian regime. Quwwatly's close ties with Saudi Arabia, and his wish to depose him, could also explain why the colonel initially turned to Iraq.[7] However, Za'im's eager advances were met coldly in Baghdad, which refused to formally commit to any sort of pact.[8] While unenthusiastically met in Iraq, France, Saudi Arabia and Egypt courted the Syrian leader. France exerted itself to secure the regime's recognition abroad and assured him of its support. On 21 April, Za'im held a secret meeting with King Faruq of Egypt. The Egyptian monarch was able to win over the Syrian colonel completely. Within a few days of the visit, Egypt, Saudi Arabia and Lebanon recognised the new regime in Damascus.[9]

It is important to take stock of the events before 21 April, for they had a profound impact upon the relationship between the Lebanese leadership and Za'im. While elements opposed to the government openly welcomed the coup, Lebanese government circles and opinion-makers received news of the coup with great alarm and apprehension. They feared that the coup would initiate a series of intrigues that could eventually threaten Lebanon.[10]

The first public statement from Prime Minister Solh stressed that the coup d'état was an internal Syrian affair. The Premier declared that the Lebanese government would not take any measures against Syria. He pressed Lebanese opinion-makers to restrain themselves so as not to inflame the situation. Although the Solh government had been officially notified of the establishment of a new regime in Syria, the Lebanese Premier did not include any statement recognising Za'im's leadership. In fact, during the first few days the attitude of the Lebanese government was distinctly uncooperative. In view of the traditional ties between Syrian and Lebanese Arab nationalists, this was to be expected. Relations between Riad el-Solh, whose strength even in Lebanon was derived to a certain extent from the support he enjoyed from the Syrian Arab nationalists, and the colonel were particularly strained. This did not inhibit the Syrian dictator from making advances towards the Lebanese government. In his first communiqué, Za'im had included a passage assuring the Lebanese government of friendly ties and improved economic bilateral relations.[11] Shortly afterwards, and as an additional sign of good faith, Za'im sent an envoy to Beirut to meet with President Khuri and Premier Solh. The envoy, Farid Zein al-Din, impressed upon the Lebanese that the new leadership in Damascus would maintain traditional friendly ties with Beirut. He also transmitted Za'im's commitment to amicably resolve all pending economic issues between the two states. The Lebanese leadership's only response was a recommendation to Za'im that the safety of Quwwatly be ensured. Similar recommendations were made by King Faruq and King 'Abdel 'Aziz bin Saud.[12]

One day later Za'im responded to Solh's declaration. The colonel thanked Lebanon for its friendly position towards Syria. He indicated his desire to strengthen and develop the economic union between the two states and explained that for this purpose he had appointed Hassan Joubara as Minister of Economy.[13] A few days later 'Adel Arslan, the newly appointed Syrian Foreign Minister, visited the Grand Serrai and met with Lebanese Deputy Prime Minister Gabriel el-Murr. Arslan informed Murr that his government had authorised the export of 1500 slaughtered animals, for the purpose of alleviating the meat shortage in Lebanon. The Syrian minister reiterated his government's commitment to meet all of Lebanon's needs. Shortly after the meeting, directives were given to lift Syrian restrictions on the transport of foodstuffs and livestock to Lebanon.[14] Although Syrian advances were greeted cordially by the Lebanese, official recognition on the latter's part was not immediately forthcoming. Za'im angrily complained to Lebanese Deputy Sami el-Solh – and other members of the Lebanese opposition who visited him, among them 'Abdul Hamid Karameh and Camille Sham'oun – about the Lebanese government's attitude. According to the colonel, Beirut's stance was characterised by an apprehensive silence. He complained that Beirut had received a number of Syrian undesirables and declared his refusal to cooperate with Riad el-Solh.[15]

The Lebanese leadership countered Syrian advances by dispatching the chief of staff of the Ministry of Foreign Affairs to Damascus then, on 17 April, the Foreign

Minister. On the evening of the following day, the Lebanese President and Riad el-Solh met with the British ambassador, Houston Boswall, and related the Lebanese government's attempts to regulate relations with Syria. Bshara al-Khuri pointed out how all his emissaries had returned rather bewildered. The Lebanese Minister of Foreign Affairs had found it impossible to get Za'im to stick to one subject for more than a few seconds at a time and said that while they were talking he kept on breaking off the conversation to pull out dossiers proving that Riad el-Solh had been plotting against his life. The Lebanese President pointed out that Za'im was very difficult to do business with. As an example he described how Hassan Joubara had called on him, bringing a message from Za'im to the effect that, while he hoped for friendly relations with Lebanon, he could not possibly cooperate with Riad el-Solh. The same evening, upon receiving new instructions, Joubara had called on the Lebanese Premier and assured him that the colonel was satisfied and would be prepared to cooperate with him. At that time Za'im was regarded in Beirut as a Hashemite loyalist. As a result, the Lebanese President informed the British diplomat that – provided Iraq was prepared to respect the Lebanese National Pact and thus the integrity of Lebanon – the Lebanese government would be ready to cooperate with Iraq, even to the extent of acquiescing in the Fertile Crescent scheme. The British ambassador was informed that the Prime Minister would be going to Baghdad in response to four invitations and that he might also go to Amman. This conversation was based on the following considerations: Khuri and Solh realised that Lebanon was too weak to influence external events and they regarded Za'im as an irresponsible dictator who posed a danger to Lebanon – not to mention the Lebanese regime, which the two men represented.[16]

Due to the successful intervention of the Egyptian King, Khuri and Solh's fears were alleviated. On 24 April 1949, the Lebanese authorities, in conjunction with Cairo and Riyadh, issued a communiqué officially recognising the new regime in Damascus. The recognition was seen as a confirmation that Syria had not moved into the sphere of influence of Amman and Baghdad. It was a political victory for Egypt and Saudi Arabia. After recognition, the Lebanese Prime Minister decided to visit Damascus, where he formed a very poor impression of Colonel Za'im. By that time, even opposition members in favour of early recognition, in order to avert the dangers of the Greater Syria or Fertile Crescent scheme, did not conceal their unease regarding Za'im, whom they regarded as an adventurer.[17]

Notwithstanding the Lebanese political elite's sentiments towards the Syrian leader, Za'im moved to untangle some of the major points of dispute between Lebanon and Syria. On the evening of 21 April, Za'im, acting in his 'legislative capacity', had ratified the Franco-Syrian Monetary Agreement and the TAPLINE agreement.[18] He thereby removed two issues that were the cause of much discord between Lebanon and Syria. Syrian public opinion towards the two agreements had changed by that time. Za'im's swift action was applauded. It was believed that the BSL would now be able to supply Syrian merchants with their needs in French francs and other hard currencies. It was also thought that the ratification of the Monetary Agreement would put an end to the suffering of the merchants, who had to go to Lebanon for their money transfers and exchanges. There were also calls to reconsider economic relations with Lebanon. Opinion-makers advocated that the Syrian people were not in a hurry to return to a kind of parliament that passed bills that only served to advance the financial interests of a few of its members or to increase their popularity. 'Why else would an agreement endorsed by financial and economic experts lie for months in the General Assembly?'[19] Similarly, opinion-makers in Lebanon expressed their relief that Syria resisted Hashemite advances and praised Za'im's resolve to retain the republican character of Syria: 'His foreign policy meets that of his previous government and, for our part, we cannot but rejoice.' The colonel's swift ratification of the Monetary Agreement and the TAPLINE agreement were also commended for, without Syrian agreement, the TAPLINE project could not materialise. Political circles in Beirut expected that, as Syrian messages assured, arrangements would swiftly follow to resolve all pending economic issues between the two states. The differences between the Lebanese and Syrian leaderships were conveniently forgotten.[20]

Between the end of April and mid-May, Syro-Lebanese economic negotiations recommenced with great vigour, mainly due to the formation of a government in Syria.[21] Discussions focused on the old issues of contention concerning customs revenues, export-import regulations, the supply of Syrian foodstuffs, grain and livestock to Lebanon and parity in the value of Lebanese and Syrian currencies.[22] These discussions took place amidst Syrian opinion-makers' calls upon its leadership to take advantage of its legislative and executive authority to realise an 'economic coup'. The leadership was urged to be rid of old, complicated regulations and legislation and extensive bureaucratic red tape. The government was pressed to address the economic crisis, in particular the chronic shortage of currency. Highlighted was the fact that Italy, Greece and Lebanon had not received Syrian olive oil or grain exports in 20 months. It was maintained that any economic coup, in order to succeed, required the reformulation of the economic partnership with the Lebanese. Lebanon should be given the choice of either limiting its imports or the liquidation of the Syro-Lebanese partnership.[23] However, before the Lebanese and Syrian Ministries of Economy and Finance could work out the aforementioned issues, Za'im closed the Syrian border with Lebanon.

The Syrian leader was driven to that extreme by the Lebanese authorities' arrest of a Syrian officer, Captain Akram Tabbara. Tabbara was under orders to apprehend and arrest Kamel Hussein el-Youssef, a Lebanese national, whom the Syrians accused of smuggling provisions, arms and intelligence to the Israelis. On 10 May, the Syrian officer and his unit caught up with Youssef in a remote area in southern Lebanon. Youssef resisted arrest and a gun battle ensued in which he was fatally wounded. A companion of Youssef who managed to escape alerted the Lebanese police, who intercepted and arrested the Syrian unit. The following day, the Syrian Foreign Minister visited the Lebanese President and Prime Minister and demanded the immediate extradition of the Syrian soldiers. 'Adel Arslan, referring to the *fraternité d'armes*, reminded his Lebanese counterpart that Syria was in a state of war with Israel and that the operation against Youssef took place in a combat zone close to the border. The Lebanese cabinet convened. Beirut held that it was not bound by any extradition agreement with Syria and that the Syrian soldiers would be judged by Lebanese courts, since the incident took place on Lebanese soil. Beirut was not only concerned with the violation of Lebanese sovereignty, but also feared that Damascus intended to liquidate all members of the Syrian opposition in Lebanon.[24]

On 18 May, Radio Damascus announced that the Syrian government regarded the Lebanese authorities' refusal to return the Syrian soldiers as a challenge to its sovereignty. Consequently, the Syrian government had decided to prohibit the import and export of any goods, to and from Lebanon. The broadcaster added that the government intended to take measures to prevent Syrian citizens from spending their summer in Lebanese resorts and concluded by emphasising that there would be no normalisation of bilateral relations until the soldiers were unconditionally returned. Premier Solh telephoned 'Adel Arslan, who informed him that the Syrian food embargo on Lebanon was a personal directive from Za'im. A Lebanese spokesperson expressed his government's surprise at the Syrian measures, intended to coerce Lebanon to adopt the Syrian point of view. He declared that Lebanon could not be held responsible for the damage the Syrian economy was bound to incur. The Syrian response was immediate. According to the Syrian spokesperson, in a communiqué addressed to the Lebanese people, Syria was not sending livestock and food supplies to Lebanon so that they end up in Israel. He added that Syrian troops were operating to defend Lebanon against the common enemy in agreement with, and at the request of, the Lebanese authorities. The killing of Youssef was an expression of the will of the two peoples. In another announcement, a Syrian spokesperson threatened that 'the few measures Syria took were sufficient because it still treats Lebanon in a manner of a little brother, who is being guided and not punished, so that he will eventually be back with his family'.[25]

The Syrians' harsh reaction took the Lebanese completely by surprise. Although the Lebanese government was criticised for insisting upon prosecuting the Syrian officer and his men instead of turning a blind eye, all Lebanese political circles dismissed Za'im's reaction as hyperbolic. Lebanese authorities were forced into a situation from which they would find it difficult to back down. A new phenomenon in Syro-Lebanese relations emerged, that of spokespersons exchanging allegations in the name of the two states. Lebanese Arab nationalists received Syrian allegations concerning the Lebanese government's involvement with Youssef with some dismay. There were also objections to Syrian communiqués addressing the Lebanese people instead of the government, which was seen as infringing upon Lebanese sovereignty. Many Lebanese saw it to be odd that the Syrian leadership was willing to sacrifice Syro-Lebanese ties over such a minor incident. The main impression in Beirut was that the Tabbara Affair was a pretext to cover other Syrian aims, mainly to blackmail Lebanon into assuming Damascus' economic policies. There were calls to work towards a solid framework upon which Syro-Lebanese relations could be based: 'It is not possible to leave those relations at the mercy of a minister or prime minister's temper. In the space of 15 months we had three or four crises, which could have been easily avoided.'[26]

By 21 May, the restriction of Syrian food exports to Lebanon was still in force. The Syrian authorities had reinforced the supervision of the borders to prevent the smuggling of foodstuffs. A day earlier, the Syrian government had warned all merchants, owners of transport vehicles and drivers that anyone caught smuggling food supplies to Lebanon would face prosecution by military tribunal. These measures not only included Syrian-registered vehicles but Iraqi, Jordanian and any others that passed through Syrian territory. On the Syrian–Lebanese border, a number of these vehicles had already been turned back to their points of origin. The restriction of Lebanese food supplies resulted in shortages and higher prices. Given this state of affairs, the Lebanese Foreign Minister contacted his Syrian counterpart a number of times to resolve the dispute. Discussions revealed that the matter of the Syrian officer was not the only source of tension. Syro-Lebanese differences over economic policies also resurfaced. At that time, it became known that Za'im had delegated Syrian Finance Minister Joubara to set down a plan for economic separation from Lebanon – including the establishment of customs barriers – should Lebanon remain adamant in adopting liberal economic policies. The Syrians publicised Joubara's assurances to Za'im that all necessary measures had been taken should separation become a reality. Only a signature was needed for implementation.[27]

Egypt and Saudi Arabia intervened to break the impasse. Their ambassadors to Lebanon, Wajih Rustum and 'Abdel 'Aziz bin Zayed, held endless discussions with both parties and managed to convince Za'im and Solh to establish a Syro-Lebanese legislative committee to solve the dispute. However, Beirut insisted that the joint committee would not meet before the Syrian embargo was lifted, maintaining that it would not negotiate under duress. In fact, officials in the Lebanese capital had taken precautionary steps to import any food shortages and decided to prohibit the export of local and foreign goods, aside from combustibles, to Syria. In response the Syrian government issued a communiqué announcing that all Syrian nationals wishing to travel to Lebanon would need a permit. Meanwhile, the Lebanese drivers syndicate notified the government that the Syrian authorities had ordered the confiscation of Lebanese vehicles on Syrian soil. On 24 May, after interventions by Saudi Arabia, Egypt, France, Britain and the United States, Za'im lifted the embargo. The following day at 10:00 am, the Syro-Lebanese committee met in a tent at the Jdaydeh border crossing. At the meeting 'Adel Arslan frankly informed the Lebanese delegation that the legal issues were of no concern to Za'im and that he was only concerned with the immediate release of the Syrian officer and his troops. The Syrian minister would leave it to the Lebanese side to formulate the legalities however it liked. The Syrian delegation also presented the Lebanese with a memorandum in which it outlined economic proposals aimed at protecting its industry. The memorandum stated that Syria insisted upon prohibiting imports of all foreign goods. Customs on imported grain – estimated at 64 per cent – was also demanded. The tabled proposal did not include a Syrian commitment to guarantee Lebanon's needs of grain. No agreement was reached. The committee met again on 26 May and decided to resort to arbitration. To that end, Egyptian and Saudi Arabian envoys formed a committee of prominent legal experts.[28]

The process of arbitration was suddenly interrupted when news reached the Lebanese capital that on 28 May a Syrian national who had been residing in the Lebanese town of Zahle for over 11 years, with no known political affiliation or criminal record, was abducted by Syrian security officers. Lebanese Foreign Minister Franjieh contacted his Syrian counterpart inquiring about the reasons behind the abduction and demanded the detainee's immediate release. Franjieh assured Arslan that if the Syrian government wanted the Syrian national, the Lebanese authorities were ready to hand him over. In the evening of the same day the Syrian Foreign Ministry informed Beirut of the detainee's release. Syria's 'arm-twisting policy' towards Lebanon continued. Aside from the abduction of a Syrian national on Lebanese soil, the Syrian army was massing troops on Lebanon's northern border. Syrian security forces were also prohibiting the entry and exit of all supplies.[29]

It was in this tense atmosphere that the arbitration committee heard the testimony of the representatives of the two governments.[30] Lebanese and Syrian representatives presented their governments' positions, after which the committee declared that it could not disregard the special penal procedures in Syria and Lebanon, which both states inherited from the Ottoman and Mandate eras and which remained in force. The arbitration committee noted that the manner in which the two states handed over criminals – regardless of whether they were Lebanese or Syrian – further reinforced the fact that neither regarded the other as a foreign state. Both states had voluntarily accepted the limitation of their sovereignty in penal affairs. The arbitration committee recommended that – in order to preserve the neighbourly and brotherly relations between the two states, and after considering the circumstances of the death of Kamel Hussein el-Youssef on Lebanese soil – the Lebanese government repatriate the officer and his unit to Syria, where they would stand before a military tribunal. Both states were called upon to express their regrets and were advised to conduct an agreement to prevent similar incidences from occurring in the future. On 2 June Captain Tabbara and his men were released to stand trial in Damascus. A Syrian court convened 14 days later and released the captain. With Tabbara's release, commercial and transport restrictions between the two states were lifted.[31]

Diplomatic circles maintained that the incident highlighted Lebanon and Syria's peculiar relations. In addition to a joint customs administration, there were practically no border controls, a fact that made the action of Tabbara unusual only in its denouement. The final recommendations of the arbitration commission, that Lebanon and Syria formalise regulations to deal with such matters, was a recognition of this state of affairs. Further, it was reported, the two states had no regular diplomatic channels with each other. The occasional governmental border meetings and visits to the other capital by cabinet ministers had more often led to misunderstandings than agreements. The personal antipathy existing between the leadership of both countries complicated matters further. The governments of both states were advised to establish formal diplomatic representation, which could prevent future difficulties and mend the economic rupture between Beirut and Damascus.[32]

Political observers in Beirut held that the Jdaydeh meeting and subsequent arbitration, even if the arbitrators were Egypt and Saudi Arabia, was another dangerous precedent in Syro-Lebanese relations. The two states were behaving like foes. Arbitration was leading bilateral relations in a manner where colonialism had failed in the past. Arbitration was seen as further evidence of the lack of harmony in Syro-Lebanese relations. It was strongly believed that the two states were well on their way to separation.[33] It should be noted that, while the Syrians had officially lifted the embargo, a number of economic boycott measures remained in force. Few if any goods were exchanged between the two states, but travellers commuted across borders freely. As a result of the embargo, prices of local products in Syria – grain, foodstuffs, vegetables and fruits – dropped considerably. The price of these goods remained unchanged in Lebanon, since the Lebanese authorities had managed to import their supplies from other states.[34]

With the aim of calming the atmosphere between Beirut and Damascus, Prime Minister Solh declared in parliament that 'the ties between Syria and Lebanon are made by God, and supported by each Syrian and Lebanese heart. Incidents from here and there do not diminish these ties.' The Premier's remarks were well received in Damascus, characterising disagreements between brothers as natural.[35]

As mentioned above, negotiations were not restricted to the release of the Syrian officer and his unit but also encompassed the future of economic ties. The Lebanese cabinet convened in extraordinary session on Sunday 22 May, and decided that certain imports would be subject to permits, a measure long demanded by Damascus. It should be noted that the Lebanese initiative came during the discussions of Arslan and Franjieh. The Lebanese cabinet's decision was accompanied by measures encouraging local production. The municipal tax (*dkhuliya*) was cancelled and electricity as well as fuel were to be subsidised. The Minister of Economy reserved the right to specify which imports were to require permits. Lebanese factory owners had requested the prohibition of all imports, but the government preferred to limit them. Factory owners had demanded the cancellation of the *dkhuliya* tax and customs on imported raw material. The government decided to cancel the *dkhuliya* tax and put the question of customs to one side until bilateral relations with Syria were normalised.[36]

Lebanese merchants strongly objected to the government's latest measure, regarding it as benefiting only Syria and going against the country's role as the mediators of East–West trade. In numerous petitions, rallies and visits to the heads of state, representatives of the various merchant associations argued that import restrictions would harm the consumer, who would be forced to purchase low-quality goods at high prices as set by factory owners. It was also argued that the local industry was not competitive with foreign imports and on foreign markets, even with government subsidies. Merchants threatened the government to transfer their capital to the east of Jordan and shut down their operations in Lebanon.[37]

The government's decision divided the country between those in favour of supporting the industrialists and those supporting the merchants. Political elites in Beirut strongly criticised the government's improvised policies.[38] While Lebanese Arab nationalist circles weighted merchants' threats with those of the industrialists, the latter threatened to go on strike and sack 50,000 workers. Industrialists also complained that their installations, which had cost the economy L£250 million, risked going under. Most Arab nationalists held that Lebanon should not adopt an economic policy not in tune with Syria's. Furthermore there were calls that the Arab League should study the potential of Arab trade and commerce.[39] The League was also called upon to work towards the removal of customs barriers and open Arab states to intra-regional trade and commerce. For Lebanese nationalists the country's freedom was linked to the laissez-faire economy, and thought of it as Lebanon's *raison d'être*. Illustrating his disbelief in Lebanon's industrial future, Michel Chiha wrote that 'no one more than us is favourable to industry, but to an industry that holds in its destiny prosperity and life and not restrictions, privation and death... Under normal circumstances it is not in obstacles to commerce that we should seek to solve the difficulties of industry.'[40]

While Lebanese industrialists and merchants were debating the fate of the Lebanese economy, Syrian opinion-makers were reiterating their demand that their leadership avoid short-term agreements with Lebanon. They argued that the Lebanese should be made to decide between complete and lasting unity or separation. The Syrian leadership was advised to build on the momentum of the Tabbara Affair. It was maintained that the Lebanese should be made to agree to Syrian conditions in order to maintain the economic union.[41]

At that time Syria was increasingly suffering from a surplus of goods and a scarcity of currency. Syrian silos were filled with unsold grain. Long lines of farmers were queuing at the doors of merchants, hoping to secure loans for the next year's harvest. Lebanese importers were flooding Syrian markets with cheap textiles, threatening to drive Syrian factories out of business. Unemployment was high. The difference in the value of Lebanese and Syrian currencies had grown and was fluctuating between 10 and 15 per cent, giving Lebanese exporters an additional advantage.[42] A strong Lebanese currency allowed them to purchase goods cheaply from Syrian markets and export them. The dominant perception among the Syrian economic and political elites was that the Lebanese were not only competing with Syrian importers and threatening Syria's nascent industry but also driving Syrian exporters out of business. Syrian public opinion expected stringent measures from their leadership, just as it had dealt with the Lebanese on the Tabbara Affair. Za'im reacted, sending two memoranda to Beirut, accompanied by a public declaration saying 'we have presented them our conditions which retain their interests as well as ours. If they do not wish to accept them or if they wish to retain the Common Interests in its current deplorable state that is driving Syria into poverty, we will be forced to establish customs barriers.'[43]

In early June, the Syrian government had sent its Lebanese counterparts a note, asking them to choose from among three separate plans before the end of the month: complete economic union; economic independence with identical customs tariff and free exchange of nationally produced goods; revision of the present system, particularly the creation of joint machinery for the control of exports and the limitation of imports.[44] The Syrian leadership took great care to disseminate the government's memoranda, proposals and veiled threats to Lebanon, which were well received by the Syrian public. The majority of Syrians believed that, now that Syria had achieved reforms in security, law and education, Za'im was orchestrating the long-awaited 'economic coup'.[45]

Syria's proposals to the Lebanese Ministry of Economy drove the latter to issue invitations to the directors of local and foreign banks, associations, the chambers of commerce and industry. The invitations included a request to study the Syrian memorandum and the proposals accompanying it, in order to formulate the Lebanese response. The representatives of the commercial associations in Tripoli and Sidon demanded economic union regardless of the price, while the commercial associations of Beirut and Zahle expressed their reservations concerning the limitation of imports. There were views that the proposal of economic union did not take into account the fact that each of the two states' economies was structured differently. Lebanese citrus fruit producers demanded that the union with Syria be retained since Syria imported large quantities of citrus fruit as well as bananas. After the meeting, the Lebanese Economy Minister noted that the Lebanese people fell into three categories: the producer (agrarian or industrial), the merchant and the consumer. The government had the duty to consider the interests of all three categories, in particular that of the consumer, which formed the majority.[46]

On 23 June, the heads of Lebanon's different parliamentary committees met. Minister of Economy Takla presented the Syrian proposals. There was a consensus that agreement was possible after a few amendments were made to the Syrian proposals, especially concerning the joint economic commission. However, the unification of export-import regulations was regarded as harmful to both states because Lebanon was a state of imports, re-export and transit trade, while Syria was a producing-exporting state.[47] The following day, one day before a plebiscite was to be held in Syria to confirm his presidency, Za'im headed to Shtura to meet with the Lebanese President and Prime Minister. In an hour-long meeting, Solh was able to convince the Syrians to extend their deadline an additional two weeks. Aside from economic bilateral relations, Za'im assured Khuri as well as Solh of his goodwill and respect towards Lebanese independence and sovereignty. Za'im expressed his eagerness to promote the fraternal relations of both states and apologised for past incidents, claiming that they took place without his prior consent.[48]

In Bloudan, on 5 July, the Syrian and Lebanese Ministers of Economy met to hammer out an economic agreement. The meeting between Takla and Joubara focused on each of the three Syrian proposals. Both ministers reconvened after three days in Shtura, where they signed an agreement unifying the monetary systems as well as internal tariffs. The two currencies were to be given parity. The agreement also included clauses protecting national industrial and agrarian products. More important, a 50 per cent tax was to be imposed on all foreign imports. With regard to grain, the Lebanese were able to include a clause exempting taxation on grain imports, in the event of a price rise or should the Syrian harvest be insufficient. The Syrians also agreed to the Lebanese demand that grain transport between the two states be unrestricted and without customs. A ton of grain was set at the international price. As soon as the news spread that both states had reached an agreement, the difference in the exchange rates of the two currencies dropped to 7 per cent.[49]

Observers viewed the Syro-Lebanese economic agreement as a step towards a new era of cooperation between the two states. High-ranking delegations were exchanged carrying congratulations on what the Syrian and Lebanese leaderships had achieved.[50] This was the impression in Damascus, at least, the Lebanese leadership being preoccupied with putting down an attempted coup by *al-Hizb al-Suri al-Qawmi* (the Syrian National Party), headed by Antun Sa'ada.[51]

On the night of 9 June, armed confrontations took place in Beirut between Sa'ada's men and the Phalangists, a radical Lebanese nationalist party founded by Lebanese Maronite Pierre Gemayyel. Gemayyel's men attacked the Syrian Party's newspaper offices and printing works. Later on the newspaper offices and printing works were raided by the police. The government claimed that Sa'ada was conspiring with the Zionists and plotting a coup.[52] The Lebanese President and Prime Minister were certain that the Za'im–Sa'ada alliance was bound to overthrow the existing Lebanese regime.[53] A large number of Sa'ada's men were arrested but he fled to Syria, where he managed to gain the support of Za'im.

Like the Lebanese leadership, Za'im in turn was convinced that Shukri al-Quwwatly, a close friend of Riad el-Solh, was plotting to regain power in Syria. The Syrian leader saw in Sa'ada an opportunity to bring down Riad el-Solh and offered him arms.[54] A series of attacks were launched by the Syrian nationalists during the first week of July.[55] But on the night of 6 July Syrian authorities turned Sa'ada over to the Lebanese.[56] Within 48 hours, the leader of the Syrian National Party was interrogated, sentenced and executed. The execution was carried out at dawn on 8 July 1949. His party was dissolved on 16 July. Numerous arrests followed and a number of his followers were sentenced to death.[57]

Why Za'im handed Sa'ada over remains open to speculation.[58] It could be argued that after the signature of the Syro-Lebanese economic agreement, relations between Beirut and Damascus – especially Solh and Za'im – witnessed remarkable improvement. It was noteworthy that only two days after Sa'ada was handed over to the Lebanese authorities, and on the same day of his execution, Ministers Takla and Joubara signed the economic agreement. Moreover, on 17 July, Solh paid a visit to the Syrian leader.[59] A visit by the Lebanese Premier would not have been forthcoming had Za'im been planning his downfall. Judging from the chronology of events, the Sa'ada card was indeed used by the Syrian leadership to pressure the Lebanese into signing an economic agreement limiting their imports – a Syrian demand dating from 1943.[60]

Three days after Solh's visit to Damascus, Syria signed the armistice agreement with Israel. By that time, Za'im had alienated most of the forces that had brought him to power. Earlier in May he had dissolved all political parties and, with his open resentment towards Iraq, he lost the support of the People's Party. The Ba'th Party protested the press restrictions and the growing army of informers, warning him against taking part in inter-Arab disputes. In response, Za'im jailed Michel 'Aflaq and the leaders of the People's Party. After a referendum, Za'im proclaimed himself President on 25 June and called upon his senior aide and confidant, Mohsen al-Barazi, to form a government.[61] All of these elements, and the betrayal of Sa'ada, earned the Syrian leader the resentment of his nationalist and politically inclined army officers. The Iraqi government was also anxious to see the Syrian leader replaced by someone more amicable to itself. Sami al-Hinnawi, commander of the First Brigade, was seen as their man. Taking advantage of the national and regional forces opposed to Za'im, Hinnawi seized power on 14 August 1949. Za'im and Barazi were shot. An officer loyal to Antun Sa'ada carried out the sentence.[62]

Za'im's forced removal was well received by Syrian opinion-makers, who criticised him for entering the power game of Arab rivalries and alienating Iraq, Jordan and Lebanon. He was also criticised for wishing to grow closer to the West while cutting his ties with the East. Syrian newspaper owners revealed how the ousted dictator used to require them to attack Lebanon and threaten it with occupation.[63] Za'im's corruption scandals filled the Syrian press.[64]

Sami al-Hinnawi lifted the ban on political parties. He declared that the army would withdraw from politics and delegated Hashim Atasi, a symbol of resistance against the French Mandate, to form a cabinet. Opinion-makers in Lebanon received the second coup with some relief, particularly since the military reinstated a civilian government. Moreover, Hinnawi's claims to have no political ambitions added to his popularity in Beirut. His adherence to the republican political system and the Arab League Charter were also commended.[65]

B. THE INTERLUDE OF SAMI AL-HINNAWI

The day after the coup, the Lebanese Prime Minister sent a telegram to his Syrian counterpart on behalf of the President congratulating him on his succession to office. With Hinnawi's seizure of power, Lebanon's ruling elite was very much concerned with the future of agreements signed, or rather ratified, by Za'im, particularly the TAPLINE agreement and the Franco-Syrian Monetary Agreement. It was generally known that among Za'im's reasons for imprisoning Michel 'Aflaq and some Ba'th Party members was the latter's stringent opposition to these agreements. Akram al-Hawarni and other key Syrian cabinet members held similar views to 'Aflaq's. It was obvious to political observers in Beirut that the Syrian cabinet was in a difficult position. What would the Syrian ruling elite tell their anxious people, especially their enthusiastic young student followers? Would the Syrian government refrain from recognising the ratified agreements – and in so doing invite Great Power anger in difficult and sensitive times when Syria was in need of their support? On the other hand, were the Syrian government to recognise the agreements, who would guarantee that Syria would not witness demonstrations – especially since the restrictions on freedom had been lifted? Would this be the formula for another coup?[66] To counter such fears and rumours, the Syrian cabinet declared that the current government's primary task was to ensure the return of constitutional life to Syria by holding parliamentary elections. Not wishing to carry the responsibility of nullifying any agreements, the current government left their fate to the new parliament.[67]

However, certain matters could not await parliamentary elections. The Syrian economy was in complete stagnation. An economic programme was absent as were developmental construction projects.[68] The gap in the value of Lebanese and Syrian currencies was growing and open to speculation. In addition, a number of public and private institutions in Lebanon refused to accept the Syrian lira.[69] Realising the precarious situation of the Syrian economy as well as the strains placed on it from the coups, Minister of Finance Khaled al-'Azem did not waste any time. Only two days after the coup, on 16 August 1949, Hassan Joubara – re-assigned as the Syrian head of the HCCI – briefed 'Azem on discussions between the Lebanese and Syrian governments and the agreement reached on 8 July. On 27 August the Lebanese and Syrian Ministers of Finance and Economy met, the first such summit to be held with the new Syrian government. To the disappointment of the Lebanese, Za'im's downfall caused the interruption of talks meant to implement policies and projects envisaged in the accord. Beirut saw the long-awaited agreement as a framework upon which to rebuild the crumbled economic bridge with Syria. Among the most important issues discussed on 27 August were closing the gap between the two currencies, the exchange of bank and postal transfers and a unified import-export policy. Customs and the amendment of some articles in the Bloudan Agreement were also raised. No consensus was reached and the discussions were postponed.[70] Syrian opinion-makers condemned the inconclusiveness of the meeting. It was pointed out with some dismay that the content and results of such meetings had not changed for years. As the gap in the two currencies' exchange rates grew, further curtailing the activities of Syrian import-export houses, the government was called upon to lift the restrictions of grain exports to Lebanon so that Syria could earn some desperately needed Lebanese liras.[71]

During September, the attention shifted from the economic sphere to the Lebanese presidential elections, and on 21 September the incumbent Bshara al-Khuri was sworn in for a second six-year term. Khuri's re-election aroused neither great enthusiasm nor pessimism. The President's inauguration was to have been followed immediately by the resignation of the cabinet and the forming of a new government. The resignation was postponed, however, due to opposition in the chamber towards the appointment of non-members of parliament to ministerial positions – stimulated by the prospect that Riad el-Solh might include one or two opposition leaders in his cabinet – and to unexpected difficulties in filling some of the posts. The sudden devaluation of sterling, the arrival of King 'Abdallah on 24 September and the death of Emile Eddé on 27 September were the excuses presented to the people and diplomatic circles.[72] On 1 October, the press published the names of Riad el-Solh's new cabinet, but a few days later the Prime Minister was forced to announce a 'second edition' of it. The reshuffle was necessary because Elias Khuri refused to take the Interior Ministry. Solh, unable to fill this key post with a politician he could sufficiently trust, decided to keep it for himself. To compensate the Maronites, Charles Helou – Lebanese ambassador to the Holy See – was introduced to the cabinet as Minister of Justice; to give him a wider field of influence, Helou was also made head of the newly created Ministry of Information. Philip Takla became Foreign Minister, Jubran Nahas took over the Ministry of Economy while Hussein Oweini was put in charge of Finance. Despite these attempts to maintain the confessional balance, however, the distribution of portfolios was generally interpreted as marking a weakening of Maronite influence. Be this as it may, diplomatic circles noted that the key positions had been 'retained by the old gang'. The Lebanese chamber convened on 15 October and Solh announced his programme. In its foreign policy, the government would act within the framework of the Arab League, spare no efforts on behalf of Palestine, strengthen links with the other Arab states and maintain friendly relations with all countries.[73]

With the conclusion of the presidential elections and the formation of the new government, the focus of Lebanese policy-makers shifted to Syria, where the ruling elite was seriously considering unifying with Iraq. Beirut worried about the effect of such sentiments upon the Arab status quo and the repercussions such a union would have on Syro-Lebanese ties. Inter-Arab relations had not yet recovered from the intrigues of the previous coup, although Nuri al-Sa'id had visited Alexandria and made numerous declarations to reassure the Egyptian and Saudi capitals that Iraq had no ambitions in Syria. Nevertheless, Hinnawi's coup threw Syria back into inter-Arab and international rivalries. As in the first coup, King 'Abdallah of Jordan and Premier Nuri Sa'id of Iraq were the first to congratulate the colonel and to sent their emissaries to Damascus. The polarisation of inter-Arab relations prevented the Arab League from playing an active mediating role.[74]

Furthermore, advances towards Baghdad by a number of Syrians close to the new regime did not bode well for the cause of regional stability. Hinnawi's brother-in-law, As'ad Tallas, who became under-secretary of foreign affairs, actively sought an agreement with Iraq. Advances towards Baghdad were reinforced on 29 September when – in a bid to gain popularity – the National Party issued a communiqué calling for union with Iraq.[75] A day before the announcement, Syrian Foreign Minister Nazim al-Qudsi arrived in Beirut. His mission was to solicit Lebanese views concerning Syria's union with Iraq and Jordan. Qudsi explained to his Lebanese counterpart that the unity project was confined to the removal of customs barriers, passports and might also include the unification of Syrian and Iraqi military commands.[76] The position of union advocates was further strengthened by a visit of the Iraqi Regent, Prince 'Abd al-Illah, to Damascus on 5 October.

The Lebanese ruling elite was closely following events in Syria and a day after 'Abd al-Illah's Syrian visit, Hassan Joubara visited Beirut to discuss bilateral monetary affairs and other pending economic issues. However, Lebanese officials preferred to discuss the fate of the Common Interests in case of the Syrian and Iraqi union. Joubara refrained from addressing Lebanese inquiries, maintaining that he would transmit them to his government. The following day, Nazim al-Qudsi arrived from Damascus to assure his Lebanese counterpart that the Syrian–Iraqi union project was still in the discussion phases. Qudsi pointed out that unification would be executed in stages, the first stage being a customs union that would not preclude Syro-Lebanese economic unity. The Syrian Foreign Minister hinted that Damascus would not have any objection to Lebanon putting economic ties on a contractual basis (i.e. treaties and agreements), instead of economic union.[77]

On 31 October, Lebanese Finance Minister Oweini headed to the Syrian capital, where he met with Atasi and 'Azem. The Syrian Minister of Finance presented Oweini with a copy of a decree issued in Syria, which lifted all restrictions on the export of locally produced agricultural and industrial goods to Lebanon. He requested that the Lebanese study the decree and indicated that he expected a response within a week.[78] But debate over the nature of Syria's relationship with Iraq continued to dominate all other issues before the Syrian parliamentary elections of 15 November.[79] On the eve of these elections, the National Party decided to boycott the contest.[80] The People's Party managed to win 51 of 114 parliamentary seats.[81]

Although the People's Party won a clear majority in the elections, the Syrian–Iraqi union scheme did not materialise. The reasons were numerous. A great number of the People's Party partisans wished to safeguard Syria's republican system and were not eager to have a monarchy in Syria. Moreover, the Syrian government was internally divided and subject to numerous external pressures, causing it to remain indecisive.

Within the Syrian cabinet 'Aflaq and Hawrani were the major opponents of Iraqi union. The Syrian Muslim Brothers, who had formed the Islamic Socialist Front early in November 1949, also opposed the union scheme. There were also fears that union would see Iraq's treaty commitments with Britain apply to Syria. To come under the suzerainty of another colonial power when only recently liberated from France was not to the liking of most of the Syrian population. The Syrian army, whose sentiment was republican, would not condone it.[82] In addition, a great number of the ruling elite did not wish to compromise their relations with Saudi Arabia, the latter openly offering $16 million in aid to Syria if it retained the republican system of government.[83] Opponents of the Syro-Iraqi union were not only found in the army. Many declarations in favour of the republican system were made in various parts of the country by bodies of students and prominent personalities. It was for these reasons that the numerous secret talks between Baghdad and Damascus led to nothing concrete.[84]

Towards the end of November the focus returned to relations between Beirut and Damascus. Tensions arose when a memorandum expressing Damascus' point of view on how to close the gap between the Lebanese and Syrian currencies went unanswered. The memorandum requested the Lebanese authorities to pay for the grain it imported from Syria in Syrian liras. This would lower the amount of Syrian lira on the Lebanese market by half and thus reduce the difference between the two currencies. In response, 'Azem suspended all scheduled meetings between Lebanese and Syrian officials.[85] Matters were further complicated by a sudden rise in value of the Lebanese lira against the Syrian currency (reaching 12 per cent),[86] coupled with Lebanese officials permitting the export of large quantities of olive oil. The sanctioning of olive oil exports without consulting Syrian authorities was ill received in Damascus.[87] The Syrian memorandum remained unanswered.

The Lebanese decided to refrain from responding until the Syrian parliament convened and a new cabinet was formed. However, the announcement of Lebanese intentions increased the activities of the speculators, which in turn drove leading Syrian businessmen and economists to hold a meeting on 2 December 1949. The meeting resulted in a number of recommendations that the government was urged to implement immediately. These were as follows.

1. To distribute large numbers of French francs among Syrian importers

2. To restrict all Syrian imports to the port of Latakiya

3. To call on Syrian merchants not to purchase goods from Lebanese markets except in case of extreme necessity, in order to reduce the demand for Lebanese currency and the supply of Syrian currency in the Lebanese market

4. To issue a memorandum to the Lebanese government demanding a decision on all pending issues. The Lebanese government's response should be given a certain time limit. Should no response be forthcoming, Syria would take the necessary measures without hesitation.[88]

Opinion-makers in Damascus were very much in support of their merchants' recommendations and wrote in their editorials that '[i]f the Lebanese markets are flourishing at the expense of the Syrian consumer and the Syrian merchant is nothing but a middle man or wage earner (*ajir*) to the Lebanese merchant, the time has come to liberate ourselves, consumers and merchants, from this slavery which has gone on for too long'.[89]

C. THE LIQUIDATION OF THE CUSTOMS UNION

The Syrian government responded to Lebanese tardiness in its usual manner. On 8 December, Premier 'Azem held a press conference in which he revealed the Syrian cabinet's decision to prohibit the transport of grain to Lebanon. The embargo was to come into effect on 10 December. The Syrian action came as a shock and caused considerable perturbation. The Lebanese government sent a letter to Damascus protesting the measure and pointing out that it was contrary to the 8 July agreement.[90] The following day, the Syrian government sent a representative, Husni Tillou, to Beirut. Tillou, who was received by Solh, explained that the Syrian measure was temporary and came in response to the lack of rain, which had hurt the harvest. He noted that this had led profiteers to hide grain supplies, causing a rise in prices from 23 to 24 piastres per kilo, while in Lebanon a kilo of grain sold for between 20 and 22 piastres. The Syrian official pointed out that Syria had already exported more grain to Lebanon than the country needed. Unconvinced of the Syrian representative's justifications, Solh responded that the Lebanese government would be compelled to counter the Syrian measure by lifting restrictions on grain imports. The Premier stressed that the differences in the two currencies' exchange rates would widen as a result of the Syrian measure. The Syrian act was widely regarded as a serious threat to continued economic union.[91]

Lebanese authorities' first response was to instruct the head of the Lebanese delegation to the HCCI, Musa Moubarak, to raise customs fees on all grain imports.[92] Moreover, the Lebanese government sent a memorandum of protest to Damascus. The memorandum did not restrict itself to matters of grain but evoked other circumstances where Syria was not conforming to the accords it had signed. The suspension of grain shipments to Lebanon without prior notice was contrary to the Bloudan Agreement and was not the only unilateral act taken by the Syrians. Syria's prohibitions of pharmaceuticals originating from Lebanon constituted another flagrant violation. The accord clearly stipulated that the transport of merchandise between the two states was entirely free and was not subject to any controls. The same went for travellers coming from Iraq and Turkey carrying entry visas to Lebanon, who were denied transit through Syria.[93]

The Syrian public received news of the grain embargo against Lebanon with great enthusiasm. It was generally perceived that Syria was taking the right position for the first time, one that would lead to the liberation of the Syrian economy from the hands of a 'few Lebanese capitalists'. It was pointed out that Syria had kept its commitments and supplied Lebanon with 100,000 tons of grain as stipulated in the agreements. In fact, Lebanon had imported 122,000 tons from Syria. Syrian public opinion was convinced that the Lebanese wished to control Syrian grain with the aim of exporting it abroad for profit. There were also numerous allegations that Lebanese mediators were smuggling Syrian grain to Israel.[94]

The Lebanese public was very critical of the Syrian grain embargo. There was a consensus that the act – whose announcement coincided with the Syrian parliament's first sitting of the session – was politically motivated. It was assumed it aimed to discredit the Lebanese ruling elite and to force it to adopt Syrian economic policies. In Lebanon, the predominant belief was that the Syrian ruling elite wished to gain popularity at the expense of the Lebanese, or that it wished to create an incident that would rupture the Common Interests. The last analysis was based on the fact that, should Lebanon decide to import grain on its own, it would be in violation of the 8 July agreement. By that time, the Bloudan Agreement was the only accord keeping the Common Interests together. Speaking confidentially to Western diplomatic circles, Lebanese officials said the grain issue had to be settled or the government would face the wrath of the Lebanese public.[95] Lebanese nationalists expressed their regrets about the Syrian position and pointed out that Lebanon could easily purchase its grain elsewhere. Damascus' previous efforts to apply coercion had not worked and ended with considerable losses to the Syrian economy.[96] Even Lebanese Arab nationalists and Syrian unionists had become sceptical of future bilateral relations: 'Syria has forced us to reconsider, again, the Syro-Lebanese economic partnership.'[97]

On 14 December, 'Azem held a press conference in which he declared that the Syrian government had proposed the establishment of a joint Syro-Lebanese committee with the mandate of purchasing Syrian grain. The Syrian proposal also entailed prohibiting the unrestricted export of grain, since merchants in both countries were monopolising the trade and asking exorbitant prices. The Syrian

Minister of Finance added that the unrestricted export policy had also resulted in the loss of a large quantity of grain to suspicious sides [Israel]. 'Azem pointed out that the Lebanese government had refused this proposal and insisted that an unregulated export policy remain in force. He justified Syria's measure against Lebanon as arising from an expectedly bad harvest and said that in spite of this Syria had supplied the Lebanese with their grain needs. 'Azem insisted that the Syrian government would not have any objections if the Lebanese decided to import grain from abroad. The Syrian minister noted that there were a number of unresolved issues – among them the appointment of a Syrian director to the Customs Directorate, a position the Lebanese refused to relinquish. He also emphasised that, although there was a customs union between the two states, each one retained different economic legislation. Any customs union that was not based on an economic union, 'Azem opined, was destined to fail. To illustrate his point, he noted that, when the Syrian government decided to forbid the import of cars or luxury items, Lebanon immediately permitted their import, with the goods then ending up on the Syrian market. He added that Syrian efforts to develop the port of Latakiya faced Lebanese protest. He accused the Lebanese of working for the failure of this project. 'This is why we say that if Lebanon wants customs separation from Syria, we do not object to such desires. Our desire is to establish a united customs union based on one economic policy.'[98]

'Azem's press conference set the tone for how Syria intended to deal with Lebanon. The Syrian Premier's firm stance was supported by the Syrian public at large. The Lebanese response came a few days later, through Lebanese Foreign Minister Takla. He detailed the content of the Bloudan Agreement, highlighting the fact that Lebanon had agreed to impose a 50 per cent tax on overseas grain imports, provided that Syria not hinder the transport of grain to Lebanon. He stressed that the Syrians agreed that the Lebanese would be free to import if there were a harvest shortfall or a price rise. Takla declared that, in deciding to suspend grain shipments without prior notice, Syria was in violation of the Bloudan Agreement and had thus given the Lebanese the right to import grain without the prior approval of the HCCI. Takla rejected the Syrian Finance Minister's allegations that Syrian grain exports to Lebanon were ending up in Israel. The Lebanese Foreign Minister pointed out that Israel imported its grain by sea at prices much lower than Syrian grain.[99]

In spite of the fact that Syrian officials were turning truckloads of grain back at the border,[100] grain prices remained unaffected. Merchants' warehouses were filled and it was generally known that supplies would last six months. Moreover, grain continued to be smuggled from Syria to Lebanon, thus contributing to price stability there.[101] But before the new crisis played itself out, a new coup diverted the attention of Syrian and Lebanese policy-makers.

The People's Party's victory led the Syrian public to accept policies aiming at securing union with Iraq. There was a clash between unionists and anti-unionists, however, over the wording of an oath to be taken by the head of state and members of the constituent assembly. The draft, prepared by Hashemite sympathisers, made no mention of Syria's republican regime. This oversight drove the chamber's anti-unionists, led by Akram al-Hawrani, to oppose the oath. However, since the People's Party commanded the majority in parliament, the bill passed. The passage of the oath was seen as the chamber's vote for union.[102] It should also be remembered that Sami al-Hinnawi was known to be under strong Hashemite influence. Everything was falling into place for unionists, which drove Hawrani and his childhood friend Adib al-Shishakli to take action. After winning over key officers in the army, on 19 December 1949 Shishakli ordered his tanks to take Damascus. The aim of the coup was to make absolutely sure that Syria's political system remained republican and to prevent union with monarchical Iraq.[103]

After securing power, Shishakli paid visits to Cairo and Riyadh with the aim of repairing the damage his predecessor had done to the countries' relations. He even paid a sudden courtesy visit to Beirut. Shishakli complained to Riad el-Solh that Syrian politicians in Lebanon were working openly for Iraqi–Syrian union. He requested their extradition to Syria, a request Solh turned down. The Syrians made arrangements to have the Iraqi unionists kidnapped. When the Lebanese Prime Minister learned about these plans, he increased the secret police presence around the activists – much to Shishakli's annoyance.[104]

Shishakli and Hawrani were outsiders on the Damascus political scene, representing extra-parliamentary pressure groups among the army and the left. The colonel's ambitions at that time were limited compared to those of his predecessors. Shishakli regarded the role of the army as that of arbiter or facilitator that could bring the politicians to order at times of national crisis. He did not see the army as an instrument of government. Hence, his first move was to retain the legitimate rulers, permitting them to pursue cabinet formation in the established manner. But as a security measure he set up the army general staff as an authority to rival that of parliament. Consequently, any government had to strike a balance between the claims of the assembly, where the People's Party retained the majority, and those of an increasingly politically minded army. After numerous attempts to form a government, on 27 December 1949 Khaled al-'Azem managed to form a cabinet that reflected the new status quo. Addressing parliament, eight days after forming the government, 'Azem proclaimed that his government would defend the republican regime and support the Arab collective security pact which was under discussion at the League of Arab States.[105]

As regards Syro-Lebanese bilateral relations, 'Azem openly acknowledged that these relations were frozen. In fact, communications between Beirut and Damascus where restricted to the exchange of memoranda. On 16 January 1950, Damascus responded to the Lebanese letter of protest that was sent in mid-December. In the letter, Damascus rejected allegations that Syria was breaking its commitments and charged the Lebanese of such practice. Lebanese policies continued to antagonise Damascus. During that time, Beirut had turned down a Syrian proposal to prohibit the import of cars. An inconclusive 29 January meeting of the Lebanese and Syrian Ministers of Finance received strong criticism from Syrian opinion-makers, who called on their government to separate from the Lebanese economically prior to any negotiation with Beirut:

> Negotiating with Lebanon is fruitless as long as this partnership is there, because retaining it is recognizing that we are unable to separate. And that is our major weakness in front of Lebanon... If we negotiate for 20 years without announcing separation, Lebanon will continue to belittle us and retain the upper hand, serving its own interests at our expense.[106]

Expressing the views of the Syrian merchants, 'Aref al-Laham commented on the causes leading to the Syro-Lebanese crisis. He said the Syrian economy was facing recession, excessive supply relative to demand, high inflation and unemployment. Laham explained that Syria had spent most of the wealth it had earned during the war years encouraging various industries and developing agriculture. He pointed out that Syria was producing ten times as much grain as prior to the war, that the food industry had expanded, that there was self-sufficiency in textiles and that the surplus was being exported.

The head of the Syrian chamber of commerce maintained that, due to the worsening condition of the global economy, the Syrian market would be increasingly exposed to the invasion of foreign goods that were more competitive than locally produced items – due to the latter's high production and labour costs. Consequently, he endorsed the Syrian government's efforts to employ protectionism on all locally produced goods. Laham warned the economic policy being imposed on Syria by Lebanon was disastrous, insisting that it would undoubtedly lead the national economy to ruin and destruction. He attacked Lebanese merchants and called upon the Syrian government to either impose its economic policy on Lebanon or separate from it. But he affirmed that it would not come to separation: 'It is expected that if Syria goes ahead with threatened separation, the Lebanese will succumb to our wishes.'[107]

In Lebanon the mood was more conciliatory. Lebanese Arab nationalists maintained that, without a secure livelihood, Lebanon could either lose its independence, its Arab identity or face partition. The Syrians were advised to ask themselves if it were in their interests to subjugate Lebanon to economic pressure, thereby endangering its existence. Would such a prospect guarantee Lebanon's falling into a Syrian orbit and request unification, it was asked, or would it seek foreign assistance and consequently end up in a foreign orbit?[108] Significantly, Lebanese nationalists, while emphasising that no customs union would come before Lebanese political freedom, declared that the two countries were in need of one another and that a Syro-Lebanese economic conflict would be detrimental to both. In response to 'Aref al-Laham's article, Khalil Gemayel asked what had happened to Arab fraternity and reiterated his conviction that economic partnership was more advantageous to Syria and Lebanon than separation.[109]

Instead of attacking Damascus, radical Lebanese nationalists criticised the Lebanese government. In particular, the Lebanese nationalists attacked a statement of Prime Minster Solh in which he explained that events in Syria had delayed economic negotiations between the two states. They held that the political turmoil that unfolded in Syria did not prevent the consistent pursuit of a vast industrial and commercial plan in Lebanon. Political and economic circles in Lebanon were under the impression that Damascus' new masters had what Mardam Bey and Za'im lacked: they were selling their grain to Turkey and Saudi Arabia, inviting foreign companies to bid in the Latakiya Port development tender, developing the railroad system, developing irrigation projects and erecting barriers in the face of Lebanese goods. The Lebanese leadership was even accused of being incompetent and lazy. 'To allow us to talk to the Syrians as equals there should at first exist a thing that has been absent for the past three years: A government in Lebanon that is truly Lebanese.'[110]

With Syrian public opinion's bitterness towards Lebanon at its height, Khaled al-'Azem accelerated steps to realise the development of the port of Latakiya, the emblem of Syrian 'economic liberation' from its neighbour.[111] While visiting Latakiya on 14 February, where he laid down the cornerstone of the port development project, 'Azem stated that the improvement of the port did not necessarily mean that Syria intended to separate from Lebanon. He added that, should separation occur, the port would be ready and would serve as a transit centre for Iraq and other neighbouring states.[112] Upon his return from Latakiya, the Syrian Prime Minister went to Homs, then took the coastal road through Lebanon's northern city of Tripoli, from which he headed to Shtura. There he rested for two hours neither meeting nor being received by a single Lebanese official.[113] Instead, the Syrian Prime Minister was met by the press and gave a statement in which he indicated that the Syro-Lebanese economic relations could not remain as they were. 'Azem reiterated that both states should follow a common, unified economic policy. This should not be limited to customs tariffs but extended to identical taxation systems for each state. He pointed out that Syrian proposals had been transmitted to the Lebanese government. When asked for the reasons that he did not take the initiative to meet with the Lebanese leadership to address these matters, he responded that all the Syro-Lebanese meetings, which had taken place at various levels, had had no results. The Syrian Premier rejected allegations that he was the champion of separatism, indicating that there was nothing in his past that justified such rumours, but added that separation was a thousand times preferable to the 'actual pseudo partnership'.[114]

'Azem's comments were followed by strong statements from the Syrian Ministers of Finance and Economy. Ma'ruf al-Dawalibi held that a legislative economic union with Lebanon no longer existed while the administrative union remained. Dawalibi revealed that the Syrian government had proposed separate economic agreements to facilitate economic cooperation but the Lebanese had refused. He emphasised that Syrian citizens were all suffering from Lebanese policies. 'Abd Rahman al-'Azem even went further and declared that the existing agreements with Lebanon, intended to induce cooperation, were being abused by the Lebanese and encouraged competition between the two states.[115] Hassan Joubara arrived in Beirut on 21 February carrying a response to a proposal in which the Lebanese government had expressed its desire to negotiate with Syria on all pending economic issues. Joubara informed the Lebanese leadership that the Syrian government would only be prepared to negotiate with Beirut if the latter agreed to adopt a unified economic policy and to the establishment of an economic union.[116]

Joubara's message prompted a wide range of consultations among the Lebanese political and economic elite. It was realised that economic separation was becoming a reality. Although there was a consensus to make as many concessions as possible to avoid the break-up of the union, there was also agreement that, should Damascus remain adamant in its demands, Lebanon would have no choice but to establish its economy on a basis that corresponded to its interests. The meeting addressed the dispute between Lebanese industrialists and merchants. The merchants were clamouring for the removal of the protectionist tariffs that were imposed after the 8 July 1949 Bloudan Agreement. The Lebanese government preferred to await the clarification of relations with Syria and recommended that a committee comprised of representatives of the government and the chambers of commerce, industry and the various merchant associations be established to study the dispute. The Lebanese government undertook not to make any decision before the committee studied the demands of the merchants and industrialists. The dispute between the Lebanese merchants and industrialists was also related to Syro-Lebanese differences, particularly since the core of the disagreement between the two states was the Syrian demand to impose heavy restrictions on imports in order to protect Syrian goods.[117]

Aside from Joubara's visit, Syro-Lebanese dialogue had become restricted to the dailies. In Beirut it was speculated that Syria had been decided on separation since 10 December 1949. Riad el-Solh attempted to dispel such notions by declaring in the Lebanese general assembly that if customs separation took place between the two states, it had to be ratified by the legislative assemblies of Syria and Lebanon, which was unlikely. However, the Premier's statements had the opposite effect on the Lebanese public. His statements were compared to the positions he took during the disputes with Syria on the Monetary Agreement and the Tabbara Affair. During one of those incidents it was recalled how, while striking his hand on the podium from which he was addressing parliament, the Lebanese Premier declared, 'Never will we envisage separation…we will bring the Syrians back to reason, against their will if necessary.'[118] Solh's 10 December remarks on 'separation' betrayed how the times had changed.

Such statements irritated 'Azem, who claimed in his memoirs that this was representative of the manner in which his Lebanese counterpart dealt with the Syrians. According to 'Azem, whenever Syrian and Lebanese interests conflicted, Solh would do his utmost among his old friends in power to secure benefits for Lebanon at Syria's expense. Solh, he said, had the mentality of a 'Lebanese merchant' who would sell the Syrians assurances that Lebanon would never be a centre or path for colonialism, in return for which Solh acquired material benefits for Lebanon and political benefits for himself.[119]

Indeed, the official statements emanating from both capitals aggravated the already strained relations. Asked about the likelihood of a summit in Beirut, Damascus or Shtura between himself and his Syrian counterpart, the Lebanese Prime Minister responded that 'there is no meeting in sight in the near future'. He asserted that Lebanon did not break any economic agreement conducted between the two states. Similarly on 25 February, two days after Solh's statement, 'Azem declared that no new developments concerning Syro-Lebanese relations had occurred. On 27 February, Lebanese emissary Takiddine el-Solh arrived in the Syrian capital. In a long meeting with the Syrian Premier he presented 'Azem with a memorandum in which the Lebanese government proposed a meeting or the exchange of memoranda on issues of dispute. The Premier responded that the Syrian government had expressed its point of view on numerous occasions and that he did not see any benefit from a further exchange of memoranda.[120]

While refusing to entertain Lebanese advances, Khaled 'Azem was engaged in mobilising Syrian industrialists and merchants. A day after receiving the Lebanese emissary, 'Azem inaugurated an economic conference, which brought together representatives of the Syrian chambers of commerce, industry and agriculture. Deliberations were held for two days in which various reports on trade agreements, future development plans for agriculture, tourism and industry were addressed. Although the subjects were diverse, the future relations with Lebanon dominated the proceedings. The customs union as well as prospects of economic and monetary union were assessed. The conference's final recommendations to the Syrian government were complete monetary, customs and economic union with Lebanon or complete separation, which should be immediate. At its meeting of 4 March, the Syrian cabinet decided to draw up a new memorandum that reflected the conference's findings and present it to Lebanon.[121]

A few days later, the Syrian memorandum, or rather ultimatum, arrived in Beirut. It listed Syrian grievances and designated 1948 as the year when each of the two states began following their own monetary, taxation and customs policies. The memorandum asserted that it was due to this state of affairs that the balance of interests in the economic partnership was disrupted, with severe consequences for Syria. It claimed that Syria could have restricted the transfer of capital to Lebanon and decreased expenditures in the defence of its currency, however, it chose not to resort to such measures in order not to weaken the customs union.

According to the memorandum, it might have been possible to avoid the current crisis had the agreement of 8 July 1949 been implemented in its significant articles, mainly those that called upon the two governments to work together to unify local taxation policies and to take joint measures to establish parity between the two currencies. The Syrian ultimatum emphasised that because these principles were not implemented, because the Lebanese government didn't concern itself with the agreement of 8 July 1949, Syria suffered a disruption of the balance of trade and payments. The ultimatum concluded that due to the absence of a united economic policy – that would unite customs regulations and monetary, import and export as well as other economic policies – and the neglect of Syria's rights to take part in the administration of the HCCI, the Syrian government was forced to demand either complete economic union or separation with Lebanon. Beirut was given until 20 March 1950 to respond.[122]

There were hopes in Beirut that the Syrian refusal to meet with the Lebanese leadership would be circumvented by the upcoming meeting of the Arab League that was scheduled to convene in Cairo on 21 March 1950. However, the Syrian leadership, not wishing to delay the matter further through Arab mediation, shattered such hopes by fixing the deadline of the Lebanese response one day prior to the Arab League summit. Pending the termination of the deadline, and while awaiting the Lebanese response, Syrian officials refused to engage their Lebanese counterparts in any formal or informal dialogue. The Syrian Premier had given strict instructions along these lines to his cabinet members. This could clearly be seen by the Beirut visit of Syrian Justice Minister Faydi al-Atasi. As it was a personal business trip, he said, he refused to meet with any Lebanese officials or to make any comment to the press.[123]

The Syrian ultimatum to the Lebanese government was followed by a press conference. On 9 March 1950, Khaled al-'Azem gave a detailed presentation of the Syrian memorandum, and stressed that any deviation from total economic union would entail a termination of the customs union. Highlighting the deadline of the Lebanese response, 'Azem attempted to dispel any notions that Lebanon would be able to develop and sustain itself regardless of Syria's fortune or misfortune. He expressed his belief that Lebanon's economic activity was based on Syria's well-being and that a protectionist economic policy was ideally suited for both states. Under a protectionist economic policy, Lebanese merchants would import and market Syrian goods and Syria would not do without Lebanese intermediary services in marketing its products abroad. The head of the Syrian cabinet concluded his statement by emphasising that his government's latest measure was a result of popular demand and were recommendations of the economic conference. He expressed his gratitude of the strong support his government received from the merchant, labourer, farmer and factory owner.[124]

Syria's latest measure was not without negative ramifications for its economy, specifically on those sectors the Syrian Prime Minister was thanking. There were criticisms of Syria's refusal to export grain to Lebanon, a policy strictly adopted since autumn 1949. As was the practice, the lack of rain was the justification for the grain embargo. But rain was abundant and the harvest turned out to be plentiful. In addition, an agreement that would have seen Syria supply Turkey with 50,000 tons of grain did not materialise. Unable to find foreign markets, the Syrian farmer suffered. Moreover, stagnation in the Syrian markets was worsening, leading to a fall in prices, especially in foodstuffs. In addition, the difference between the Lebanese and Syrian currencies rose to 14 per cent.[125] The gap was expected to widen further, particularly since it was the time of the month when the Syrian merchants would head to the Lebanese markets to conduct their business. A number of officials in Damascus welcomed the higher Lebanese exchange rate, since they hoped that this would prevent Syrian merchants from purchasing goods from Beirut.[126]

On 10 March 1950, the Lebanese cabinet convened to study its response to the Syrian ultimatum, which was carried the following day to the Syrian capital by a Lebanese emissary, Muhammad Ali Hemadeh, the director of social affairs at the Lebanese Foreign Ministry. The Lebanese response highlighted that the Syrian memorandum took the appearance of a warning and was coupled with statements that did not conform to the spirit of cooperation and friendship. Beirut reiterated its faithfulness to the customs union with Syria and claimed to have made numerous sacrifices to retain the bonds. The importance of the Lebanese memorandum lies in the fact that it listed, for the first time, Lebanese grievances with numerous Syrian practices. Also significant was the fact that these grievances were official and made public. From the Lebanese point of view, the most important issues were as follows.

1. Lebanon agreed to the *Mira* system although it constituted a clear contradiction to the system of the customs union and its primary condition: the free movement of goods between the two states. Lebanon also remained silent on the imposition of a 15-piastre Syrian government tariff on each kilo of grain bound to Lebanon.

2. For every instant that the Syrian government prohibited grain supplies to Lebanon, the Lebanese government was satisfied to draw the Syrian government's attention to the matter without threatening separation. [The Syrian grain embargos were] unjustified and at times coincided with periods when there was only sufficient grain in Lebanon to feed the population for 15 days. On other occasions, [the Lebanese government] did not retain enough hard currency to afford importing the country's needs from abroad.

3. It never occurred to the Lebanese government to demand separation every time the Syrian government or one of its ministers prohibited the export of food supplies such as *samneh*, oils or livestock to Lebanon. The Lebanese government never thought of similar retaliation.

4. The Lebanese government remained silent to its Syrian counterpart's demand that car agents and importers had to open branches of their offices in Syria, although this was in direct infringement to the role of Lebanon as a mediator of Syrian imports.

5. The Lebanese government agreed to lift customs on industrial machines and equipment. It also lowered customs on primary industrial material for industries in Syria and Lebanon.

6. The Lebanese government imposed import restriction on 40 items to limit their import and protect local industry, while the Syrian authorities did not bind themselves to these measures and continued issuing import licences for these items.

7. The Lebanese government imposed a 50-piastre customs fee on sweets and chocolates while the Syrian counterpart only put a 15-piastre customs fee.

8. The Lebanese government implemented all the articles of the agreement of 8 July 1949, and agreed to lift customs on materials made from cotton and silk. The Higher Council of the Common Interests was in the process of implementing the remaining conditions of this agreement related to customs.

9. The Lebanese government implemented the agricultural policy that was drawn up by Syria, and hence agreed to impose a 110 per cent customs fee and a 50 per cent fee on imports of grain and its derivatives, in spite of Lebanon's need for grain. The Lebanese government took these measures to protect Syrian products. While the Syrian government undertook to facilitate the export of grain to foreign countries, a short period after signing the mentioned agreement.

10. Finally, when the Syrian government expressed its desire to increase the number of its nationals serving in the Common Interest, the Lebanese government agreed to establish entrance examinations to this directorate. Only Syrians would be allowed to sit for the examinations.[127]

The memorandum expressed the Lebanese government's regret that its efforts to retain the bonds of friendship did not find any response from its Syrian counterpart. The sudden restriction of grain transport to Lebanon, while Syria allowed the grain exports to foreign countries, was noted. It was emphasised that grain export restrictions to Lebanon clearly violated the 8 July 1949 agreement and the preceding agreements.

In the memorandum, the Lebanese government reminded its counterpart that both governments agreed upon the spirit and text of this agreement, however, the Syrian government saw fit to reject it at the last minute. The Lebanese government regarded the agreement as a safeguard for its currency. The Lebanese signature of the Monetary Agreement was received with hostility by the Syrian government. The memorandum underscored that reality proved the wisdom of the Lebanese policy, for after one year, on 7 February 1949, the Syrian government itself signed a Monetary Agreement with France, which was based on the same clauses as the previous agreements.

The Lebanese government conceded that, due to the limited resources at its disposal, it was unable to assist Syria sufficiently in its monetary difficulties. Nevertheless, the Lebanese government accepted receipt of customs revenues (on Lebanese soil) in Syrian currency. Damascus was reminded that the Lebanese authorities opened an account for the Syrian government whereby the latter could utilise the Lebanese currency gained from the revenue of the Common Interests. However, in spite of all Lebanese efforts, the Syrian government did not implement this agreement, which was reached on 8 July 1949.

In the memorandum, Beirut expressed its misgivings concerning the establishment of a monetary union between the two states. In the Lebanese view, monetary union required unity in the issuing of banknotes, in the elements covering the currency and in financial and economic policy. Realising monetary union also required unified legislation in each state and compelled each government to take measures that were political in nature. All these measures, the memorandum underlined, infringed upon the sovereignty of each state and weakened the Lebanese currency.

The Lebanese government urged its Syrian counterpart to reconsider its position. It reiterated its readiness to conduct consultations with the aim of reforming all issues that the experience of the last years had proven needed reform. Beirut pointed out that if the Syrian government insisted on its position and refused to negotiate, the Lebanese government absolved itself from any responsibility for the consequences and declared that it retained the right to adopt a policy that conformed to its interests.[128]

On the same day the Lebanese cabinet drafted its response to the Syrian memorandum, a luncheon in honour of Foreign Minister Philip Takla turned into a celebration of the failure of an assassination attempt upon Riad el-Solh, and a demonstration of political solidarity with the Lebanese government's economic policies vis-à-vis Syria.[129] Noteworthy was the attendance of Lebanese political, economic and press personalities with good Arab nationalist credentials. Also important was the fact that the merchants association organised the luncheon. Anis Naja, a prominent Sunni merchant, delivered a heated speech rejecting Syrian threats of separation. He said he found it ironic that during its quarter-century mandate, France had tried to prevent the collapse of the two states through their economic union. But as soon as both states were blessed with independence, they started considering separation. He placed the responsibility of such a prospect with the Syrian government and placed greater responsibility on Syrian thinkers and economists.

Naja maintained that Syria was perusing a false economic policy that would separate two brothers and create animosity between them at a time where there should be understanding, solidarity and unity. He argued that the goal of the Arab nation was to achieve an economic union, free trade, removal of tariff barriers, passports and free exchange of agricultural produce and goods. 'Where are you separatists from this noble goal? Are you aware of the dangers arising from Zionism? Are we really in need of new divisions amongst ourselves so that we lose additional land from the Arab nation as we did with our internal divisions? Or does Syria see that it secured its front with Israel only to start a new front with its brother Lebanon?' Taking the floor after Naja, Solh stated that he was under the false impression that Syro-Lebanese relations were based on national sentiment and not numbers. He strongly criticised the timing of Damascus' discussion of separation. 'It pains me greatly that the Syrian ultimatum expires on date in which LAS is scheduled to meet and it also pains me greatly that the incident with Syria comes at a time when the two states might be forced to close their borders in the face of an Arab state (Jordan), which was negotiating with Israel.'[130] In fact, sympathy for Riad el-Solh – arising from the unsuccessful assassination attempt and the restrained and dignified manner in which he was handling the threat of economic rupture with Syria – earned his government unprecedented support among Lebanese.[131]

Two days after the luncheon, which received wide press coverage in Lebanon and Syria, Lebanese representatives of the chambers of commerce and industry, in addition to numerous representatives of merchants associations, held a meeting to study the Syrian ultimatum and the Lebanese government's response to it. After the meeting, 'Abdel Rahim Sahmarani, president of the chamber of commerce and industry, made an announcement in the name of Lebanese merchants and industrialists in which he regretted Syria's rigid attitude. He declared that Lebanese merchants and industrialists hoped that all efforts be made to maintain the cooperation and union between the two countries. Sahmarani disclosed the readiness of all Lebanese associations to eliminate the obstacles preventing Syrian–Lebanese agreement. Sahmarani believed that, in the event of separation and after realising its inconveniences, it would not be long before Damascus expressed its wish to return to Syro-Lebanese cooperation.[132]

Lebanese opinion-makers strongly condemned the manner and policy of the 'Azem government towards Lebanon. Lebanese nationalist circles, in particular Michel Chiha, condemned Syria's slide into autarky and criticised its monetary situation, noting that it could not be improved by Lebanon taking part in it. Chiha asserted that Lebanon had nothing to gain from an impoverished Syria and that the latter's economic distress would gravely harm Lebanon, Syria's neighbour and immediate client. He concluded that the Syrians had to bring their internal economic affairs into order. During that process they could not expect Lebanon to follow it blindly, especially after the vicissitudes (or coups d'état) Syria had witnessed.[133] Radical Lebanese nationalist opinion-makers attributed Syro-Lebanese differences to two different concepts of life – two different philosophies and attitudes had made Lebanon and Syria of 1950 incompatible. According to radical Lebanese nationalists, there was a strong mood of isolationism in Syria. Moreover, the 'Azem government's policies were perceived to be more a matter of personal prestige for the Syrian Premier than in conformity with Syrian interests.[134] Lebanese Arab nationalist circles in Lebanon were in agreement with this assessment. It was recalled that 'Azem passed through Lebanon on his way from Latakiya but refused to pass through Beirut to meet with his Lebanese counterpart:

> He, who was expected to do so – being the son of a great noble family and representative of a neighbouring area dear to our hearts – did not meet the Lebanese prime minister nor talk to him, man to man.
>
> They say that Prime Minister 'Azem was upset from the Lebanese government, which did not congratulate him the day he assumed the premiership. He thus wanted to avenge his dignity when he passed by Beirut by not stopping to see his Lebanese counterpart. Is it in the manner of good diplomacy that personal affairs be mixed with public affairs, and is it befitting to exchange memoranda and warnings from a distance and to designate the day of 20 March 1950 the promised day of either union or separation?[135]

On 13 March 1950, 'Azem, completely disregarding Lebanese appeals, convened a cabinet meeting at 10:00 pm. After the meeting, a communiqué was issued announcing the dissolution of the two countries' customs regime. According to the communiqué, Syria demanded the establishment of a joint Syro-Lebanese committee that would supervise the liquidation of the Common Interests. The Syrian government established surveillance and customs posts and prohibited the travel of Syrian nationals to Lebanon without special permits. Syrian authorities hoped thereby to keep Syrian currency from flooding the Lebanese market. For that purpose, Damascus stationed an infantry battalion at the frontier, on the Beirut–Damascus road, and another battalion on the road near the frontier north of Tripoli. The Syrian government requested that the Lebanese Customs Directorate recall all civil servants of Lebanese nationality from Syria and to facilitate the return of all Syrian civil servants to Syria. The following day, telegrams and letters from commercial, industrial and agricultural circles started flooding the office of the Syrian Prime Minister, congratulating him on his government's measures. Five days later, on 18 March, an enthusiastic assembly overwhelmingly endorsed the Syrian government's action. With the dissolution of the customs union, Syro-Lebanese relations entered a new era.[136]

CONCLUSION

T he collapse of the Ottoman Empire in 1918 brought with it the formal establishment of a European order in the Levant. For decades, France and Britain worked on building nation states in the Middle East. In Lebanon and Syria, France imposed her rule from above, creating apparatuses, institutions and bureaucracies for two states that were politically separate but whose economic organs – all operating under the authority of the French High Commissioner – were intertwined.

Against this background, Syrian and Lebanese Arab nationalists worked to liberate the Levant from French domination. As explained in the Introduction, they were convinced that the collapse of the French order would hasten, or at least facilitate, integration and cooperation among all Arab states, and Lebanon and Syria in particular.

Paradoxically, Lebanese nationalists, especially the radicals, were also convinced that French withdrawal from the Levant would eventually be followed by the subjugation of Lebanon – the sole Christian safe haven in the Middle East – to an Arab/Islamic order. The views of the Lebanese and Syrian Arab nationalists as well as the Lebanese nationalists proved to be exaggerated.

In Chapter 1 it was shown how, until the complete withdrawal of the last French soldier from Lebanon and Syria at the end of 1946, the ruling elites in both states were very keen on sidelining any cause that might threaten the alliance that had developed in October 1943 between Lebanese Arab nationalists, Lebanese nationalists and Syrian Arab nationalists. Between 1943 and 1946, Lebanese and Syrian Arab nationalists took great care to mitigate the fears of the Lebanese nationalists, particularly the radicals. Every attempt was made to reassure them that emancipation of Lebanon from French control did not mean Arab, Muslim or Syrian domination.

During the same period, the overriding priority for Lebanese and Syrian Arab nationalists was liberation. Bilateral relations were conducted in such a manner as to prevent, or at least postpone, controversy over thorny issues. As illustrated in Chapter 1, this trend cumulated in the Agreement of the Higher Council of the Common Interests (HCCI), which came into effect in January 1944. The agreement, engineered by an alliance of Lebanese and Syrian Arab nationalists and Lebanese nationalists, took into consideration the sensitivities of the radical Lebanese nationalists, who were reassured that the HCCI was not a supra-state structure in the making or a mechanism to facilitate political union.

Syrian attempts to replace the HCCI with a more effective Syro-Lebanese organ that would firmly coordinate and control the economic and financial activities of both states continued to be rebuffed by successive Lebanese governments – despite the fact that outspoken Arab nationalists headed them. The latter argued that Lebanese unity would be compromised and that Lebanese nationalists would be pushed into a French orbit. This, in addition to other positions adopted by Lebanese Arab nationalists, was – intentionally or otherwise – misconstrued by various Syrian Arab nationalists and Lebanese nationalists. To the former it represented an abandonment of the 'Arab cause'. The latter saw it as a betrayal of the National Pact, which entailed loyalty to the Lebanese state. On one hand, the Lebanese Arab nationalist role in bringing Lebanese nationalists into the Arab orbit was taken for granted by their Arab brethren. On the other hand, their role in safeguarding Lebanese independence, sovereignty and interests was also taken for granted by the Lebanese nationalists.

Chapter 2 established how Syrian and Lebanese ruling elites prevented serious differences over customs revenues, taxation policies and grain prices from damaging the two countries' united front against France. The foreign policies of Lebanon and Syria were conducted along similar lines.

With the collapse of the French order in the Levant at the end of 1946 and the rise of an Arab order, bilateral relations between Lebanon and Syria went through a period of readjustment. As was pointed out in Chapter 3, Syrian Arab nationalists were under the impression that they enjoyed a privileged position in Lebanon and that this position entailed parallel economic privileges for their country there. In 1947, with liberation from France all but secured, Syrian Arab nationalist frustration with what they felt to be their country's economic servitude to Lebanon became more pronounced. This was to continue until the termination of the customs union. A particular source of irritation for the Syrians was Lebanon's unlimited appetite for imports. In turn, Syrian taxation policies were causing economic hardship in Lebanon. No common ground was reached. Aside from these issues, Chapter 4 related how the Syro-Lebanese economic partnership was further strained by the TAPLINE affair, where each state had attempted – unilaterally – to maximise its benefits from Aramco, even at the expense of 'brotherly relations'. The leadership in Damascus gravely embarrassed proponents of Arab nationalism in Lebanon by delaying the entire project for years in an attempt to secure an oil terminal and refinery on Syrian soil. It was Lebanese Arab nationalists, led by Riad el-Solh, who interceded between Aramco and the Syrians to resolve the deadlock. But that did not dispel the complaints of the Syrian Arab nationalists.

Significantly, criticism against Syria did not originate from Lebanese nationalists alone, but from Lebanese Arab nationalists as well. The latter were infuriated by their Syrian counterparts' drive to utilise Lebanon's need for staples, such as grain, as a means to force her into toeing the Syrian line.

Grain was the Syrian government's weapon of choice in its monetary discord with Lebanon. Chapter 5 illustrated how differences over monetary relations with France drove Syria to impose a harsh embargo on food supplies and grain, causing shortages and high prices in Lebanon. Convinced that without Lebanese Arab nationalist consent the Lebanese government would not have been able to conduct the Monetary Agreement with France, Syrian Arab nationalists alleged that their Lebanese Arab nationalist brethren betrayed the Arab nationalist cause. Lebanese Arab nationalists were portrayed as upholding Lebanese interests to the detriment of the Arab world, colluding with Lebanese nationalists in upholding French influence in the Levant. In Syrian eyes, Lebanese Arab nationalists had reneged on their pledge to prevent Lebanon from becoming a passage or centre for foreign ambitions. Syrian opinion-makers, merchants and politicians called for immediate economic separation from Lebanon.

It was the Lebanese nationalists who took the lead in defending the customs union against radical Lebanese nationalist and Syrian Arab nationalist calls for separation. At the same time, Lebanese Arab nationalists were outspokenly critical of Syrian measures against Lebanon. They argued that such practices were only reinforcing the borders between the two states. For all practical purposes, the Syro-Lebanese monetary dispute resulted in deepening the alliance between the Lebanese Arab nationalists, on one hand, and the Lebanese nationalists on the other. It also led to a convergence of interests between Syrian Arab nationalists and radical Lebanese nationalists. The monetary discord between Lebanon and Syria also revealed how the Lebanese Arab nationalists lent their political support and protection to the Lebanese economic order.

It is noteworthy that Syria's embargo against Lebanon in 1948 was popular among the Syrian public. In contrast, the 'Gentlemen's Agreement', which was brokered by the League of Arab States, was met with dismay by Syrian Arab nationalists. Lebanon was accused of taking advantage of the situation in Palestine, which called for Arab solidarity in the face of the Zionist onslaught. In the Syrian Arab nationalist view, the Lebanese unscrupulously ratified the Paris Accord and presented Syria with a fait accompli. Decision-makers in Damascus were being called upon to cease signing temporary agreements and to liberate Syria from 'economic slavery' to Lebanon.

The Syrian government proceeded to tighten its control over foreign trade and exchange transactions and urged its Lebanese counterparts to do the same. Any attempt to tighten government control over the economy was successfully averted by the Lebanese economic elite. It should be noted that the Syrian government failed to take Lebanon's internal make-up into consideration. Lebanese nationalists argued that a protectionist economy would inevitably lead to an autocracy. For them, it was difficult to conceive of a Lebanon where different communities had to cooperate and live together, in which the state would become omnipotent. In a multi-religious environment, Lebanese nationalists wondered, which sect would control the state?

By the end of 1948, sentiments concerning the futility of negotiating with Lebanon had come to a head in Syria. By that time, the Lebanese government had lifted all restrictions on imports and hard currencies. A Syro-Lebanese crisis was averted mainly because Syria had slid into political turmoil, which was largely attributed to the deteriorating economic situation as well as the devastating defeat in Palestine. Aside from these internal challenges, Syria had also become a stage for international as well as intra-Arab rivalry.

Chapter 6 demonstrated how the aforementioned factors combined to bring the military to power in Syria, which only served to further complicate Syro-Lebanese relations. The affinity between Lebanese and Syrian ruling elites was undermined, and with it the modest impact these personal ties had on bilateral relations. With the rise of a military order in Syria, a new factor was to emerge. Syria's new ruling elite feared Lebanon and was convinced that this was the hatching ground of plots to unseat them. In turn, Lebanese Arab nationalists and their Lebanese nationalist allies were extremely wary of Syria's new leadership, who were perceived as a threat to Lebanon's political order.

These fears combined to complicate an already complicated and strained relationship. Although it was under Syrian military rule that the Franco-Syrian Monetary Agreement as well as the TAPLINE agreement came into effect, the new rulers of Damascus drew heavily on the well-established practices of embargoes to coerce Beirut to adopt Syrian positions, whether on old outstanding economic disputes or on differences that were more political in nature – such as the Tabbara Affair. Such practices continued to enjoy wide popularity in Syria, even among outspoken Syrian Arab nationalists.

With the coming of the second and third coups, led respectively by Sami al-Hinnawi and Adib al-Shishakli, the gap between the Lebanese and Syrian currency exchange rates continued widening to the advantage of the Lebanese merchants. This gap was noticed by Syrian public opinion, whose disenchantment with Lebanon reached new lows by the end of 1949.

Khalid al-'Azem, who assumed the Syrian premiership at the end of 1949, built on anti-Lebanese sentiments and vigorously pursued a heavy-handed policy towards Lebanon. He was known to have strong personal antipathy to the Lebanese leadership, in particular Riad el-Solh. But it was popular support, from the various merchant and industrial associations in particular, which provided him with the solid ground to retain an uncompromising stance towards Lebanon. 'Azem was dismissive of Lebanese Arab nationalist warnings that the inflexible Syrian position could drive Lebanon to an anti-Arab orbit. 'Azem also refused to entertain Lebanese nationalist assertions that in spite of the flaws of the economic union, which could be addressed, the union served the interests of both states. On 7 March 1950, the

Syrian Premier sent his ultimatum to Lebanon setting 20 March as the deadline for the Lebanese response. 'Azem selected the deadline carefully to precede an Arab League summit by one day. He therefore closed the door upon any Arab mediation efforts, while giving instructions to Syrian officials to refrain from informal or formal contact with their Lebanese counterparts.

For all practical purposes, and as the Syrian ultimatum indicated, the Syro-Lebanese economic partnership ended in 1948 with the monetary separation of the two states. It is significant to note that, at the political level, there was a basic understanding between the two states on both cardinal issues and objectives. The two states remained active members of the League of Arab States; their common position vis-à-vis the Greater Syria scheme and, later, the Arab-Israeli conflict persisted. However, where bilateral functional relations were concerned, the state of affairs was much different.

From 1947 and until March 1950, the defining feature of Syro-Lebanese bilateral relations was temporary solutions dictated by ephemeral political and regional considerations. Never were long-term points of contention seriously addressed. Rather they accumulated, unresolved, particularly as each state began to develop and retain distinct interests.

As this book demonstrates, the beliefs of the Arab nationalists in Syria and Lebanon were identical in theory, but when it came to negotiating bilateral relations between these two Arab countries, behaviour was conditioned by circumstances and national interests that contradicted Arab nationalist sentiments.

Arab states, especially Lebanon and Syria, still exhibit weaknesses when addressing contentious issues. Dispute resolution mechanisms remain weak to this day. Where Syro-Lebanese relations were concerned, political and ideological expectations proved exaggerated if not misleading. In today's global village, greater efforts are needed to create instruments to facilitate intra-Arab cooperation. These efforts must address issues of functional cooperation, and create mechanisms that would bring the interests of all Arabs into harmony.

NOTES

INTRODUCTION

1 Abou Khaldun Sati' al-Husri, *Ara' wa ahadith fi al-qawmiyya al-'arabiyya*, Beirut: Markaz dirasat al-wihda al-'arabiyya, 1986, 33–35.

2 George Antonius, *The Arab Awakening: The Story of the Arab National Movement*, Beirut: Khayat's College Book Cooperative, 1938, 248–249.

3 Nabih Amin Fares, *Haza al-'alam al-'arabi: dirasa fi al-qawmiyya al-'arabiyya wa fi'awamel al-taqadum wa al-ta 'khur wa al-wihda wa al-tafriq fi al-'alam al-'arabi*, Beirut: Dar al-'ilm li al-malayin, 1953, 124.

4 Michel 'Aflaq, *Fi sabil al-ba'th*, Beirut: Dar al-tali'a, 1963, 119 and 341.

5 James Gelvin, *Divided Loyalties: Nationalism and Mass Politics in Syria at the Close of Empire*, Berkeley: University of California Press, 1998, 15.

6 Gelvin, *Divided Loyalties*, 237–239.

7 Joseph Elias, 'Al-Qabass al-Madi', in *al-A'mal al-Mukhtara, Najib al-Rayyes*, Beirut: Dar Riad al-Rayyes, 1994, 30.

8 Joseph Sokhn, *Horizons Libanais*, Beirut, 1983, 138–139 and 144–145 and Henry Abu-Fadel (ed.), *A'lam al-Orthodox fi Lubnan*, Beirut: Lajnat al-dirassat al-orthodoxiya fi lubnan, 1995, 62 and 66.

9 Walid 'Awad, *'Abdallah al-Mashnuq yatazakar*, Beirut: al-Ahliya li al-nashir, 1981, 10.

10 Nadim Shehadi, *The Idea of Lebanon*, Oxford: Centre for Lebanese Studies, 1987, 8 and Fawaz Traboulsi, *Silat bila wasil, Michel Chiha wa al-idiolojya al-lubnaniya*, Beirut: Riad al-Raiyyes, 1999, 28.

11 Interview with Ghassan Tweini, 23 December 2003.

12 Kamal Salibi, *A House of Many Mansions: The History of Lebanon Reconsidered*, Berkeley: University of California Press, 1988, 29 and Meir Zamir, *The Formation of Modern Lebanon*, London: Croom-Helm, 1985, 94–95. Radical Lebanese nationalists argue that, though universally recognised for more than two thousand years as a cohesive region, Syria was historically not a polity. It never acquired political form as a single state or entity containing Syria and nothing else. For most of its history, Syria was usually the province of an empire based elsewhere. Unlike Syria, the radical Lebanese nationalists argued, Lebanon had always enjoyed a certain degree of autonomy. See Daniel Pipes, *Greater Syria: The History of an Ambition*, Oxford: Oxford University Press, 1990.

13 See also C. Ernest Dawn, 'The Origins of Arab Nationalism', *The Origins of Arab Nationalism*, edited by Rashid Khalidi et al., 3–30, New York, 1991. In contrast to Dawn and Khoury, Rashid Khalidi has persistently highlighted the part played by a circle of

professionals, particularly journalists, in the development and promotion of Arab nationalism. See Rashid Khalidi, 'Abd al-Ghani al-'Uraisi and *al-Mufid*: The Press and Arab Nationalism before 1914', in *Intellectual Life in the Arab East, 1890–1939*, edited by Marwan Buheiry, 84–91, Beirut, 1981; 'Society and Ideology in Late Ottoman Syria', in *Problems of the Middle East in Historical Perspective: Essays in Honor of Albert Hourani*, edited by John Spagnolo, 119–131, Reading, England, 1992.

14 The *mutasarrifiya*, also known as Smaller Lebanon, came about as a result of the Ottoman–European settlement of the 1860 civil war in Mount Lebanon. It extended from the outskirts of Tripoli in the north to the boundaries of Jezzine in the south, including parts of the Beqa. The *mutasarrifiya* was much more independent from Istanbul than neighbouring Syrian provinces. This autonomous status was taken as a historical and political basis for the foundation of modern Lebanon. See Walid Phares, *Lebanese Christian Nationalism: The Rise and Fall of an Ethnic Resistance*, London: Lynne Rienner Publishers, 1995, 59–62; and John P. Spagnolo, *France and Ottoman Lebanon*, London: Ithaca Press, 1977, 81.

15 Jean Karl Tanenbaum, *France and the Arab Middle East, 1914–1920*, Philadelphia: The American Philosophical Society, 1978.

16 Stephen H. Longrigg, *Syria and Lebanon under the French Mandate*, London: Oxford University Press, 1958, 144.

17 For the text of the Sykes–Picot Agreement see J. C. Hurewitz, *The Middle East and North Africa in World Politics: A Documentary Record*, vol.2: *The British-French Supremacy, 1914–1945*, New Haven: Yale University Press, 1979, 60–64, 118–128, 158–166.

18 Gelvin, *Divided Loyalties*, 136.

19 Gelvin, *Divided Loyalties*, 143, 144 and 152.

20 See Eliezer Tauber, *The Formation of Modern Syria and Iraq*, Essex: Frank Cass, 1995.

21 Here, special reference should be made to al-Fatat, a clandestine Arab society, the Arab Independence Party (*Hizb al-istiqlal al-'arabi*) and the Syrian National Party (*al-Hizb al-watani al-suri*). For more on the popular committees, societies and parties in Syria (and Lebanon) see Eliezer Tauber, *The Formation of Modern Syria and Iraq*, Essex: Frank Cass, 1995, 8–9, 17, 48–58.

22 Marwan Buheiry (ed.), *Intellectual Life in the Arab East 1890–1939*, Beirut, 1981, 79–80.

23 J. P. Spagnolo, 'French Influence in Syria prior to World War I: The Functional Weakness of Imperialism', *Middle East Journal*, 23 (1969), 57–61. See also Peter Shambrook, *French Imperialism in Syria, 1927–1936*, Reading: Ithaca Press, 1998, 5–34.

24 On Maysalun, see Sati' al-Husri, *Yawm maysalun: safha min tarikh al-'arab al-hadith*, Beirut: Maktabat al-Kashaf, 1947.

25 Philip Khoury, *Syria and the French Mandate: The Politics of Arab Nationalism, 1920–1945*, Princeton, NJ: Princeton University Press, 1987, 19–20; Zamir, *The Formation of Modern Lebanon*, 1985, 12, 151–152, 107–108; Stephen H. Longrigg, *Syria and Lebanon under the French Mandate*, London, 1958, 116–117; Meir Zamir, *Lebanon's Quest: The Road to Statehood 1926–1939*, London: I.B. Tauris, 1997, 3.

26 Zamir, *The Formation of Modern Lebanon*, 59, 80–81, and 'Faysal and the Lebanese Question, 1918–1920', *Middle Eastern Studies*, 27, (1991), 404–426.

27 Khoury, *Syria and the French Mandate*, 168–169.

28 Zamir, *Lebanon's Quest*, 105–109.

29 Interview with Raghid el-Solh, 11 December 2003.
30 On the Eddé–Khuri dualism, see Kamal Salibi, *The Modern History of Lebanon*, London: Weidenfeld, 1965, 215–216; see also Bshara el-Khuri, *Haqa'iq lubnaniya*, Beirut: Awraq Lubnaniya, 1961, 189–190; Camille Chamoun, *Mémoires*, Beirut: Centre de Documentation et de Recherches, 1980, 8; and Zamir, *The Formation of Modern Lebanon*, 219–222. On the National Bloc, see Sami Moubayed, *The Politics of Damascus, 1920–1946*, Damascus: Tlass House, 1999, 68–76.
31 Zamir, *Lebanon's Quest*, 193.
32 Raghid el-Solh, *Lebanon and Arabism: National; Identity and State Formation*, London: I.B. Tauris in association with the Center for Lebanese Studies, 2004, 223–224.
33 Sa'id Murad, *Al-Harakah al-wahdawiyya fi lubnan bayn al-harbayn al-'alamiyayn*, Beirut: Ma'had al-inma' al-'arabi, 1986, 153, 180; Carolyn Gates, *The Historical Role of Political Economy in the Development of Modern Lebanon*, Oxford: Centre for Lebanese Studies, 1989, 13–16 and Gates, *The Merchant Republic of Lebanon: Rise of an Open Economy*, London: I.B. Tauris, 3–17.
34 Najla W. Atiyah, *The Attitude of the Lebanese Sunnis Towards the State of Lebanon*, PhD. Diss, Univ. of London, 150–151; Michael Johnson, 'Confessionalism and Individualism in Lebanon, Critique of Leonard Binder (ed.), Politics in the Lebanon', in *Review of Middle Eastern Studies*, 1 (1975), 85–86.
35 Raghid el-Solh, *Lebanon and Arabism*, 87–88.
36 Eyal Zisser, *Lebanon: The Challenge of Independence*, London: I.B Tauris, 2000, 174.
37 Steven Heydemann, *Authoritarianism in Syria: Institutions and Social Conflict, 1946–1970*, Ithaca: Cornell University Press, 1999, 42.
38 See Nadim Shehadi, *The Idea of Lebanon*; Carolyn Gates, *The Merchant Republic of Lebanon; The Historical Role of Political Economy in the Development of Modern Lebanon*, and her 'Laissez-Faire, Outward-Orientation, and Regional Economic Disintegration: A Case Study of the Dissolution of the Syro-Lebanese Customs Union', in *State and Society in Syria and Lebanon*, edited by Youssef Chouveiri, 74–83, Exeter, 1993.

CHAPTER 1

1 Salma Mardam Bey, *Syria's Quest for Independence 1939–1945*, Reading: Ithaca Press, 1994, 56–60.
2 On 17 August 1943 the newly elected Syrian parliament convened and elected Shukri al-Quwwatly to be President. Quwwatly's consultations with political leaders saw the creation of a new nationalist government. Its members were: Sa'dallah al-Jabiri (Prime Minister), Jamil Mardam Bey (Foreign Minister), Lutfi al-Haffar (Interior), 'Abd al-Rahman al-Kayyali (Justice), Nasuhi al-Bukhari (Education and Defence), Khaled al-'Azm (Finance), Mazhar Raslan (Public Works and Ravitaillement) and Taufiq Shamiyya (Agriculture and Commerce). See *al-Bashir*, 19 August 1943.
3 Albert Hourani, *Syria and Lebanon: A Political Essay*, London: Oxford University Press, 1946, 290–291 and Khoury, *Syria and the French Mandate*, 613.
4 Beirut to Foreign Office, 10 March 1943, FO 371/35176 and Beirut to Foreign Office, 9 June 1943, FO 371/35177.

5   For details on the Syrian national elections, see Khoury, *Syria and the French Mandate*, 598–603.

6   *Al-Bashir*, 23 September 1943.

7   From Commander in Chief Middle East to the War Office, 9 September 1943, FO 371/35181.

8   Khuri, *Haqa'q lubnaniya*, vol. II, 289–299.

9   On the results of the Lebanese elections in addition to reports of malpractices by Lebanese pro-French elements aligned to the Eddé camp, see 'Results of the Lebanese elections', 1 September 1943, FO 371/35181.

10 Beirut to Foreign Office, 15 October 1943, FO 371/35182.

11 *Fata al-'Arab* as quoted in *al-Bashir*, 9 and 10 September 1943 and *al-Qabass*, 10 October 1943.

12 Lebanese Arab nationalist opinion-makers called for furthering the Syro-Lebanese economic union, demanding the unity of economic policy and legislation between the two states. Both governments were called upon to make common cause in fighting the rising cost of living. See *Beirut*, 6, 7 October 1943.

13 Beirut to Foreign Office, 6 October 1943, FO 371/35182.

14 Beirut to Foreign Office, 9 October 1943, FO 371/35182. See also *Beirut*, 26 November and 2, 22 December 1943.

15 Beirut to Foreign Office, 22 October 1943, FO 371/35183.

16 *Al-Qabass*, 21 October 1943.

17 Beirut to Foreign Office, 2 November 1943, FO 371/35182.

18 As quoted in Raghid el-Solh, *Lebanon and Arabism*, 213.

19 Upon the publication of the French communiqué, the Syrian Prime Minister informed the French delegate in Damascus of his government's reservations vis-à-vis the French position and pointed out that 'if any government had a bone to pick with Lebanon it was Syria, but when the Syrian government had learned of the Lebanese Prime Minister's declaration concerning the maintenance of present frontier they had decided to support the government fully'. From Beirut to Foreign Office, 8 November 1943, FO 371/35183.

20 From Beirut to Foreign Office, 21 November 1943, FO 371/35190.

21 As quoted in Zisser, *Lebanon: The Challenge of Independence*, 79.

22 *Al-Qabass*, 23 November 1943.

23 Beirut to Foreign Office, 20 December 1943, FO 371/35196.

24 On the crisis of 1943 from the perspective of Anglo-French discord, see A. B. Gaunson, *The Anglo-French Clash in Lebanon and Syria, 1940–45*, New York: Macmillan, 1987, 123–143.

25 Beirut to Foreign Office, 30 November 1943, FO 371/35194 and Beirut to Foreign Office, 22 December 1943, FO 371/35196.

26 From Beirut to Foreign Office, 2 December 1943, FO 371/35194. A noteworthy comment in one of the British Legation's dispatches indicated that the press was reporting political speeches and developments with an 'astonishing' openness. See Beirut to Foreign Office, 22 December 1943, FO 371/35196.

27 Khoury, *Syria and the French Mandate*, 89 and 137.

28 United States National Archives (henceforth USNA), RG 59, 890D.51/81, 'Report on Measures to Check Inflation in Syria and Lebanon', 7 July 1943.

29 Beirut to Foreign Office, 23 December and 24 December 1943, FO 371/35196; *al-Nahar*, 23, 24 December 1943 and *al-Qabass*, 24 December 1943.

30   *Al-Qabass*, 24, 28 December 1943 and *Beirut*, 22 December 1943. For the complete agreement between France and Syria and Lebanon see *al-Qabass*, 28 December 1943.

31   Antoine Hokayem, 'Al-'alakat al-lubnaniya al-suriya, 1918–1950', in *Al-'alakat al-lunnaiya al-suriya: muhawala takwimiya,* Antelias: Al-haraka al-thakafiya, 2001, 52.

32   *Al-Qabass*, 24 December 1943. Editorial by Najib al-Raiyyes.

33   *Beirut*, 23 December 1943.

34   It was decided that the administration of the different directorates would be divided between Syria and Lebanon and that the service of three of the high-ranking French officials be retained to assist Syrian and Lebanese officials in the administration. The Syrian and Lebanese governments retained the right to jettison the French administrators when the two governments saw that their services were no longer needed. *Al-Qabass*, 30 December 1943.

35   *Al-Nahar*, 31 December 1943.

36   *Al-Nahar*, 4 January 1944; *al-Bashir*, 5 January 1944 and *al-Qabass*, 4, 6 January 1944. The early stage of the transfer of the Common Interests encompassed the directorates of Customs, *Régie*, Lighthouse and the Concessionary Companies. For further details see *al-Nahar*, 5, 8 January 1944 and *al-Bashir*, 9 January 1944.

37   *Al-Nahar*, 5 January 1944.

38   *Al-Bashir*, 29 January 1944.

39   *Al-Bashir*, 1 February 1944.

40   *Al-Qabass*, 1 February 1944.

41   *Al-Bashir*, 1 February 1944 and *al-Qabass*, 2 February 1944. Khuri attached the text of the bill sent to the Lebanese parliament in his memorandum to the Maronite Patriarch. For the complete text, see *al-Bashir*, 1 February 1944.

42   *Al-Bairaq*, 1 February 1944 and *al-Bashir*, 2 February 1944.

43   *Al-Qabass*, 3 February 1944 and *al-Bashir*, 4 February 1944.

44   *Al-Bashir*, 4 February 1944. Sami el-Solh argues that restricting customs legislation to the parliaments of Lebanon and Syria, to the exclusion of the HCCI, subjected bilateral relations to the political interests of the deputies. Sami el-Solh, *Ahtakimu ila al-tarikh*, Beirut: Dar al-Nahar, 1970, 82.

45   *Al-Qabass*, 8 February 1944.

46   *Al-Qabass*, 6 February 1944.

47   *Al-Bashir*, 5, 6 February 1944; *al-Qabass*, 6 February 1944 and Nabil Franjiyah, *Hamid Frangie, L'autre Liban*, Beirut: Fiches du monde arabe, 1993, 149–150.

48   *Al-Qabass*, 6 February 1944. Editorial by Najib al-Raiyyes.

49   *Al-Bashir*, 19 March 1944.

50   *Al-Nahar*, 10 April and 13 May 1944.

51   Elias Saba, 'The Syro-Lebanese Customs Union: Causes of Failure and Attempts at Reorganization.' *Middle East Economic Papers*, 1960, 92. Saba argues that the Syro-Lebanese customs union agreement's fundamental deficiency was that it did not regulate other aspects of economic cooperation, such as monetary and fiscal policies. According to Saba, this proved to be a major factor in the dissolution of the customs union. Khaled al-'Azem blames the signatories of the agreement – namely Jabiri and Mardam Bey from Syria and Riad el-Solh and Takla from Lebanon – for destroying the 'hundreds of years'-old economic union between both states by limiting bilateral

economic relations to customs affairs only. Khaled al-'Azem, *Mudhakkarat Khaled al-'Azem*, vol. II, Beirut: al-Dar al-mutahida li al-nashr, 1973, 8.

52 Raghid el-Solh, *Lebanon and Arabism*, 223–224.

53 For a complete list of the directorates transferred, see *al-Qabass*, 8 June 1944.

54 USNA, RG 59, 890E.00/7–2744, 'Transfer of the Common Interests', 27 July 1944.

55 *Al-Nahar*, 16 January and 3, 4 February 1945. It should be noted that the Syrian and Lebanese currencies were in effect the same, that is both were issued from *Banque de Syrie et du Liban*. They only could be distinguished as being either Syrian or Lebanese by a stamp that indicated their national character.

56 The French demand for a *Convention Universitaire* dated from the 1930s. It stipulated a privileged cultural position for France in Syria and Lebanon. The French thought that by fostering a cultural affinity, political influence would filter through. Under such a convention, all Syrian and Lebanese state schools should teach French as a compulsory subject, starting in the primary stages. French textbooks should be used and French cultural missions should be given predominance over other cultural missions.

57 For the complete minutes of the negotiations between the French and the Lebanese, see Salma Mardam Bey, *Syria's Quest for Independence*, 150–165.

58 Beirut to Foreign Office, 3 February 1944, FO 371/40110.

59 USNA, RG 59, 890E.00/8–4444, 'Syrian/Lebanese Protest Regarding Apparent French Penetration to the Right of Legislation', 4 August 1944.

60 On the inter-Arab states' discussions surrounding the Alexandria Conference, see Raghid el-Solh, *Lebanon and Arabism*, 245–251.

61 USNA, RG 59, 890E.00/11–2444, 'Monthly Political Review', 24 November 1944.

62 Beirut to Foreign Office, 27 January 1945, FO 371/45553. 'Abdel Hamid Karameh was delegated to form the government. The members of the new cabinet were Henri Phar'oun, Minister for Foreign Affairs; Karameh took over the portfolios of defence and finance; Deputy Premier Nicolas Ghosn headed the Ministries of Commerce, Posts and Telegraph; Wadi' Na'im was given the Ministries of Interior and National Education and Ahmad el-As'ad took over the Ministries of Public Works and Health. The Karameh government promised 'reform, honesty and work'. For further details see USNA, RG 59, 'Beirut to Secretary of State', 890E.002/1–2145, 21 January 1945 and 'Political Review, January 1946', 890E.00/2–1745; 17 February 1945.

63 For a detailed analysis of the reaction to the Alexandria Protocol, involving France, Britain and Arab states as well as Lebanese sensitivities, see Raghid el-Solh, *Lebanon and Arabism*, 251–257.

64 Sham'oun listed the pillars upon which Lebanese and Syrian policy rested: 1. To assist in the war effort of the United Nations; 2. To achieve complete independence; 3. To have the best of relations with all the Arab states; 4. To reject the special position of any foreign state. For the complete text of the statement, see USNA, RG 59, 'Sham'oun's Statement to the London Press'; 890E.00/2–21145; 21 February 1945. See also *al-Qabass*, 9 February 1945 and *Beirut*, 8 February 1945.

65 *Al-Bashir*, 9, 12 February 1945 and *L'Orient*, 9 February 1945.

66 *Al-Qabass*, 11 February 1945.

67 *Al-Qabass*, 11 February 1945.

68 *Al-Qabass*, 11, 13 February 1945.

69 *Al-Qabass*, 11 February 1945.

70 *Al-Bashir*, 14 February 1945 and From Beirut to Foreign Office, 19 February 1945, FO 371/40110.

71 Beirut to Foreign Office, 16 March 1945, FO 371/45553 and *al-Bashir*, 20, 22 February 1945. For further details on the Arab Conference in Cairo and its repercussions on Lebanese politics, see Raghid el-Solh, *Lebanon and Arabism*, 263–280.

72 Beirut to Foreign Office, 26 April 1945, FO 371/45553; USNA, RG 59, 890D.01/4–2445, 'Damascus to Washington', 24 April 1945 and *al-Nahar*, 6 April 1945.

73 Tweini signed his editorial in the following manner: 'These are the words of Abou Ghassan the Arab, who is fully devoted to his small Lebanese and his large Arab nation.' *Al-Nahar*, 7 April 1945.

74 *Al-Bashir*, 10, 12, 14 April 1945. For the charter, see *al-Qabass*, 25 March 1945 and *al-Nahar*, 28 March 1945.

75 USNA, RG 59, 890D.00/5–245, 'Monthly Political Review – Syria, for April 1945', 2 May 1945; *al-Nahar*, 6 April 1945 and *al-Bashir*, 7 April 1945. Jamil Mardam Bey was appointed Deputy Prime Minister while retaining foreign affairs and defence. Sabri al-'Asali, an Arab nationalist, was given the ministry of the interior.

76 USNA, RG 59, 890D.00/5–245, 'Monthly Political Review – Syria, for April 1945', 2 May 1945; Salma Mardam Bey, 192–195, Shambrook, *French Imperialism in Syria*, 280–283 and *al-Nahar*, 20, 21, 22 April 1945.

77 Beirut to Foreign Office, 17 May 1945, FO 371/45553; *al-Nahar*, 15 February 1945 and *al-Qabass*, 20 February 1945. What came to be known as the 'Yarn Agreement' between Syria and Lebanon was reached on 12 February 1945. It stipulated that Lebanon would put its yarn surplus at Syria's disposal in return for delivery of Syria's textile surplus. Another agreement was signed at the end of March 1945 whereby Lebanese yarn would be bartered for Syrian textiles. Both agreements were not implemented because the factory owners in Aleppo refrained from implementing the agreements and from handing over their textile share to their government, finding the black market more profitable. See *al-Bashir*, 24 February and 14 March; *al-Qabass*, 20, 27 March and 11 April and *al-Nahar*, 17, 18, 23 March and 11, 27 April 1945.

78 Beirut to Foreign Office, 29 May 1945, FO 371/45554; USNA, RG 59, 890E.01/5–445, 'Beirut to Secretary of State', 4 May 1945 and *al-Nahar*, 22 May 1945.

79 USNA, RG 59, 890E.01/5–1345, 'Beirut to Secretary of State', 13 May 1945 and Salma Mardam Bey, 204.

80 USNA, RG 59, 890E.01/5–2045, 'Beirut to Secretary of State', 20 May 1945; *al-Nahar*, 22–23 May 1945 and Salma Mardam Bey, 206.

81 *Al-Bashir*, 24 May 1945.

82 *Al-Nahar*, 23 May 1945. Editorial by Jubran Tweini.

83 *Al-Bashir*, 26 May 1945.

84 *Al-Qabass*, 24 May 1945.

85 Khoury, *Syria and the French Mandate*, 616–617.

86 *Al-Nahar*, 1 June 1945. For a detailed eye-witness report of the damage the French caused in Damascus, see *al-Nahar*, 5 June 1945. For a detailed account of the Damascus bombing see USNA, RG 59, 890D.01/6–3045, 'The Bombardment of Damascus, May 29–31', 30 June 1945.

87 For details of British policy in Syria see W. Roger Louis, *The British Empire in the Middle East 1945–1951*, Oxford, 1984, 147–172. On Anglo-French antagonisms marking the

aforementioned crisis, see Gaunson, *The Anglo-French Clash in Lebanon and Syria*, 163–181.

88 Due to the disorders, at the end of May the British army established the *Mira* to replace the *Office des Céréales Panifiables* (OCP), which was the Anglo-French-Syro-Lebanese grain collection agency, established to ensure the proper general collection and sale of local grains. After the disturbances, French participation was no longer acceptable to Syria. Although run by British officers, Lebanon and Syria completely financed the *Mira*. Noteworthy was the fact that there was no controversy between Damascus and Beirut as regards either payment or price. For the mandate of the *Mira*, see USNA, RG 84, 'Replacement of OCP by MIRA', 18 July 1945.

89 The Arab League Resolution to Lebanon and Syria was as follows: 1. The transitional government of France is an aggressor on Syria and Lebanon and bears the sole responsibility for those killed and displaced 2. The presence of French forces will continue to be the cause of violence and threatens the relationship of the two states with France; the Arab League supports the withdrawal of the French forces from Syria and Lebanon 3. What are known as the *Troupes Spéciales* should be handed over to the Lebanese and Syrians 4. Council of the Arab League decides to take the appropriate action, as stipulated in the sixth paragraph of its charter (to defend any aggression falling on any of the Arab states). *Al-Nahar*, 9 and 10 June 1945; see also *al-Qabass*, 29 May 1945.

90 *Al-Nahar*, 23 and 24 June 1945.

91 USNA, RG 59, 890D.00/8–845, 'Monthly Political Review – Syria, for July 1945', 8 August 1945; USNA, RG 84, OSS: Research and Analysis Branch, no. 1090.122, 'Situation Report: Near East', 4 August 1945.

92 USNA, RG 84, OSS: Research and Analysis Branch, no. 1090.122, 'Situation Report: Near East', 4 August 1945.

93 USNA, RG 84, 'Maronite Statements Regarding the Need for French Protection', 13 August 1945 and USNA, RG 84, 'France and Lebanese Christians Attitude towards Independence', 24 August 1945.

94 USNA, RG 59, 890E.00/7–545, 'Monthly Political Review of Lebanon, June 1945', 5 July 1945.

95 *Al-Nahar*, 12 June 1945.

96 *Al-Nahar*, 5 June 1945.

97 *Al-Nahar*, 2, 3 and 19 October 1945.

98 Claiming to be overworked and tired, Karameh submitted his resignation during the month of August 1945. Khuri delegated Sami el-Solh to form a new government.

99 *Al-Nahar*, 27 and 28 October 1945.

100 The President's visit to the South served to strengthen his political position. At that time it was maintained that he was the strongest man in Lebanon. This was mainly because there was a weak Prime Minister in office. USNA, RG 59, 890E.00/11–845, 'Monthly Political Review of Lebanon, October 1945', 8 November 1945. See also *al-Nahar*, 27 and 28 October.

101 Beirut to Foreign Office, 1 August 1945, FO 371/45554.

102 Beirut to Foreign Office, 8 January 1946, FO 371/52857 and Beirut to Foreign Office, 16 January 1946, FO 371/52857 and *al-Nahar*, 14 December 1945.

CHAPTER 2

1   Beirut to Foreign Office, 3 November 1945, FO 371/45554; *al-Nahar*, 11, 18, 25 and 27
     July 1945.
2   See *al-Nahar*, 17 August 1945.
3   USNA, RG 59, 890E.5151/1–2446, 'Control of Dollar Import Licenses', 24 January 1946.
4   *Al-Nahar*, 27 December 1945. The agreement was as follows: all goods for unrestricted
     export from the country of origin were exempted from import licences except for those
     goods whose importers required hard currencies, whose materials needed to be
     subjected to import licences for local manufacturing, or that were subject to the
     'controlled distribution regulation' All goods whose export was unrestricted were
     exempted from export licences. Import and export levies were collected in advance,
     according to existing rules and regulations. The Minister of National Economy
     determined which goods were subject to import and export licenses and foreign
     exchange currencies. See Adnan Nashaba, *Al-Mu'ahadat al-duwaliya al-suriya al-
     thuna'iya min al-'am 1923 ila 1955*, Beirut: Matba'at al-adab, 1955, 52.
5   Beirut to Foreign Office, 16 January 1946, FO 371/52857; USNA, RG 59, 890E.51/1–546,
     'Distribution of the Levant States Common Interests Receipts', 5 January 1946. See also
     L'Orient, 2 January 1946; *al-Nahar*, 29, 30, 31 December 1945 and 1 January 1946.
6   *Al-Qabass*, 18 January and 9 June 1946. See also Mohammed Amine el-Hafez, *La
     structure et la politique économique en Syrie et au Liban*, Beirut, 1953, 203 and Gates,
     'Dissolution of the Syro-Lebanese Customs Union', 77.
7   *L'Orient*, 31 January 1946.
8   *L'Orient*, 8 February 1946.
9   *Beirut*, 16 October 1943.
10   Beirut to Foreign Office, 5 March 1946, FO 371/52857 and *L'Orient*, 7 March 1946.
11   USNA, RG 59, 890E.50/3–1846, 'Beirut to Secretary of State', 18 March 1946. Diplomatic
     circles in Beirut urged Syrians to permit the import of grain and wheat flour in order
     to lower the cost of living in both Syria and Lebanon. It was noted that Canadian
     white flour could be sold in Beirut for 28 piastres a kilo while poor-quality Syrian
     flour was being sold at 125 piastres. USNA, RG 59, 890E.50/1–2446, 'Beirut to Secretary
     of State', 24 January 1946.
12   *Al-Qabass*, 13 and 14 February 1946 and *L'Orient*, 20 January and 9 February 1946.
13   See *L'Orient*, 5 March 1946. Withdrawal negotiations had started between French and
     British military delegations in Beirut. It was reported that the withdrawal from Syria
     was scheduled to commence 11 May and would be completed 30 April 1946. *Al-Nahar*,
     20 February and 5 March 1946.
14   Beirut to Foreign Office, 13 and 29 March 1946, FO 371/52857 and *al-Qabass*, 12, 13,
     15 March 1946. See also Franjiyah, *Hamid Frangie*, 245.
15   *Al-Qabass*, 14 March 1946.
16   Beirut to Foreign Office, 10 April 1946, FO 371/52857.
17   *Al-Qabass*, 21 March 1946. In fact, there was a secret agreement between Faris al-
     Khuri and Hamid Franjieh that the latter should negotiate on Syria's behalf. If the
     agreement between the Lebanese and French was favourable, Syria would recognise
     it. Mohammad Farhani, *Faris al-Khuri wa ayam la tunsa*. Beirut: Dar al-ghad, 1964,
     120–121.

18 Beirut to Foreign Office, 10 April 1946, FO 371/52857and *al-Qabass*, 24 March 1946.

19 *L'Orient*, 13 March 1946. The increase of taxation caused an upsurge in prices of the following items: 11 per cent increase on crude oil and cotton. An increase from 11 per cent to 25 per cent on cotton and wool threads and silk and fabricated threads, used for clothing. Goods that witnessed an increase from 35 to 40 per cent were dairy products and textiles. Increasing from 35 to 50 per cent were numerous items such as vegetables, alcoholic beverages, matches. An increase from 40 to 50 per cent covered all kinds of silk products and perfumes. *Al-Nahar*, 20 March 1946.

20 *L'Orient*, 15 March 1946.

21 *Al-Nahar*, 6, 7 and 12 April 1946.

22 The most important clauses of the bill – or rather terms of reference of the *Mira* – were as follows: the Syrian administration would provide the Lebanese authorities with the necessary amounts of grain in accordance with each state's quota. Should a harvest turn out to be insufficient to meet demand, the *Mira* council had the right to import the necessary amounts of grain. The harvest was to be exempted from taxation and fees. No alteration should occur on prices. The 2.5 per cent levied from grain bound for Lebanon should be returned to the *Mira* administration of Lebanon to cover general expenses. *Al-Qabass*, 30 April and 3 July 1946; *al-Nahar*, 10 May, 7 and 20 June 1946 and Beirut to Foreign Office, 16 May 1946, FO 371/52857.

23 USNA, RG 59, 890E.002/5–2346, 'Beirut to Department of State', 23 May 1946 and 890E.00/6–646, 'Monthly Political Review for May 1946', 6 June 1946. Other members of the government were given the following ministries: Interior, Saeb Salam; Defence, Majid Arslan; Justice, Ahmad Husseini.

24 USNA, RG 59, 890D.00/4–2946, 'Damascus to Secretary of State', 29 April 1946 and 890D.00/5–546, 'Damascus to Secretary of State', 5 May 1946 and Beirut to Foreign Office, 16 May 1946, FO 371/52857.

25 Beirut to Foreign Office, 31 May 1946, FO 371/52857; Beirut to Foreign Office, 13 June 1946, FO 371/52858 and *L'Orient*, 5, 8, 11 and 21 June 1946. For the May agreement, see Nashaba, *Al-Mu'ahadat al-duwaliya al-suriya al-thuna'iya*, 45.

26 *Beirut*, 6, 11, 18 and 21 June 1946.

27 *Al-Qabass*, 18 and 28 June 1946.

28 *L'Orient*, 25 June 1946.

29 *Al-Qabass*, 28 June 1946. For further details on the grain production issue see USNA, RG 59, 890E.50/1–1246, 'Syrian Ministry of National Economy Program for Economic Development', 12 January 1946.

30 *Al-Qabass*, 26 June and 10 July 1946.

31 *Beirut*, 13, 14 July 1946.

32 *Al-Qabass*, 30 June 1946.

33 Beirut to Foreign Office, 19 August 1946, FO 371/52858; USNA, RG 59, 890D.00/8–346, 'Monthly Political Review – Syria, July', 13 August 1946; USNA, RG 59, 890E.50/7–2646, 'Beirut to Secretary of State', 26 July 1946 and *al-Qabass*, 26 July 1946.

34 *L'Orient*, 26 July 1946.

35 The meeting was described as 'stormy'. Agreement was reached on the following points: a. The Syrian *Mira* agreed to deliver to the Lebanese 100,000 tons of cereal, against payment of 13 million liras to be remitted in two instalments; b. Taxes on fuel in both countries were to remain the same; c. A Syro-Lebanese committee was to be appointed

to examine and report on the issue of import and export licences; in 1949 a Syrian customs representative would become the director of customs. Beirut to Foreign Office, 5 and 15 October 1946, FO 371/52858; USNA, RG 59, 890E.50/9–1646, 'Beirut to Secretary of State', 16 September 1946; USNA, RG 59, 890E.50/9–2446, 'Beirut to Secretary of State', 24 September 1946 and *Le Commerce du Levant*, 14 and 18 September 1946.

36 *Al-Nahar*, 15 December 1946.
37 USNA, RG 59, 890D.50/5–1046, Untitled, 10 May 1946 and USNA, RG 59, 890E.50/ 5–2946, Untitled, 29 May 1946.
38 *Al-Qabass*, 26 July 1946. On 16 July 1946, the Lebanese government issued a decree in which it limited profits on imports to 20 per cent. It was hoped that this decree would lower the cost of living and reduce prices. However, as in previous decrees, the Lebanese government did not have any enforcement mechanism in place. Moreover, it did not coordinate with the Syrian government to undertake similar measures. See USNA, RG 59, 690E.006/7–1846, 'Lebanese Decree No.2148', 18 July 1946.
39 *Al-Qabass*, 28 July 1946.
40 *Beirut*, 31 July 1946.
41 *Al-Qabass*, 4, 9 and 21 August 1946.
42 *L'Orient*, 25, 29 July and 3 August 1946. It was generally known that the Economic Higher Council was an initiative tabled by Sami el-Solh and adopted by al-'Azem.
43 *L'Orient*, 7 April 1946.
44 *L'Orient*, 7 April 1946.
45 *Beirut*, 3, 4 August 1946.
46 *L'Orient*, 24 August 1946.
47 *Al-Qabass*, 27 August 1946.
48 Ibid.
49 *L'Orient*, 6 September 1946.
50 *Al-Nahar*, 10 September 1946.
51 *Al-Qabass*, 12 September 1946. Editorial by al-Raiyyes.
52 *Al-Qabass*, 12 September 1946.
53 *Al-Nahar*, 14, 15, 26 September and 1 October 1946; *Le Jour*, 26 September 1946; *L'Orient*, 1 October 1946. Sa'di al-Mulla was appointed by Bshara al-Khuri to form a government during the month of May 1946; see *L'Orient*, 23 May 1946.
54 USNA, RG 59, 890D.50/10–1546, 'Beirut to Washington', 15 October 1946; *al-Nahar*, 16–17 October 1946; *L'Orient*, 16, 18 and 23 October 1946 and *al-Qabass*, 16 October 1946.
55 USNA, RG 59, 890D.50/10–2446, 'Beirut to Washington', 24 October 1946.
56 USNA, RG 59, 890E.00/11–546, 'Monthly Political Review, October, 1946', 5 November 1946; *al-Nahar*, 19 October 1946 and *L'Orient*, 1 November 1946.
57 *L'Orient*, 26 October and *al-Nahar*, 25 October 1946.
58 *L'Orient*, 5 November 1946.
59 *L'Orient*, 5 November 1946.
60 *Al-Nahar*, 21 November 1946.
61 USNA, RG 59, 890E.00/12-1246, 'Beirut to Secretary of State', 12 December 1946; *al-Qabass*, 25 December 1946; *L'Orient*, 15, 20, 24 and 28 December 1946 and *al-Nahar*, 10 and 12 December 1946.

62 For a detailed biography of each member of the new Lebanese cabinet, see USNA, RG 59, Department of State, Division of Biographic Information, 'Biographies of the Lebanese Cabinet of Riad Bey Al-Sulh', 13 February 1947.

63 Beirut to Foreign Office, 30 December 1946, FO 371/52858; USNA, RG 59, 890E.002/12–1046, 'Beirut to Secretary of State', 10 December 1946.

64 *L'Orient*, 25 December 1946.

65 *L'Orient*, 28 December 1946. The formation of Riad el-Solh's third cabinet was strongly influenced by Khuri, who wished to guarantee his re-election. The cabinet was designated as the 'Presidential Compromise' since this government would supervise the upcoming elections, and hence have considerable influence upon the composition of the new parliament – which in turn would select the next President. Khuri went to great lengths to include nearly every major faction leader. On the other hand, the Mardam government was designated a 'Coalition Government', though in light of the absence of political personalities it was expected to rely for its parliamentary majority on the support of Jabiri and his followers. USNA, RG 59, 890E.002/12–2046, 'Beirut to Secretary of State', 20 December 1946 and Beirut to Foreign Office, 23 January 1947, FO 371/62119.

66 *Al-Qabass*, 26 December 1946.

67 This phrase was first coined in Abdul Latif Tibawi, *A Modern History of Syria, Including Lebanon and Palestine*, London: Macmillan, 1969, 379.

CHAPTER 3

1 *Al-Qabass*, 3 January 1947. Editorial by Najib al-Raiyyes.

2 *Al-Bashir*, 7 January 1947. Editorial by Salah Labaki.

3 USNA, RG 59, 890D.01/1–2247, 'From American Legation (Beirut) to Secretary of State', 23 January 1947.

4 USNA, RG 59, 890D.01/1–2247, 'From American Legation (Beirut) to Secretary of State', 23 January 1947.

5 USNA, RG 59, 890D.01/1–2247, 'From American Legation (Beirut) to Secretary of State', 23 January 1947.

6 Tabitha Petran, *Syria: A Modern History*, London: Ernest Benn, 1972, 85–86.

7 *Al-Nahar*, 4 March 1947 and *al-Qabass*, 18 March 1947.

8 Members of the Lebanese delegation to Damascus were Premier Raid el-Solh, Minister of Justice 'Abdallah al-Yafi, acting Minister of Finance and Minister of Foreign Affairs Henri Phar'oun and Minister of Economy Kamal Jumblatt. *Al-Nahar*, 1 January 1947.

9 The Syrians had received a copy of these proposals, drawn up by Jumblatt, on 31 December 1946. French authorities were very supportive of Jumblatt's proposals. Due to the chronic shortage of dollars, France was urging both governments to institute tighter import controls, increase exports and reduce foreign expenses. USNA, RG 59, 890E.51/3–2547, 'From Beirut to Secretary of State', 25 March 1947 and Beirut to Foreign Office, 23 January 1947, FO 371/62119.

10 Damascus to Foreign Office, 6 February 1947, FO 371/62119; *Le Jour*, 3, 4 January 1947, *al-Nahar*, 4 January 1947 and *al-Qabass*, 5 January 1947. At the meeting, Lebanon was represented by Finance Minister 'Abdallah Al-Yafi, Minister of Foreign Affairs

Henri Phar'oun, Minister of Economy Kamal Jumblatt, and Colonel Suleiman Naufal, the secretary general of the Ministry of Economy. The Syrian delegation was composed of Sa'id Ghazzi, Minister of Finance and head of the Syrian delegation to the HCCI Hikmat al-Hakim, and Leon Murad, secretary general of the Ministry of Economy.

11 *Al-Qabass*, 22 May 1947.

12 *Al-Nahar*, 1 and 2 March 1947.

13 For a detailed account on the income accruing to the Syrian Treasury from taxes on certain consumer items see *al-Qabass*, 5 and 7 January 1947. Syrian opinion-makers argued that a 50 per cent tax reduction on sugar, tobacco and combustibles lost the government 10.5 million liras in tax revenues, while the poor and average income groups' expenses would have been lowered by half. It was stressed that if low grain prices were added to these savings – from sugar, tobacco and combustibles – these price reductions would assist the government in its fight against the rise in prices – losing a total of 10 million liras from a budget of 120 million liras. *Al-Qabass*, 5 and 7 January 1947.

14 Beirut to Foreign Office, 6 February 1947, FO 371/621710 and *Le Commerce du Levant*, 1 January 1947.

15 *Al-Qabass*, 3 January 1947.

16 *Al-Qabass*, 3, 5 January 1947.

17 USNA, RG 59, 890D.00/1–647, 'Damascus to Secretary of State', 6 January 1947.

18 *Al-Qabass*, 5 January 1947.

19 *Al-Qabass*, 7 January 1947.

20 *Al-Qabass*, 9 January 1947. A delegation of Syrian merchants complained to the foreign trade directorate that Lebanese customs prohibited the shipment of Syrian goods because of Lebanese laws forbidding their export. See *al-Nahar*, 4 January 1947 and *al-Qabass*, 1 January 1947. See also *al-Qabass*, 3 January 1947 on the 'Mistreatment of our [Syrian] merchants in Beirut'.

21 *Al-Bashir*, 10 January 1947. Editorial by Salah Labaki.

22 Beirut to Foreign Office, 6 February 1947, FO 371/61710. Announcing his satisfaction with the results of the Syro-Lebanese discussions, Prime Minister Solh declared that the price of 20 litres of petrol would be set at 600 piastres (down from 755) and diesel at 325 piastres (down from 500). The price of one ton of cement was set at 60 liras. *Al-Nahar*, 11, 12 and 13 January 1947; *Le Jour*, 10 and 11 January 1947; *al-Qabass*, 10, 11 and 14 January 1947.

23 *Al-Qabass*, 15 January 1947.

24 *Al-Qabass*, 17 January 1947.

25 *Al-Qabass*, 21 January 1947.

26 For further discussion of the weaknesses of industry see Gates, *The Merchant Republic of Lebanon*, 61–77.

27 *Al-Qabass*, 14 January 1947.

28 As quoted in *Le Commerce du Levant*, 15 January 1947.

29 As quoted in *Le Commerce du Levant*, 15 January 1947.

30 *Le Commerce du Levant*, 18 January 1947. Editorial signed by R.A.

31 *L'Orient*, 21 January 1947. Editorial by George Najjar. In his editorial Najjar compared the Syro-Lebanese economic union to that of Belgium and Luxembourg. He also presented in detail the advantages and disadvantages of economic separation between Lebanon and Syria.

32 *Al-Bashir*, 22 January 1947.

33 *Le Jour*, 22 January 1947. As preparations were under way for another Syro-Lebanese summit in Shtura, scheduled for 20 January 1947, the prices of grain in Damascus witnessed an increase. Merchants were taking advantage of the lifting of transportation restrictions on grain, monopolising the grain trade in spite of the fact that the government's stores were filled. At that time, a ton of grain had risen from 360 to 480 liras. Consequently, the Syrian Prime Minister ordered the formation of a committee to investigate grain theft. Moreover, the head of the Syrian *Mira* resigned. On Monday (20 January 1947), the Lebanese and Syrian delegations, headed by the Prime Ministers, met in Shtura to deliberate on the progress made on the common measures against the high cost of living. It was decided to further reduce tariffs on vital consumer items, particularly petrol, kerosene and cement. See *al-Qabass*, 17, 22, 23 January 1947 and *al-Nahar*, 22 January 1947. For a detailed list of reduced tariffs on all consumer goods see *al-Qabass*, 22, 23 January 1947 and *al-Nahar*, 23 January 1947.

34 *Le Jour*, 23 January 1947.

35 *Le Jour*, 9 February 1947.

36 The Société Libanaise d'Economie Politique was the institutional organ of the 'New Phoenicians', a powerful circle drawn mainly from Beirut's mercantile/financial bourgeoisie. This circle included such influential figures as Michel Chiha, Henri Phar'oun, Alfred Kettaneh and Gabriel Menassa. Their primary objective was to promote and safeguard the laissez-faire economic orientation of the Lebanese economy. Gates, *The Historical Role of Political Economy in the Development of Modern Lebanon*, 18 and *The Merchant Republic of Lebanon*, 82 and 95–96.

37 Beirut to Foreign Office, 6 March 1947, FO 371/61710; *Le Commerce du Levant*, 8 February 1947 and Gabriel Menassa, *Plan de reconstruction de l'économie libanaise et de réforme de l'état*, Beirut Société libanaise d'économic politique, 1948, 355.

38 *Al-Qabass*, 19 February 1947.

39 *L'Orient*, 22 February 1947.

40 *Al-Qabass*, 11 January 1947. At that time the allocation of the Common Interests' revenues remained at 56 per cent for Syria and 44 per cent for Lebanon.

41 *Al-Qabass*, 17 February 1947.

42 *Le Jour*, 22, 23 and 24 February 1947; *L'Orient*, 22 and 23 February 1947; *al-Bashir*, 20 February 1947, *Beirut al-Masa'*, 24 February 1947; *al-Qabass*, 21, 23, 25 and 26 February 1947.

43 Editorial by Khalil Gemayel in *Le Jour*, 23–24 February 1947.

44 USNA, RG 59, 890D.00/3–547, 'Monthly Political Review – Syria, for February 1947', 12 March 1947 and *al-Nahar*, 4 March 1947.

45 *Al-Nahar*, 15 and 16 February 1947.

46 *Al-Nahar*, 21 February 1947 and *al-Qabass*, 5 March 1947.

47 Beirut to Foreign Office, 23 April 1947, FO 371/61710.

48 Damascus to Foreign Office, 22 March 1947, FO 371/62119.

49 USNA, RG 59, 890E.50/3–1047, 'Beirut to Secretary of State', 10 March 1947. The decision to establish the Higher Economic Council was taken on 2 January 1947 during a meeting in Beirut between the Lebanese and Syrian Prime Ministers.

50 *Al-Qabass*, 9, 11 and 16 March 1947.

51 For all the recommendations of the Higher Economic Council see *al-Nahar*, 14 March 1947 and *al-Qabass*, 14 March 1947.

52 *Al-Nahar*, 19 March 1947. Towards the end of April the members of the Higher Economic Council went on strike in protest the Syrian and Lebanese governments' refusal to consider their recommendations. *Al-Nahar*, 26 and 27 April 1947.

53 *Al-Qabass*, 21 March 1947. The price of a ton of steel, for example, used to range between 350 and 400 liras, but after Sa'id Ghazzi's decision a ton of steel rose in price to 700 liras. Syrian merchants and contactors journeyed to Beirut to purchase what they needed.

54 *Al-Qabass*, 21 March 1947.

55 *Al-Qabass*, 13 February 1947. It should be noted that there were numerous incidences in which Syrian merchants were mistreated at the hard currency bureau, where they were not allowed to purchase hard currency because they were Syrian. This in turn led to similar actions against Lebanese merchants in Damascus. See *al-Nahar*, 6 June 1947.

56 *Al-Qabass*, 13 February 1947.

57 *Al-Qabass*, 13 and 19 February 1947.

58 Editorial by al-Raiyyes in *al-Qabass*, 2 March 1947. See also *al-Qabass*, 4 March 1947.

59 *Al-Qabass*, 25 March and 22 April 1947.

60 *Al-Qabass*, 9 April 1947.

61 USNA, RG 59, 890E.51/3–2547, 'From Beirut to Secretary of State', 25 March 1947.

62 *Al-Qabass*, 9 April and 16 May 1947.

63 USNA, RG 59, 890E.6476/9–447, 'Cement Distribution in Lebanon', 4 September 1947.

64 *Al-Nahar*, 21 March 1947 and *al-Qabass*, 27 November 1947.

65 For further reference on Aramco as well as TAPLINE see Irvine H. Anderson, *Aramco, the United States and Saudi Arabia: A Study of the Dynamics of Foreign Oil Policy 1933–1950*, Princeton: Princeton University Press, 1981.

CHAPTER 4

1 USNA, RG 84, 'Summary of negotiations for a pipeline concession in Syria and Lebanon', Memorandum to the Minister, Jidda, 15 March 1947.

2 Ibid.

3 Ibid.

4 USNA, RG 59, 890E.6363/3–1847 'Beirut to Secretary of State', 18 March 1947 and *al-Qabass*, 16 March and 1 April 1947.

5 *Al-Qabass*, 20 March 1947.

6 *Al-Qabass*, 1 April 1947.

7 Lenahan had negotiated with the Syrian government and had twice met with the Syrian President between 3 and 6 March 1947. In fact, the Syrians insisted that the terminal must be in Syria, and that Aramco must build a port in Syria, thus completely excluding Lebanon. Lenahan rejected the Syrian proposition. Then the Syrians offered the compromise of a joint Syro-Lebanese port near Tripoli, revenues to be split between the two countries. Lenahan retorted that he was not authorised to negotiate an agreement that departed significantly from the accord signed with the Lebanese. USNA, RG 84, 'Summary of negotiations for a pipeline concession in Syria and Lebanon', Memorandum to the Minister, Jidda, 15 March 1947.

8   *Al-Bashir*, 4 April 1947 and *al-Qabass*, 6 April 1947.

9   *Al-Qabass*, 21 March 1947.

10 *Al-Qabass*, 20 March 1947.

11 *Al-Qabass*, 16 March 1947.

12 *Beirut al-Masa'*, 14 April 1947.

13 *Al-Qabass*, 20 March 1947.

14 USNA, RG 84, 'Summary of negotiations for a pipeline concession in Syria and Lebanon', Memorandum to the Minister, Jidda, 15 March 1947.

15 Ibid.

16 *Al-Qabass*, 30 March and 16 May 1947.

17 *Al-Qabass*, 9 April 1947.

18 *L'Orient*, 13 April 1947.

19 *Al-Bashir*, 11 April 1947.

20 *Le Jour*, 12 April 1947. Editorial by Michel Chiha.

21 *Al-Qabass*, 11 April 1947.

22 USNA, RG 59, 690.90E31/4–1247, 'From Beirut to Secretary of State', 23 April 1947; *al-Nahar*, 11, 12 April 1947 and *Le Jour*, 11 April 1947. For the official communiqué see *al-Qabass*, 13 April 1947.

23 *Le Jour*, 13 and 14 April 1947. Editorial by Khalil Gemayel on the Shtura talks.

24 It was noteworthy that both governments did not have accurate statistical data concerning grain. Any attempts to acquire accurate figures by dealing directly with local mukhtars were flawed because Lebanese and Syrian farmers tended to withhold accurate information, believing that it would be used as a basis for tax schedules. USNA, RG 59, 890E.50/7–2247, 'From Beirut to Secretary of State', 22 July 1947.

25 *Beirut al-Masa'*, 14 April 1947.

26 *Al-Nahar*, 16 April 1947.

27 Beirut to Foreign Office, 18 June 1947, FO 371/61710.

28 *Beirut al-Masa'*, 14 April 1947. Regarding the monetary issue, the Syrians agreed with the Lebanese motion to postpone discussing this item until the visit of the expert Paul Van Zeeland.

29 *Le Jour*, 12 April 1947. Editorial by Michel Chiha.

30 *Le Commerce du Levant*, 14 June 1947. In his article, Chiha maintained that of the 225,000 tons of grain needed by Syria and Lebanon, 200 to 210,000 tons were available according to official estimates. He emphasised that a 15- to 25,000-ton grain deficit was no cause for alarm. Chiha's view, that there were no reasons to fear shortages, was supported by a statement of the governor of Aleppo, who maintained that, in spite of the shortage of rain, the *Mira* – with the amounts in its stores and the yields of the coming harvest – would be able to collect 250,000 tons of grain. See *al-Nahar*, 3 June 1947.

31 *Beirut al-Masa'*, 14 April 1947; *Le Jour*, 13, 14 April 1947 and *al-Bashir*, 16 April 1947.

32 Beirut to Foreign Office, 21 May 1947, FO 371/61710 and *Le Jour*, 19 April 1947. The headline of *Le Jour* read 'Agreement on Saudi Oil, Syria delivers 15,000 tons of grain'.

33 For the meetings see: *al-Qabass*, 23, 29 April and 1, 16 May 1947 and *Le Jour*, 18, 19, 26 April and 1, 9, 15 May and 3 June 1947. See also *al-Nahar*, 26, 27, 29 April and 2 May 1947. Regarding the grain issue, the Lebanese were insisting that all tariffs, usually added when the grain was sold to Lebanon, be removed. It should be noted that

a census conducted by the *Mira* reported that there was enough grain for Syrian and Lebanese consumption. See *al-Qabass*, 13 May 1947.

34 Beirut to Foreign Office, 25 June 1947, FO 371/62119 and USNA, RG 59, 890D.61311/5–2647, 'Damascus to Washington', 26 May 1947. See also *al-Qabass*, 20, 22 May and 3 June 1947.

35 USNA, RG 59, 1945–1949, 890E.00/5–2647, 'Beirut to Secretary of State', 26 May 1947; *Le Jour*, 27 May 1947; *al-Qabass*, 25, 27, 28 May 1947 and *al-Nahar*, 29 May 1947. On the May 1947 Lebanese elections see also Zisser, *Lebanon: The Challenge of Independence*, 128–138.

36 USNA, RG 59, 890E.00/5–2847, 'Beirut to Secretary of State', 28 May 1947.

37 *Al-Qabass*, 29 May 1947.

38 *Al-Qabass*, 1 June 1947. Editorial by Najib el-Raiyyees.

39 Ibid.

40 The members of Solh's new cabinet were: Minister of Foreign Affairs Hamid Franjieh, Minister of Justice Ahmad Husseini, Minister of Defence Amir Majid Arslan, Minister of Public Works Gabriel Murr, Minister of Finance Muhammad Aboud and Minister of Economics Suleiman Naufal. The new government undertook to conduct a national census and to introduce a new electoral law. These would be the first steps in drawing the country away from confessionalism. USNA, RG 59, 890E.01/6–1847, 'Beirut to Secretary of State', 18 June 1947 and 'Lebanon: Summary No.11, month ending 30 June 1947', 24 July 1947, FO 371/61710.

41 For final results and analysis of the Syrian elections see Confidential US State Department Central Files, Syria: Internal Affairs and Foreign Affairs, 1945–1949, 890D.00/7–2947, 'Elections, the final results', 29 July 1947 and 890D.00/8–1147, 'Full list of elected deputies', 11 August 1947. See also *al-Qabass*, 16, 20, 27 July 1947 and *al-Nahar*, 10 and 11 July 1947.

42 *Le Jour*, 12 July 1947.

43 *Le Jour*, 22 July 1947. Editorial by Michel Chiha.

44 USNA, RG 59, 890D.00/7–1547, 'Beirut to Secretary of State', 15 July 1947; Damascus to Foreign Office, 18 July 1947 and 25 August 1947, FO 371/62119.

45 The breach between Sharabati and Mardam Bey – known to have played a double game with the Islamists and Quwwatly supporters – emerged during the election campaign. Sharabati was reported to have told the American military attaché that Syria needed a new Prime Minister. USNA, RG 59, 890D.00/9– 1347, 'Monthly Political Review – Syria, July 1947', 13 August 1947.

46 For further information on the Syrian position regarding the TAPLINE see Al-'Azem, *Mudhakkarat Khaled al-'Azem*, vol. II, 94.

47 *Al-Nahar*, 6 and 7 August 1947.

48 *Al-Qabass*, 26 August 1947.

49 Beirut to Foreign Office, 'Summary for the month no.13, ending 31 August 1947', FO 371/61710 and *Beirut al-Masa*, 1 August 1947.

50 *Al-Nahar*, 9, 10, 12 and 13 August 1947.

51 *L'Orient*, 14 August 1947.

52 *L'Orient*, 8, 14 August 1947.

53 *Le Commerce du Levant*, 9 August 1947. Editorial by Michel Chiha. It should be noted that there was in fact a cabinet crisis in Damascus throughout the first week

of October. It was only with great difficulty that Mardam Bey was able to form a government, which he was only able to achieve with Wehbe al-Hariri's agreement to join the government. Hariri was made Minister of Finance; Minister of Foreign Affairs was Munir al-'Ajlani; Minister of Economy was Sa'id Ghazzi and Minister of Defence was Ahmad Sharabati. Damascus to Foreign Office, 28 November 1947, FO 371/62119. See also *al-Qabass*, 3, 5, 7 and 8 October 1947; *al-Nahar*, 30 September and 8 October 1947.

54 Khairiya Qassmiya, *Mudhakkarat Muhsen al-Barazi, 1947–1949*, Beirut: al-Ruwwad li al- nashir, 1994, 32.

55 See *al-Nahar*, 20, 21 July; 14 August; 5, 12 September 1947; *Le Jour*, 13 August 1947. See also *al-Qabass*, 13, 14 August 1947. On the technical details of the TAPLINE see *al-Qabass*, 24 August 1947.

56 *Al-Qabass*, 2 September 1947.

57 *Le Jour*, 2 September 1947 and *al-Qabass*, 3 September 1947.

58 *Al-Qabass*, 3 September 1947.

59 *Beirut al-Masa'*, 29 September 1947.

60 Qassmiya, *Mudhakkarat Muhsen al-Barazi, 1947–1949*, 60–61 and 70–71; *Le Jour*, 18 December 1947 and *al-Qabass*, 1 December 1947.

61 For Lebanese and Syrian grain negotiations, see *Le Jour*, 19, 21, 22 September; 6, 18, 19, 20, 21, 24 October; 1, 2, 3, 19, 20 November 1947 and *al-Nahar*, 19, 20, 23, 24 September and 1 November 1947.

62 Beirut to Foreign Office, 6 January 1948, FO 371/68489.

63 In order to secure the country's needs for the next harvest, the Lebanese government reached an agreement with Damascus for the immediate purchase of 5000 tons of grain (keeping in mind that the Syrians had earlier agreed to supply their neighbour with 15,000 tons). *Al-Nahar*, 30 October 1947.

64 USNA, RG 59, 890E.5151/9–347, 'Beirut to Secretary of State', 3 September 1947.

65 Jamil Mardam Bey remained the Prime Minister, Said Ghazi was given the Ministry of Economy, while Mohsein Barazi took over the Ministry of Interior and Ahmad Sharabati became Minister of Defence. Both these men reflected Quwwatly's strong influence over the new cabinet. USNA, RG 59, 890D.00/10–2747, 'Syrian Politics and Cabinet Reshuffle', 27 October 1947.

66 USNA, RG 59, 890E.032/10–2347, 'From Beirut to Secretary of State', 28 October 1947.

67 Beirut to Foreign Office, 'Beirut Summary for the month of December 1947 No.16', February 1948, FO 371/68489 and USNA, RG 59, 890D.50/11–1747, 'Damascus to Washington', 17 November 1947.

68 See *al-Qabass*, 1 and 12 December 1947.

CHAPTER 5

1 A summary for income (public and private sectors) computations for the years 1948 to 1950, see Albert Yusuf Badre, *National Income of Lebanon*, Beirut, 1953.

2 USNA, RG 59, 890E.032/1–2048, 'Beirut to Secretary of State', 28 January 1948.

3 Ibid.

4   See Moshe Ma'oz, 'Attempts at Creating a Political Community in Modern Syria', *Middle East Journal*, 22 (1972), 389–404.

5   Beirut to Foreign Office, 31 January 1949, FO 371/75527.

6   Moshe Ma'oz, *Syria and Israel: From War to Peacemaking*, Oxford: Clarendon Press, 1995, 17.

7   Ma'oz, *Syria and Israel*, 18–20.

8   *Le Commerce du Levant*, 31 December 1947.

9   *Al-Qabass*, 6 January 1948.

10 USNA, RG 59, 890D.50/1–848, 'Syro-Lebanese Economic Relations Discussed in Parliament', 8 January 1948.

11 *Le Commerce du Levant*, 14 January 1948. On the issue of the directorship of the customs directorate see also *al-Bashir*, 27 June 1947. The Jesuit daily claimed that Syria was in fact striving to replace the HCCI with a joint Syro-Lebanese ministerial committee through which it would reach complete economic control over Lebanon that would inevitably lead to political control.

12 See *al-Qabass*, 10, 18, 20, 28, 29 January 1948; *al-Nahar*, 9, 16, 24, 29 January 1948 and *Le Jour*, 9, 10, 17, 28 January 1948.

13 *Al-Qabass*, 11 January 1948.

14 George Farshakh, *Hamid Franjieh wa Jumhuriyat al-Istiqlal*, Beirut: Al-Mu'asasa al-'arabiya li al-dirassat wa al-nashr, 1997, 207 as quoted in Hokayem, 'Al-'alakat al-lubnaniya al-suriya, 1918–1950', 66.

15 Gates, *The Merchant Republic of Lebanon*, 20.

16 Gates, *The Merchant Republic of Lebanon*, 42.

17 Gates, *The Merchant Republic*, 42–43 and 'Azem, *Mudhakkarat Khaled al-'Azem*, vol. II, 79–88.

18 For further details on the accord, especially the guarantees given to the Lebanese and Syrian governments by Catroux, see USNA, RG 59, 890E.51/29, 'From Beirut to Secretary of State', 16 February 1944.

19 For details on the 1947 Franco-Lebanese monetary negotiations led by Franjieh, see Franjiyah, *Hamid Frangie*, 274–316.

20 *Al-Qabass*, 27 January 1948. Editorial by 'Aref Laham. To argue that the sentiments of monetary separation from France were restricted to the Arab nationalists in Syria is not accurate, as numerous editorials by Laham illustrate.

21 Hokayem, 'Al-'alakat al-lubnaniya al-suriya, 1918–1950', 67 and *al-Qabass*, 1, 3 February 1948.

22 'Azem, *Mudhakkarat Khaled al-'Azem*, vol. II, 89; Franjiyah, *Hamid Frangie*, 293–304; Damascus to Foreign Office, 1 January 1948, FO 371/68808; *al-Nahar*, 2 February 1948 and *al-Qabass*, 1 February 1948.

23 Roger Gehchan, *Hussein Aoueini: un demi-siècle d'histoire du Liban et du Moyen-Orient (1920–1970)*, Beirut: Fiches du monde arabe, 2000, 112.

24 *Le Jour*, 3 February 1948 and *al-Qabass*, 30 January and 3 February 1948. It should be noted that the Syrian and Lebanese currencies were essentially the same in appearance; only a stamp indicated if a note was Lebanese or Syrian.

25 Gehchan, *Hussein Aoueini*, 111 and *al-Nahar*, 2 February 1948. The Solh government was later on criticised for restricting its consultations to financiers and bankers, particularly stakeholders at the BSL. Unlike the Syrian government, which

consulted representatives from the various sectors of the economy. *Al-Qabass*, 3 February 1948.

26 *Le Jour*, 1 and 2 February 1948.

27 *Al-Qabass*, 3 February 1948.

28 Beirut to Foreign Office, Undated, FO 371/68489; *L'Orient*, 3 February 1948 and *Le Jour*, 2 and 4 February 1948.

29 *Al-Nahar*, 5 February 1948.

30 *Le Jour*, 3, 12 and 19 February 1948. On the economic drawbacks of the Franco-Lebanese Monetary Agreement, see Elias Saba, 'The Syro-Lebanese Customs Union: Causes of Failure and attempts at Reorganization', *Middle East Economic Papers*, 1960, 91–108; Saba, 'Lebanon's Liberal Foreign Exchange System', *Middle East Economic Papers*, 1960, 98–112 and Saba, *The Foreign Exchange Systems of Lebanon and Syria 1939–1957*, Beirut, 1961.

31 *Le Jour*, 4 and 24 February 1948. In fact the Syrians did not go to the Hague. Van Zeeland had in fact advised the Syrians not to take this option since even if the court ruled in Syria's favour, Damascus would still have to negotiate with Paris to reach an agreement. Gehchan, *Hussein Aoueini*, 96.

32 *Le Jour*, 1 April 1948.

33 *Al-Qabass*, 13 February 1948.

34 *Le Commerce du Levant*, 14 February 1948.

35 Franjiyah, *Hamid Frangie*, 304; *al-Nahar*, 4, 6 and 7 February 1948. For the official text of the Lebano-Franco Monetary Agreement see *Le Jour*, 7 February 1948; *al-Nahar*, 7 February 1948 and *Le Commerce du Levant*, 7 February 1948.

36 *Al-Nahar*, 2 and 4 February 1948 and *L'Orient*, 1 February 1948. Syrian capital flight into Lebanon was also prompted by the hostilities in Palestine. Large sums of Jewish capital funds were transferred from Syria into Lebanon, where anti-Jewish feeling was thought to be less extreme, a reflection of Lebanon's religious, social and political tolerance. See Saba, 'The Syro-Lebanese Customs Union', 98–99.

37 *Al-Qabass*, 3 February 1948.

38 At the following exchange rates: 885 piastres for £1; 298 piastres for $1; 97 piastres for 1 French franc.

39 *Al-Nahar*, 4 February 1948. Syria offered Egypt 85,000 tons of grain at the price of $170 per ton. Egypt agreed in principle to the Syrian offer but demanded that the price be reduced to $140. Syria also offered its olive oil to the United States, 15,000 tons for $345 per ton. The Americans responded that this price was higher than the market's value.

40 *Al-Qabass*, 4 February 1948. For further details on the repercussions of Syria's withdrawal from the Franc zone see Edmund Asfour, *Syria: Development and Monetary Policy*, Cambridge, MA: Harvard University Press, 1959, 52–54 and Gehchan, *Hussein Aoueini*, 97–98.

41 'Azem, *Mudhakkarat Khaled al-'Azem*, vol. II, 91, 103–104; Gehchan, *Hussein Aoueini*, 110 and *al-Nahar*, 4 February 1948. As a consequence to the accord, the Lebanese and Syrian currencies were no longer the same. There was now a structural difference and as a result Lebanon had to withdraw from circulation all the banknotes that carried the Syrian stamp.

42 *L'Orient*, 3 February 1948, *al-Nahar*, 5 February 1948 and *al-Qabass*, 6 February 1948.

43 *Al-Qabass*, 6 February 1948 and Gehchan, *Hussein Aoueini*, 111.

44 *Al-Nahar*, 5 February 1948.

45 *Le Jour*, 5 February 1948; *Le Commerce du Levant*, 4 February 1948.

46 As quoted in *al-Qabass*, 12 February 1948.

47 *Al-Qabass*, 4 February 1948.

48 *Le Commerce du Levant*, 4 February 1948.

49 *Al-Qabass*, 6 February 1948.

50 *Al-Qabass*, 5 February 1948.

51 For the detailed presentation of the Lebanese Prime Minister, see *al-Nahar*, 6 February 1948.

52 Sami el-Solh, *Ahtakimu ila al-tarikh*, Beirut: Dar al-Nahar, 1970, 92–93 and *al-Nahar*, 6 February 1948.

53 *Al-Nahar*, 6 February 1948.

54 In fact, in an interview in Paris with the Egyptian daily *al-Ahram*, Lebanese Foreign Minister Franjieh regarded that the strong criticism originating from Damascus were not in conformity with the Syrian position taken during the negotiations with the French nor with the instructions sent by Damascus to its delegation in Paris. *Al-Qabass*, 8 February 1948.

55 *Al-Qabass*, 6 February 1948.

56 *Al-Qabass*, 10 February 1948. In his memoirs, 'Azem highlights how Solh had turned from an Arab unionist to a Lebanese separatist in order to appease the Maronites and retain power. See 'Azem, *Mudhakkarat Khaled al-'Azem*, vol. II, 11–12.

57 Damascus to Foreign Office, 'Political Summary for the Months of February and March No.2, Damascus', Undated, FO 371/68808.

58 *Al-Qabass*, 8 February 1948. The Syrians found it unacceptable that although Damascus issued a decree in which it guaranteed the Syrian lira through the Syrian Treasury, the Lebanese government chose not to accept the Syrian currency in its customs directorates, this although Syria owned two-thirds of the customs revenue. *Al-Qabass*, 13 February 1948.

59 *Le Jour*, 10 and 11 February 1948.

60 *Le Jour*, 14 February 1948.

61 *Le Jour*, 9 March 1948.

62 *Al-Nahar*, 12 February 1948.

63 *Al-Nahar*, 14 and 15 February 1948.

64 *Al-Nahar*, 14 February 1948.

65 Al-'alaqat al-lubnaniyya al-suriyya, 1943–1958, waqa' biblioghrafiyya, vol. II, Beirut: Markaz al-tawthiq wal-buhuth al-lubnani, 1986, 79–81; Franjiyah, *Hamid Frangie*, 308–309 and Saba, 'The Syro-Lebanese Customs Union', 98. See also *al-Qabass*, 15 February 1948 and *al-Nahar*, 14 February 1948.

66 *Al-Qabass*, 13 and 17 February 1948.

67 *Al-Qabass*, 15 February 1948.

68 Charged speeches between the two Premiers were exchanged during the deliberations of the LAS. Mardam Bey claimed that 'we would be mocking ourselves if we were striving for the evacuation of foreign armies from our countries while at the same time maintaining the control by foreigners of our economies'. Solh responded that he was not in need of lessons in patriotism from anyone 'Lebanon comes at the forefront of those countries that made sacrifices [for the Arab cause]'. For the complete speeches of Solh and Mardam Bey, see Gehchan, *Hussein Aoueini*, 98–99.

69 *Al-Nahar*, 14 and 15 February 1948.

70 Beirut to Foreign Office, 'Lebanon: Annual Review for 1948', 14 February 1949, FO 371/75317 and *al-Qabass*, 20 February 1948. The text of the Gentleman's Agreement, was as follows: 1. Consultations between the two governments will start immediately to reconsider the agreement of the Common Interests, the consultations shall terminate two weeks before the end of March so that both governments will have ample time to take the necessary measures in light of what is going to be agreed upon. 2. The Syrian and the Lebanese currencies shall be accepted at the customs directories, without any difference, until 31 March 1948. 3. The provisional restrictions on the movement of goods that were put down between the two states since 31 January 1948 shall be lifted. 4. The movement of funds, above S£200, between both countries shall require a permit from the minister of finance. Exempted are the funds moving between either central bank. The agreement was signed in Cairo, 17 February 1948 by Mardam Bey and Solh. *Al-Nahar*, 21 February 1948 and *Le Jour* and *L'Orient*, 20 February 1948. See also Gehchan, *Hussein Aoueini*, 112–113.

71 Beirut to Foreign Office, 'Beirut Summary for the Month of February, 1948', Undated, FO 371/68489.

72 *Al-Qabass*, 24 and 26 February 1948.

73 *Al-Qabass*, 26,29 February and 2 March 1948.

74 *Le Jour*, 4 March 1948.

75 *Al-Nahar*, 16 March 1948. The majority of Lebanese merchants preferred receiving Lebanese lira in return for Syrian purchases and those who accepted the Syrian currency, did so by deducting 0.8 per cent from the value of the Syrian lira. Lebanese merchants refused to sell their goods on credit based on Syrian lira. In addition, all Syrian merchants paid their fees to the Lebanese customs in Syrian lira, to the extent that since the issuing of a memorandum by the Lebanese head of customs allowing the acceptance of Syrian lira in all its directories, the customs treasury did not receive a single Lebanese lira.

76 'Tel Aviv under Arab Shell fire' read the headline of *al-Qabass* in its 4 March 1948 edition.

77 *Le Jour*, 2 March; *al-Qabass*, 2, 3 March; *al-Nahar*, 2 and 3 March 1948. What the official communiqué did not mention, according to Lebanese observers, was Syria's (old) insistence that the customs revenue be divided between the two states according to their surface area and population. However, the Lebanese maintained that revenue distribution should be based on the consumption ratio of each state.

78 USNA, RG 59, 690D.90E31/3–248, 'Beirut to Secretary of State', 2 March 1948.

79 *Al-Nahar*, 16 March 1948 and *al-Qabass*, 17 March 1948.

80 *Le Jour*, 3 and 4 March 1948.

81 *Al-Qabass*, 24 March 1948. Prime Minister Solh was apparently annoyed with the remarks made by the Syrian press. In that regard he stated that 'I have noticed that the Syrian press wishes to hasten events and is calling for economic separation to take place as soon as possible, but what will this achieve?' in *al-Nahar*, 25 March 1948.

82 *Al-Qabass*, 16 and 17 March 1948.

83 *Al-Qabass*, 21 March 1948.

84 *Al-Nahar*, 24 March 1948. It was strongly advocated by al-Nahar that 'the time has come for our government to put an end to its hesitation on its talks with Syria, which have, to the present time, not resulted in anything practical. We had enough of statements which either side makes in the context of the brotherly bonds between the

two states, we hope that these statements will be changed from the area of sentiments to the area of reality.'

85 *Al-Nahar*, 28 March 1948.

86 USNA, RG 59, 690D.90E31/4–248, 'Beirut to Secretary of State', 2 April 1948 and 'Beirut Summary for the month of March, 1948', Undated, FO 371/68489. For the details of the negotiations see also *al-Qabass*, 26, 28, 31 March and 2 April 1948. See also *al-Nahar*, 31 March and 3 April 1948; *L'Orient*; *Le Jour*, 31 March, 2 and 3 April 1948 and *Beirut al-Masa'*, 5 April 1948.

87 Beirut to Foreign Office, 'Lebanon: Annual Review for 1948', 14 February 1949, FO 371/75317 and USNA, RG 59, 890D.00/9–445, 'Monthly Political Review – Syria, June 1948', 30 June 1948.

88 USNA, RG 59, 890D.515/5–1848, 'Beirut to Washington', 18 May 1948. See *al-Qabass*, 28 May and 29 June; *al-Nahar*, 13 and 29 June 1948 for the complete texts of the extensions of the agreement. It should be mentioned that during the month of June alone, Syrian and Lebanese delegations, headed by Mardam Bey and Solh, met four times in Shtura. According to 'Azem, the Gentlemen's Agreement was detrimental to the value of the Syrian currency vis-a-vis the Lebanese lira because it forced the Syrians to purchase Lebanese liras in order to pay their customs dues to the HCCI. See 'Azem, *Mudhakkarat Khaled al-'Azem*, vol. II, 104.

89 *Al-Nahar*, 29 June 1948.

90 USNA, RG 59, 890E.51/6–848, 'Beirut to Secretary of State', 10 June 1948.

91 USNA, RG 59, 890E.51/6–948, 'Beirut to Secretary of State', 16 June 1948.

92 USNA, RG 59, 890E.5151/8–1048, 'Automatic Convertibility Lebanese Pound – French Franc Modified', 10 August 1948.

93 On 17 August 1948, Quwwatly was re-elected for a second five-year term as President. Jamil Mardam Bey was delegated to form the government and took great care to include three nationalist party members (Lutfi al-Haffar, Sabri al-'Asali and Michel Ilyan) to ensure a large working majority in parliament.

94 *Al-Qabass*, 8 June 1948.

95 In fact, Franco-Syrian monetary negotiations recommenced in the summer of 1948. See 'Azem, *Mudhakkarat Khaled al-'Azem*, vol. II, 91–94. It should be mentioned that the Syrian ruling elite's change of heart regarding the Paris Accord affected the formation of the new Syrian cabinet. Minister Wehbe al-Hariri, who was opposing the signature of any financial agreement with France, had to change his attitude in order to be allowed to join the new cabinet. *Al-Nahar*, 26 and 27 August 1948. The key ministerial positions went to the following: Jamil Mardam Bey, Prime Minister and Minister of Defence; Michel Iliyan, Minister of Economy; Wehbe al-Hariri, Minister of Finance; Minister of Justice, Said Ghazi; Minister of Interior, Sabri al-'Asali; Minister of Foreign affairs, Mohsen al-Barazi. The new Syrian cabinet was announced on 23 August 1948.

96 Beirut to Foreign Office, 'Beirut Monthly Summary for August 1948', Undated, FO 371/68489 and USNA, RG 59, 890E.5151/8–3148, 'Report of the Parliamentary Finance Committee on the Franco-Lebanese Monetary Agreement', 31 August 1948. See mentioned document for complete report of the Finance Committee.

97 USNA, RG 59, 890E.5151/9–148, 'Ratification of the Franco-Lebanese Monetary Agreement', 1 September 1948. For the complete defence of the accord of Oweini before parliament see Gehchan, *Hussein Aoueini*, 101–102.

98 USNA, RG 59, 890E.5151/9–248, 'Ratification of the Franco-Lebanese Monetary Agreement', 3 September 1948 and *al-Nahar*, 28 August 1948.

99 *Al-Nahar*, 1 September 1948.

100 *Al-Qabass*, 5 September and *Le Jour*, 5 and 6 September 1948.

101 *Le Commerce du Levant*, 8 September 1948. See also Beirut to Foreign Office, 'Beirut Summary for the Month of September, 1948', Undated, FO 371/68489 and Damascus to Foreign Office, 'Political Summary for the Month of September, 1948, Damascus', Undated, FO 371/68808.

102 *L'Orient*, 4 September 1948.

103 *Le Jour*, 31 August 1948.

104 *Al-Nahar*, 5 September 1948. Editorial by Ghassan Tweini.

105 *Le Commerce du Levant*, 8 September 1948.

106 In *al-Qabass* as quoted in *al-Nahar*, 8 September 1948. See also *al-Qabass*, 25 August 1948. In that issue the title read as follows: 'The Syrian currency is being humiliated in Lebanon.'

107 *Al-Qabass*, 5 September 1948. See also Awad Barakat, *Recent Economic Development in Syria*, Middle East Economic Papers, Beirut: 1954, 3–4.

108 *Al-Qabass*, 7 and 19 September 1948.

109 *Al-Nahar*, 12 September 1948.

110 USNA, RG 59, 890E.50/9–1348, 'Beirut to Secretary of State', 13 September 1948.

111 Aside from Prime Ministers Mardam Bey and Solh as well as numerous experts, Lebanese and Syrian delegations were composed of the following ministers: Hussein Oweini and Philip Takla. The Syrian delegation included Michel Ilyan, Sa'id Ghazzi and Wehbe al-Hariri.

112 *Al-Nahar*, 22, 23, 24, 25, 26, 29 September and 1, 2, 3 October; *al-Qabass*, 21, 22, 24, 28, 30 September and 1 October 1948; *Le Jour*, 22–23, 25, 26, 28, 30 September and 1 October 1948.

113 USNA, RG 59, 890D.90E31/10–548, 'Beirut to Secretary of State,' 5 October 1948; *al-Qabass*, 3 October 1948 and *Le Jour*, 2 October 1948.

114 Gehchan, *Hussein Aoueini*, 116; *Le Jour*, 2, 3 and 4 October and *al-Nahar*, 5 October 1948.

115 On 8 October Moubarak and Joubara as well as their accompanying delegations met. A list of imported goods for the year 1947 and the 1st and 2nd quarters of 1948 was studied. So was a list of exports for the same period. These lists, from the Common Interests and Customs Directorates, revealed that the goods imported amounted to 414,057 tons, worth S£362,764,000. Of these goods, 148,018 tons worth S£83,640,000 were re-exported. Goods, which the country could do without, were selected and sent to a joint committee that was delegated to draft a regulation. *Al-Nahar*, 6, 7 and 8 October 1948 and *Le Jour*, 7 and 8 October 1948. For a detailed list of the goods see *al-Nahar*, 9 October 1948.

116 The Syrians included in the list of articles they wished restricted vehicles and refrigerators. The Syrians also demanded to apply special restrictions on grain. Lebanon considered vehicles as essential for her tourist industry and feared that the restriction of grain imports would compel her to buy from Syria at prohibitive prices. USNA, RG 59, 690D.90E31/11–1648, 'Beirut to Secretary of State', 16 November 1948; *Le Commerce du Levant*, 9 October 1948.

117 *Al-Nahar* and *Le Jour*, 12 October 1948. See also Gehchan, *Hussein Aoueini*, 117.

118 USNA, RG 59, 690D.90E31/10–1548, 'Beirut to Secretary of State', 15 October 1948; *al-Nahar*, 15 October 1948. Among the recommendations were also the unrestricted transaction in hard currencies and the protection of industry through the lifting of customs on raw materials. The conference endorsed the memorandum presented by the Beirut merchants to the President.

119 USNA, RG 59, 690D.90E31/10–2648, 'Beirut to Secretary of State', 26 October 1948; *al-Nahar*, 15 October 1948. See also *al-Qabass*, 12 October 1948.

120 *Le Jour*, 16, 17 and 18 October 1948.

121 *Le Commerce du Levant*, 20 October 1948. See also el-Hafez, *La structure et la politique économique en Syrie et au Liban*, 203.

122 *Al-Qabass*, 12 October 1948.

123 As quoted in *al-Qabass*, 19 and 20 October 1948.

124 *Al-Qabass*, 19 October 1948. Hariri was under continuous attack in Syria. He was held responsible for allowing the US dollar to reach 400 (Syrian) piastres (its value was 220 piastres). There were charges of corruption allotted to him and a number of large merchants who had sizeable debts in the Syrian currency and at the same time were known to have American dollars abroad. The loss in value of the Syrian lira was seen as serving their interests. *Al-Qabass*, 20, 21 and 24 October 1948.

125 *Al-Qabass*, 21 October 1948.

126 *Al-Qabass*, 21 October 1948.

127 Busson, dubbed the 'economic dictator of Lebanon', exerted great influence over post-war Beirut, especially after he forged an alliance between the two major French financial groups in Lebanon in addition to his close alliance with President Khuri's entourage. Busson was instrumental in persuading the Lebanese government to retain monetary ties with France. His image of Lebanon's future revealed a small Christian enclave, whose liberal economy would be a 'Singapore' of the Middle East. He was an outspoken critic of Syrian economic nationalism. Gates, *The Merchant Republic of Lebanon*, 93.

128 *Le Jour*, 22 October 1948. See also *al-Nahar*, 23 October 1948 and *al-Qabass*, 31 October 1948. It was until *al-Qabass* issue of 24 December 1948 that the daily reported that negotiations were taking place between France and Syria.

129 *Beirut al-Masa'*, 25 October 1948. Under the Franco-Syrian Monetary Agreement, which would be signed early 1949, Syria undertook to meet a share of the combined Syro-Lebanese trade deficit by settlement in scarce sterling, while Lebanon paid in relatively abundant French francs. This further increased the sensitivity of the Syrians towards Lebanese merchants, who continued to flood Syrian markets with foreign goods in return for Syria's receding hard currency. Saba, 'The Syro-Lebanese Customs Union,' 100 and Gates, *The Merchant Republic of Lebanon*, 90.

130 For all the conference's recommendations see *al-Qabass* and *al-Nahar*, 4 November 1948.

131 *Al-Nahar* and *Le Jour*, 6 November 1948. See also *al-Qabass*, 10 November 1948.

132 *Al-Qabass*, 5 November 1948.

133 USNA, RG 59, 690D.90E31/10–2648, 'Beirut to Secretary of State', 26 October 1948; Beirut to Foreign Office, 14 February 1949, FO 371/75317; Damascus to Foreign Office, 31 January 1949, FO 371/75527 and Gehchan, *Hussein Aoueini*, 118.

134 USNA, RG 59, 690D.90E31/10–2648, 'Beirut to Secretary of State', 26 October 1948.

135 USNA, RG 59, 690D.90E31/11–1648, 'Beirut to Secretary of State', 16 November 1948; 'Political Summary for the Month of November, 1948, Damascus', Undated, FO 371/68808; *al-Qabass*, 21, 23 and 26 November and 1 December 1948.

136 USNA, RG 59, 890D.002/11–2348, 'Development in Syrian Internal politics: Cabinet Crisis', 23 November 1948. The resigning cabinet members of the Nationalist bloc were Sabri al-'Asali, Michel Ilyan and Lutfi al-Haffar. *Al-Nahar*, 10 November 1948. For their statements see *al-Qabass*, 10 November 1948 and *al-Nahar*, 10 and 11 November 1948.

137 Syrian Foreign Minister Mohsen al-Barazi kept stating that there was no agreement with France and that the negotiations in Paris aimed at liquidating financial relations and not settling them. *Beirut al-Masa'*, 1 and 8 November 1948.

138 It seems that by early November the Syrian cabinet had discussed the Monetary Agreement. During that cabinet session, the cabinet in its majority approved the agreement with the abstention of Hariri. Lutfi al-Haffar asked Hariri if he were convinced of the benefits of the agreement, to which Hariri responded positively. Al-Haffar then told him that he could not dodge the agreement and that he had to assume the full responsibility of the agreement just like everyone else in the cabinet. However, Hariri remained adamant at his request, after which the three ministers resigned. USNA, RG 59, 890D.002/11–2348, 'Development in Syrian Internal politics: Cabinet Crisis', 23 November 1948 and *al-Nahar*, 10 November 1948.

139 *Al-Nahar*, 10 and 13 November 1948.

140 *Le Jour*, 2, 3, 4, 5, 7, 14 and 19 December 1948 and *al-Qabass*, 19 December 1948. It should be noted that *al-Qabass*, and most of the Syrian press, stopped appearing between 1–19 December. The key posts in the 'Azem government went to the following: Khaled al-'Azem, aside from the premiership, held the Ministries of Defence and Foreign Affairs; Hassan Joubara became the Minister of Finance, Hanin Sahnawi was appointed Minister of Economy and 'Adel al-'Azmeh, Minister of Interior. USNA, RG 59, 890D.00/12–2948, 'Program for Khaled al-Azzem Government', 29 December 1948.

141 Damascus to Foreign Office, 'Political Summary No.1 the months of January and February, 1949', Undated, FO 371/75528; *Le Jour* and *al-Nahar*, 29 January 1949 and *al-Qabass*, 30 January 1949. For the agreement see *al-Qabass*, 4 February 1949 and *al-Nahar*, 2 February 1949.

142 For the role of the 'Azem in pushing for the TAPLINE and Monetary Agreement with France see al-'Azem, *Mudhakkarat Khaled al-Azem*, vol. II, 94–98.

143 USNA, RG 59, 890D.00/2–949, 'Damascus to Washington', 10 February 1949 and 890D.00/2–1449, 'Memorandum of Conversation with HE Shukri Quwwatly', 14 February 1949. See also *al-Nahar*, 10 February 1949 and *al-Qabass*, 18 February 1949.

144 *Le Commerce du Levant*, 9 March 1949.

145 *Al-Nahar*, 14 January 1949. The Franco-Syrian Monetary Agreement under scrutiny did not much differ from the Lebanese version. *Le Jour*, 28 January 1949.

146 *Le Jour*, 28 January 1949, *al-Qabass*, 8 February 1949 and *al-Nahar*, 9 February 1949 and *L'Orient*, 8 and 20 February 1949. According to specialists the Franco-Syrian Monetary Agreement was less favourable than its Lebanese counterpart. Gehchan, *Hussein Aoueini*, 119–120. For the details of the Monetary Agreement, see *al-Qabass*, 25 January, 8 and 9 February 1949 and *Le Commerce du Levant*, 19 February 1949. For a detailed comparison between the Syro-French and the Lebanese-French Monetary Accords, see *L'Orient*, 22 February 1949.

147 *Al-Qabass*, 23 February 1949.

148 *Al-Qabass*, 13 January 1949.

149 USNA, RG 59, 890E.00 (W), 'Beirut to Secretary of State', 4 March 1949. There were numerous instances where the Lebanese customs would refuse to free Syrian goods. During most of these incidents, customs officials in Beirut told Syrian merchants that Lebanese merchants had already imported similar goods. Other incidents involved the delay of Syrian exports through the delay of customs formalities by Lebanese officials. When Syrian merchants complained to Lebanese authorities, they were told they were following instructions of the Syrian government and as such their complaints should be directed to it. Opinion-makers in Syria were asking the government if it were necessary that the Syrian merchant continue to be under the mercy of the Lebanese civil servants. *Al-Qabass*, 18 March 1949.

150 *Al-Qabass*, 1 February and 6 March 1949.

151 *Al-Qabass*, 10 February and 30 March 1949. In a meeting, the Syrian chambers of commerce and industry called for the hasty ratification of the Monetary Agreement and TAPLINE agreement. The meeting convened to address the means to prevent the transfer of Syrian capital to Lebanon. *Al-Qabass*, 11 March and *Le Jour*, 11 and 12 March 1949.

152 USNA, RG 59, 890D.6363/2–2149, 'Damascus to Washington', 21 February 1949. See also *Le Jour*, 6, 7, 8, 9 and 24 February 1949. Although the armistice discussions took place during March, the delay in the Syro-Lebanese negotiations to replace the Gentlemen's Agreement with a more lasting one was not related to the ceasefire talks. But the Syrian government decided to postpone economic negotiations till after the ratification of the Syro-French Monetary Agreement by parliament. *Al-Qabass*, 20 March 1949. For details on the armistice negotiations see *Al-Qabass*, 2, 10, 17, 22 March 1949 and *Le Jour*, 2, 19, 22, March 1949. For the text of the Lebanese–Israeli ceasefire agreement see *Le Jour* and *al-Nahar*, 24 March 1949.

153 *Le Jour*, 26 February; *al-Nahar*, 27 February and *al-Qabass*, 25 and 27 February 1949.

154 *L'Orient* and *Le Jour*, 28 February 1949.

155 *Le Jour*, 28 February 1949. Editorials by Khalil Gemayel and Michel Chiha.

CHAPTER 6

1 Patrick Seale, *The Struggle for Syria: A Study of Post-War Arab Politics, 1945–1958*, London: I.B. Tauris, 1986, 2–4. The struggle for Syria in the Syrian and Lebanese press was referred to as the struggle between the Hashemites (in the form of the Fertile Crescent or the Greater Syria schemes) versus Syrian and Lebanese independence.

2 In fact, the year before Za'im's coup saw the emergence of Iraq and Saudi Arabia as rival backers of Syrian political factions. Seale, *The Struggle for Syria*, 47.

3 The army officers were drawn to the ideas of Akram al-Hawrani (founder of the Arab Socialist Party), Antun S'ada (founder of the Parti Populaire Syrien), Michel 'Aflaq and Salah al-Din Bitar (founders of the left-wing Arab nationalist movement al-Hizb al-Ba'th al-'Arabi).

4 The 'Cooking-Fat Scandal' unfolded when it became evident that the army was supplied with fat or samnah of inferior quality, made from bone waste. Quwwatly

ordered the arrest of Colonel Antoine Bustani, chief supply officer. Za'im refused to comply with the order. Instead of backing Quwwatly, the officers sided with Za'im. For the details see Seale, *The Struggle for Syria*, 41–45.

5 *Al-Nahar*, 2 and 3 April 1949 and *Le Jour*, 4 April 1949.

6 On the negotiations between the Syrian and Iraqi military, see *al-Qabass*, 14 April 1949 and *al-Nahar*, 19 April 1949.

7 The Hashemites saw in Za'im an opportunity to realise the Greater Syria or Fertile Crescent schemes, both of which were rejected by the major Arab Powers of that time, Egypt and Saudi Arabia. *Al-Nahar*, 9 and 14, 15 April 1949.

8 The sudden visit of Iraqi Prime Minister Nuri al-Sa'id to the Syrian capital did not have any tangible results, which saved the Lebanese from an awkward position vis-à-vis Egypt and Saudi Arabia. *Al-Nahar*, 19 April 1949.

9 USNA, RG 59, 890D.01/4–2349, 'Visit of Colonel Zaim to His Majesty King Farouk', 23 April 1949 and 890D.01/4–2449, 'Damascus to Washington', 24 April 1949. It was particularly the French who found in Za'im an opportunity to regain their battered influence. Members of the French legation visited the Syrian leader almost on a daily basis. 'Adel Arslan, *Dhikrayat al-amir 'Adil Arslan 'an Husni al-Za'im*, Beirut: Dar al-kitab al-jadid, 1962, 29–35.

10 Beirut to Foreign Office, 'Beirut, Summary for the Month of March, 1949', FO 371/75318; USNA, RG 59, 890D.00/4–449, 'Beirut to Washington', 4 April 1949 and *Le Jour*, 9 April 1949 (editorial by Michel Chiha).

11 Zisser, *Lebanon: The Challenge of Independence*, 166 and Khuri, *Haqa'iq lubnaniya*, vol. III, 206.

12 Beirut to Foreign Office, 'Beirut, Summary of the Month of April 1949', FO 371/75318; *Le Jour*, 5 and 7 April and *al-Nahar*, 3 and 5 April 1949.

13 *Al-Nahar*, 6 April 1949. In an interview to *al-Nahar*, Za'im announced that any hostility towards Lebanon would be regarded as an aggression towards Syria. *Al-Nahar*, 8 April 1949.

14 *Le Jour*, 10 April 1949 and *al-Qabass*, 14, 15 and 17 April 1949.

15 USNA, RG 59, 890E.00 (W) /4–1549, 'Beirut to Secretary of State', 15 April 1949. See also *Beirut al-Masa*', 18 April 1949.

16 From Beirut to Foreign Office, 19 April 1949, FO 371/75322. See also Khuri, *Haqa'iq lubnaniya*, vol. III, 212–213. Noteworthy is how 'Adel Arslan relates Za'im's obsession with alleged attempts by the Lebanese government to topple his regime. Convinced that the coup would be prepared in Lebanon, Za'im planted over 200 spies there who used to feed him with fictitious reports. Arslan, *Dhikrayat al-amir 'Adil Arslan 'an Husni al-Za'im*, 60–62.

17 From Beirut to Foreign Office, 23 April 1949, FO 371/75322 and Khuri, *Haqa'iq lubnaniya*, vol. III, 207–208.

18 Za'im agreed to ratify the TAPLINE by 'legislative decree' on the condition that Aramco start work in Syria immediately. Aramco agreed. USNA, RG59, 890D.6363/4–649, 'Damascus to Washington', 6 April 1949. Significantly, the US military attaché in Damascus was directly involved in the coup that brought Za'im to power. According to former CIA agent Wilbur Eveland, the coup was carried out in order to obtain ratification of the TAPLINE agreement. In Irene Gendizier, *Notes from the Minefield, United States Intervention in Lebanon and the Middle East, 1945–1958*, New York: Columbia University Press, 1997, 98.

19 *Al-Qabass*, 24 and 26 April 1949 and *al-Nahar*, 22 and 24 April 1949.

20 USNA, RG 59, 890E.50/4–1149, 'Beirut to Secretary of State', April 1949; Michel Chiha and Khalil Gemayel, *Le Jour*, editorials by, 24, 27, 28 April 1949.

21 Za'im retained the premiership, Defence and Interior Ministries for himself while allocating the other main ministerial portfolios to 'Adel Arslan, who became Foreign Minister, and Hassan Joubara, who took over the Ministry of Finance. The new cabinet was deemed conspicuous for the absence of prominent political leaders and concentration of key posts under the colonel. USNA, RG 59, 890D.002/4–1749, 'Damascus to Washington', 17 April 1949 and Damascus to Foreign Office, 'Political Summary No.3 for the Period 31 March 1949 to 30 April 1949', Undated, FO 371/75528.

22 *Al-Qabass*, 29, 30 April and 1, 4, 15 May 1949.

23 *Al-Qabass*, 11, 17 and 19 May 1949. Editorials by Najib Raiyyes.

24 Andrew Rathmell, *Secret War in the Middle East: The Covert Struggle for Syria, 1949–1961*, London: Tauris Academic Studies, 1995, 46; Zisser, *Lebanon: The Challenge of Independence*, 168 and Al-'alaqat al-lubnaniyya al-suriyya, 1943–1958, vol.I, 46–47.

25 Beirut to Foreign Office, 'Beirut Summary for the Month of May, 1949', FO 371/75318; *Le Jour*, 12, 18, 19 and 20 May 1949; *al-Nahar*, 19, 20 and 21 May 1949 and *al-Qabass*, 20 May 1949. 'Adel Arslan was very critical of Za'im's open threats against Lebanon, warning him that such a policy would further alienate the two countries. Arslan, *Dhikrayat al-amir 'Adil Arslan 'an Husni al-Za'im*, 42.

26 *Al-Nahar*, 19 and 21 May 1949. Editorials by Ghassan Tweini; *Le Jour*, 21 and 22 May 1949. Editorials by Khalil Gemayel and *Beirut al-Masa'*, 23 May 1949.

27 Beirut to Foreign Office, 'Beirut Summary for the Month of May, 1949', FO 371/75318 and *al-Qabass*, 22 May 1949.

28 USNA, RG 59, 790D.90E/5–2349, 'Beirut to Washington', 23 May 1949. See also *al-Nahar*, 21, 22, 24, 25, 26, 28 May 1949; *Le Jour*, 23, 24, 25, 26, 27, 28 May 1949 and *al-Qabass*, 24, 25, 26, 27, 30 May and 2 June 1949.

29 USNA, RG 59, 790D.90E/6–149, 'Beirut to Washington', 1 June 1949. See also *al-Nahar*, 29 May and 2 June 1949 and *Le Jour*, 29 May and 2 June 1949. The Syrian army took up positions in Rashaya (in the Beqa' valley).

30 *Al-Nahar*, 31 May 1949.

31 USNA, RG 59, 890E.00/6–649, 'Saudi Arab-Egyptian Arbitral Decision', 6 June 1949. See also Khuri, *Haqa'iq lubnaniyya*, vol. III, 225; *al-Nahar*, 2, 3, 7, 16, 24 June 1949; *Le Jour*, 3, 7 June 1949. For the text of the arbitration committee see *al-Qabass*, 3 June 1949.

32 USNA, RG 59, 890E.00/6–649, 'Saudi Arab-Egyptian Arbitral Decision', 6 June 1949.

33 *Al-Nahar*, 27 May 1949. Editorial by Ghassan Tweini.

34 *Al-Nahar*, 26 and 29 May 1949. For Syrian communiqué, see *al-Nahar*, 25 May 1949.

35 *Al-Qabass*, 3 June 1949.

36 USNA, RG 59, 690E.006/5–2649, 'Import and Price Control Measures', 26 May 1949. See also *al-Nahar*, 24 May 1949.

37 *Al-Nahar*, 26, 27 May 1949. For the views of the major Lebanese merchants see *al-Nahar*, 27 May 1949.

38 *Al-Nahar*, 29 May and 19 June 1949. Editorial by Ghassan Tweini and editorial by Camille Sham'oun. For a detailed account of the Lebanese factory owners see *al-Nahar*, 29 May 1949.

39 *Beirut al-Masa'*, 23 May 1949.

40 *Le Jour*, 2 June 1949. Editorial by Michel Chiha. See also Menassa, *Plan de reconstruction*, 100 and Gates, *The Merchant Republic of Lebanon*, 90–91.

41 *Al-Qabass*, 24, 25 May 1949. Editorials by Najib al-Raiyyes. By that time, Syrian conditions to maintain the economic union with Lebanon were as follows. 1. Limit imports to levels with which Syria must agree. 2. Put tariffs on all imported goods that compete with local goods. 3. Lebanon would abstain from imports of grain or grain-based goods. In return, Syria would provide the Lebanese with grain for the same price as Syrians. 4. The general director of the customs should be Syrian for the same duration as his Lebanese counterpart had served. 5. The number of civil servants serving in the customs and the common interests directorates should be according to the share of the revenues of each state. 6. No import licence should be granted to any Syrian or Lebanese merchant, unless the Syrian and Lebanese delegates (to the Common Interests) signed that licence.

42 *Al-Qabass*, 11 June 1949. See also *al-Nahar*, 16 June 1949 and *Le Commerce du Levant*, 18 June 1949.

43 *Al-Qabass*, 14 June 1949.

44 Beirut to Foreign Office, 'Beirut Summary for the Month of June, 1949', FO 371/75318; *al-Nahar*, 15, 16 June 1949 and *Le Jour*, 11 June 1949. For the complete texts of the Syrian memoranda and proposals as well as the letter sent by Minister Joubara to his Lebanese counterpart see *al-Qabass*, 14, 15 June 1949.

45 See *al-Qabass*, 14 June 1949.

46 See *al-Nahar*, 15, 16, 17, 29, 30 June 1949 and *al-Qabass*, 30 June 1949. For the detailed presentations of the representatives of each association see *al-Nahar*, 29 June 1949.

47 *Al-Nahar*, 24 June 1949.

48 Khuri, *Haqa'iq lubnaniyya*, vol. III , 230; Zisser, *Lebanon: The Challenge to Independence*, 170 and *al-Nahar*, 25 June 1949.

49 USNA, RG 59, 690D.90E31/7–1549, 'Beirut to Secretary of State', 15 July 1949; USNA, RG 59, 690D.90E31/7–1349, 'Beirut to Secretary of State', 13 July 1949 and USNA, RG 59, 890E.00 (W)/7–1449, 'Beirut to Secretary of State', 14 July 1949. See also *al-Nahar*, 5, 6, 10, 12 July 1949 and *al-Qabass*, 7 July 1949. For the complete text of the agreement see *al-Qabass*, 12 July 1949 also in *al-Nahar*, 12 July 1949 and in *Le Jour*, 12 July 1949.

50 *Al-Qabass*, 13, 14 July 1949.

51 The party was later to be known as the Syrian Social Nationalist Party. Antun Sa'ada founded the party in 1932. On the ideology of the party see Antun Sa'ada, *Nushu' al-umam*, Beirut: 1938 and *The Principles of the Syrian Nationalist Party*, Beirut: al-Hizb al-Suri al-Qawmi al-Ijtima'i, 1949.

52 From Beirut to Foreign Office, 10 June 1949, FO 371/75320 and From Beirut to Foreign Office, 11 June 1949, FO 371/75320. See also *al-Nahar*, 11, 12, 21 June and 7 July 1949; *al-Qabass*, 19 June 1949.

53 Khuri, *Haqa'iq lubnaniya*, vol. III, 228–229 and 236–237.

54 The Lebanese Prime Minister had informed a British minister that Za'im had financed and armed Sa'ada's men, but realising that this course might drive the Lebanese government into the hands of the Hashemites, he had abandoned the party and handed its leader over to be shot. In 12 July 1949, FO 371/75320. See also Beirut to

Foreign Office, 'Beirut Summary for the Month of June, 1949', FO 371/75318; From Damascus to Foreign Office, 14 June 1949, FO 371/75320; From Damascus to Foreign Office, 9 July 1949, FO 371/75320 and Seale, *The Struggle for Syria*, 70.

55 'Syrian Police Arrested Law Breakers from Lebanon'; 'Lebanon: Sixty National Socialists Arrested'; 'Lebanon: National Socialist Party Creates Disturbances'; 'Attack on Police Station'; 4 to 5 July 2003, FO 371/75320.

56 Za'im even assisted the Lebanese authorities by closing the frontier after handing over Sa'ada. Beirut to Foreign Office, 'Political Summary for the Month of July, 1949', FO 371/75318.

57 From Beirut to Foreign Office, 7 and 8 July 1949, FO 371/75320; *al-Nahar*, 8, 9, 12, 17 July; *Le Jour*, 13, 14, 17 July and *al-Qabass*, 6, 7, 10 July 1949.

58 Explanations that led the Syrian leader to hand over Sa'ada to the Lebanese range from pressures on Damascus from regional Powers, mainly Saudi Arabia and Egypt to pressures from Western Powers see Seale, *The Struggle for Syria*, 89; Jubran Jurayj, *Ma'a Antun Sa'adeh min 8 fibrayr 1932 ila 8 tammuz 1949*, Beirut: 1984, 188–189 and Nadhir Fansa, *Ayam Husni al-Za'im: 137 yawm hazzat Suriya*, Beirut: Manshurat dar al-afaq al-jadida, 1982, 86–89.

59 For the visit see *al-Nahar*, 19 July 1949 and Damascus to Foreign Office, 'Political Summary No.6 for the Month of July 1949, Damascus', Undated, FO 371/75528.

60 *Al-Nahar*, 9 July 1949. See also Gehchan, *Hussein Aoueini*, 120–121 and Franjiyah, *Hamid Frangie*, 310.

61 Za'im's close association with Barazi earned him the animosity of Akram al-Hawarni.

62 Seale, *The Struggle for Syria*, 58–75.

63 *Al-Qabass*, 17, 18 August 1949. Editorial by Raiyyes.

64 See *al-Qabass*, 22, 23, 24 August 1949 and see also *Le Jour*, 17 August 1949.

65 USNA, RG 59, 890E.00 (W)/8–1949, 'Beirut to Secretary of State', 19 August 1949 and Beirut to Foreign Office, 'Political Summary for the Month of August 1949', Undated, FO 371/75318. See also *al-Nahar*, 18 August 1949 and *Le Jour*, 16, 17 August 1949.

66 Beirut to Foreign Office, 'Political Summary for the Month of August 1949', FO 371/75318 and *al-Nahar*, 23 August 1949.

67 *Al-Nahar*, 24 August 1949.

68 *Le Jour*, 8 September 1949.

69 'Minute by Williams', 13 August 1949, FO 371/75326 and *al-Qabass*, 23 August 1949.

70 USNA, RG 59, 690D.90E31/8–3049, 'Beirut to Secretary of State', 30 August 1949; *al-Qabass*, 18, 28, 29 August 1949 and *al-Nahar*, 27 August 1949 and Gehchan, *Hussein Aoueini*, 122. For a Syrian view on the causes that led to the differences in the value of the two currencies, after the signature of the Franco-Syrian Monetary Agreement, see 'Azem, *Mudhakkarat Khaled al-'Azem*, vol. II, 99–103.

71 *Al-Qabass*, 1 September 1949.

72 Beirut to Foreign Office, 23 September 1949, FO 371/75320; Beirut to Foreign Office, 'Political Summary for the Month of September, 1949', FO 371/75318; Beirut to Foreign Office, 'Re-Inauguration of the Lebanese President', 19 September 1949, FO 371/75320.

73 Beirut to Foreign Office, 'Political Summary for the Month of October, 1949', FO 371/75318; Beirut to Foreign Office, 5 October 1949, FO 371/75320; Beirut to Foreign Office, 6 October 1949, FO 371/75320 and Beirut to Foreign Office, 18 October 1949, FO 371/75320. For the detailed profile of the cabinet members, see From Beirut to

Foreign Office, 5 October 1949, FO 371/75320 and USNA, RG 59, 890E.002/10–349, 'Beirut to Secretary of State', 3 October 1949.

74 Beirut to Foreign Office, 10 October 1949, FO 371/75321; Beirut to Foreign Office, 31 October 1949, FO 371/7532 and *Le Jour*, 31 August 1949.

75 Damascus to Foreign Office, 'Political Summary No.8 for the Month of September, 1949', Undated, FO 371/75528.

76 *Al-Nahar*, 28 September 1949.

77 *Al-Nahar*, 7 October 1949 and *al-Qabass*, 18 October 1949.

78 For the complete text of the decree see *al-Qabass* and *al-Nahar*, 1 November 1949.

79 Damascus to Foreign Office, 'Political Summary for the Month of November, 1949', FO 371/75318. For a detailed description of how the elections were conducted in Syria, see *al-Qabass*, 16 November 1949.

80 The withdrawal of the People's Party was interpreted by some Lebanese as the defeat of the Syrian-Iraqi unionists. *L'Orient*, 16, 17, 18 November 1949.

81 The People's Party was victorious in Aleppo, Homs and other areas except for Damascus, where independent candidates, Islamic and Socialist blocs won. *Al-Nahar*, 16, 17, 18 November 1949.

82 Damascus to Foreign Office, 'Political Summary No.10 for the Month of November 1949', Undated, FO 371/75528.

83 See *al-Nahar*, 22 November 1949.

84 Damascus to Foreign Office, 'Political Summary No.11 for the Month of December 1949', Undated, FO 371/82784. See also Seale, *The Struggle for Syria*, 73–83.

85 *Al-Nahar*, 13 November 1949.

86 *Al-Qabass*, 28 November 1949.

87 *Al-Qabass*, 29, 30 November and 1, 2, 11 December 1949.

88 *Al-Qabass*, 4 December 1949.

89 *Al-Qabass*, 4 December 1949.

90 USNA, RG 59, 690D.90E31/12–1449, 'Beirut to Secretary of State', 14 December 1949; *al-Qabass*, 9 December 1949. Also in *al-Nahar*, 9 December and *Le Jour*, 10 December 1949.

91 USNA, RG 59, 690D.90E31/12–1449, 'Beirut to Secretary of State', 14 December 1949 and *al-Nahar*, 10, 14 December 1949.

92 *Al-Qabass*, 14 December 1949.

93 *Le Jour*, 11 December 1949.

94 *Al-Qabass*, 12 December 1949.

95 USNA, RG 59, 'Beirut to Secretary of State', 13 January 1950; *Le Commerce du Levant*, 14 December 1949 and *al-Nahar*, 11 December 1949.

96 *Le Jour*, 16 December 1949.

97 *Al-Nahar*, 11 December 1949. Editorial Ghassan Tweini.

98 *Al-Qabass*, 15 December 1949.

99 *Le Jour*, 15, 18 December 1949.

100 See *al-Qabass*, 11 December 1949.

101 *Al-Nahar*, 13 December 1949.

102 *Le Jour*, 20 December 1949.

103 Seale, *The Struggle for Syria*, 84–86. See also *al-Nahar*, 20 December 1949 and *Le Jour*, 20 December 1949.

104 Beirut to Foreign Office, 'Political Summary for the Month of January 1950', FO 371/82266. See also *al-Nahar*, 14, 18 January 1950.

105 Seale, *The Struggle for Syria*, 88–93. Holding the key portfolios in the new Syrian government were the following: Prime Minister and Minister of Foreign Affairs, Khalid al-'Azem (Independent); defence, Akram al-Hawarani (Republican Front); economy, Ma'ruf al-Dawalibi (People's Party); Interior, Sami Kabbara; Finance, 'Abd al-Rahman al-'Azem (Independent). For the negotiations that led to the formation of the government, see *al-Qabass*, 29 December 1949; *al-Nahar*, 21, 22, 24, 28 December 1949.

106 USNA, RG 59, 983.61/2–1050, 'Damascus Press Summary, 1–15 January 1950', 10 February 1950; USNA, RG 319, 'From Military Attaché to Dept. of the Army', 20 January 1950; Damascus to Foreign Office, 'Political Summary No.2 for the Month of February', FO 371/82784; *al-Nahar*, 8, 31 January 1950 and *al-Qabass*, 17, 18, 20, 31 January and 1 February 1950.

107 USNA, RG 59, 983.61/2–1050, 'Damascus Press Summary, January 16–31, 1950', 10 February 1950 and *al-Qabass*, 22 February 1950.

108 *Beirut al-Masa'*, 13 February 1950.

109 *Le Jour*, 15, 18, 25 February 1950. Editorials by Khalil Gemayel and Michel Chiha.

110 *L'Orient*, 8, 13 February 1950. Editorial by George Naccache.

111 Hokayem, 'Al-'alakat al-lubnaniya al-suriya, 1918–1950', 63.

112 *Al-Qabass*, 15 February 1950 and *al-Nahar*, 9, 17. About that time the Syrian government began engaging the Iraqis in a dialogue to conduct an economic agreement. See *al-Nahar*, 18 February 1950.

113 *Le Jour*, 18, 19 February 1950; *al-Nahar*, 19 February 1950 and *al-Qabass*, 20 February 1950.

114 *Le Jour*, 19 February 1950; *al-Nahar*, 19 February 1950 and al-'Azem, *Mudhakkarat Khaled al-'Azem*, vol. II, 107.

115 *Le Jour*, 21 February 1950; *al-Nahar*, 22, 24 February 1950 and *al-Qabass*, 26 February 1950. See also Gehchan, *Hussein Aoueini*, 125.

116 *Al-Nahar*, 23 February 1950 and *Le Jour*, 22, 24 February 1950.

117 USNA, RG 59, 783A.00 (W)/2–2450, 'Beirut to Secretary of State', 24 February 1950.

118 *L'Orient*, 25 February 1950.

119 'Azem, *Mudhakkarat Khaled al-'Azem*, vol. II, 12–13 and 108.

120 *Al-Nahar*, 24, 26, 28 February 1950; *al-Qabass*, 27 February, 3 March 1950 and *Le Jour*, 25 February 1950.

121 'Azem, *Mudhakkarat Khaled al-'Azem*, vol. II, 37. For the recommendations of the conference see *Le Commerce du Levant*, 8 March 1950; *al-Qabass*, 5 March 1950; *al-Nahar*, 2, 3, 7 March 1950.

122 'Azem, *Mudhakkarat Khaled al-'Azem*, vol. II, 39–40 and *al-Qabass*, 17 March 1950.

123 *Al-Nahar*, 9, 10 March 1950.

124 *Al-Qabass*, 10 March 1950. See also 'Azem, *Mudhakkarat Khaled al-'Azem*, vol. II, 38.

125 *L'Orient*, 11 March 1950.

126 *Al-Qabass*, 6, 9 March 1950.

127 *Al-Nahar*, 10, 11 March 1950 and *al-Qabass*, 13, 17 March 1950.

128 *Al-Nahar*, 10, 11 March 1950 and *al-Qabass*, 13, 17 March 1950.

129 On 9 March 1950, Tufiq Hamdan, a member of the Syrian Social Nationalist Party, shot at Solh in Beirut while the latter was paying a formal visit. For details of the assassination attempt, see USNA, RG 59, 783A.13/3–2350, 'Attempt on the Life of the Lebanese

Premier', 23 March 1950 and USNA, RG 59, 783A.13/3–1050, 'Beirut to Secretary of State', 10 March 1950.

130 *Le Jour*, 12 March 1950, *al-Nahar*, 11 March 1950. See also *al-Qabass*, 12 March 1950.

131 USNA, RG 59, 783A.00 (W)/3–1750, 'Beirut and Secretary of State', 20 March 1950.

132 USNA, RG 59, 783A.00 (W)/3–1050 'Beirut to Secretary of State', 10 March 1950 and *Le Jour*, 13 March 1950.

133 *Le Jour*, 9 March 1950.

134 *L'Orient*, 9, 15 March 1950.

135 *Beirut al-Masa'*, 13 March 1950.

136 'Azem, *Mudhakkarat Khaled al-'Azem*, vol. II, 47–51 and 59; Damascus to Foreign Office, 'Political Summary No.3 for the Month of March, 1950, Damascus', Undated, FO 371/82784 and USNA, RG 319, 'From Military Attaché, Beirut to Dept. of Army', no. 573, 15 March 1959. For the communiqué see *Le Jour*, 14 March; *al-Nahar*, 14 March 1950.

SELECTED BIBLIOGRAPHY

PRIMARY SOURCES

Official Archives

Great Britain:
Public Records Office, London.
FO 371 Lebanese, Syrian and Middle East files, 1920–1952 [In view of the separation of the British legations at Beirut and Damascus, the Beirut Combined Weekly Political Summary closed on 23 January 1947. Starting from the mentioned date, separate summaries were prepared in Beirut and Damascus.]

United States:
National Archives and Records Administration, Washington DC.
Record Groups:
59 (General Records of Department of State, central files, 1920–1954)
84 (Records of the Foreign Service Posts, regional files, 1920–1954)
165 (Office of Strategic Services, Military Attaché Reports, G-2 regional files)

Newspapers

Al-Bashir. Beirut.
Beirut. Beirut.
Beirut al-Masa'. Beirut.
Al-Istiqlal al-'arabi. Damascus.
Le Jour. Beirut.
Al-Nahar. Beirut.
L'Orient. Beirut.
Al-Qabas. Damascus.

Memoirs

Abu Mansur, Fadlallah. *A'asir Dimashq*. Beirut: 1959.
Arslan, 'Adel. *Dhikrayat al-amir Adel Arslan 'an Husni al-Za'im*. Beirut: Dar al-kitab al-jadid, 1962.
'Awad, Walid. *'Abdallah al-Mashnuq yatazakar*. Beirut: al-Ahliyya li al-nashir, 1981.

199

Al-'Azem, Khaled. *Mudhakkarat Khaled al-'Azem*. Vol. I–III. Beirut: al-Dar al-mutahida li al-nashr, 1973.

Al-Azmah, Bashir. *Jil al-hazima: bayna al-wihda wa al-infisal, mudhakkirat*. London: Riad el-Rayyes, 1991.

Babil, Nasuh. *Sahafa wa siyassa: Suriya fi al-qarn al-'ishrin*. London: Riad el-Rayyes, 1987.

Fansa, Nadhir. *Ayam Husni al-Za'im: 137 yawm hazzat Suriya*. Beirut: Manshurat dar al-afaq al-jadida, 1982.

El-Hafez, Mohammad Amine. *La structure et la politique économique en Syrie et au Liban*. Beirut: Imprimerie Khalife, 1953.

Al-Hakim, Da'd. *Awraq wa mudhakirrat Fakhri al-Barudi: khamsun 'am min hayat watan*. Damascus: Ministry of Culture, 1999.

Al-Jisr, Bassem. *Mithaq 1943, limaza kan wa limaza saqat*. Beirut: Dar al-Nahar, 1997.

Jurayj, Jubran. *Ma'a Antun Saadeh min 8 fibrayr 1932 ila 8 tammuz 1949*. Beirut: 1984.

Khuri, Beshara. *Haqa'iq lubnaniya*. Vol. I–III. Beirut: Awraq Lubaniya, 1961.

Qassmiya, Khayriah. *Mudhakart Muhsen al-Barazi, 1947–1949*. Beirut: al-Ruwwad li al-nashr, 1994.

Saqqal, Fathallah Mikha'il. *Min dhikrayat hukumat al za'im Husni al-Za'im*. Cairo: Dar al-ma'aref, 1952.

El-Solh, Sami. *Ahtakimu ila al-tarikh*. Beirut: Dar al-Nahar, 1970.

SECONDARY SOURCES

Abou al-Shamat, Hania M. *Syria under Civilian Rule*. Thesis (MA), Department of Political Studies and Public Administration, American University of Beirut, 1999.

Abouchdid, E. Eugenie. *Thirty Years of Lebanon and Syria, 1917–1947*. Beirut: Sader Rihani Print Co., 1948.

Abu Fadel, Henry. *A'lam al-orthodox fi lubnan*. Beirut: Lajnat al-dirasat al-orthodoxiyya fi lubnan, 1995.

Abu Saleh, Abbas Said. *History of the Foreign Policy of Lebanon, 1943–1958*. Thesis (PhD), Graduate School of the University of Texas at Austin, 1971.

'Aflaq, Michel. *Fi sabil al-ba'th*. Beirut: Dar al-tali'a, 1963.

Akarli, Engin Deniz. 'The Administrative Council of Mount Lebanon', in Nadim Shehadi and Dana Haffar Mills (eds.). *Lebanon, a History of Conflict and Consensus*. London: I.B. Tauris, 1988.

Al-Akhrass, Mohammad Safouh. *Revolutionary Change and Modernization in the Arab World: A Case from Syria*. Damascus: Atlas, 1972.

Antonius, George. *The Arab Awakening: The Story of the Arab National Movement*. Beirut: Khayat's College Book Cooperative, 1938.

Antoun, Richard and Quataeret, Donald (eds). *Syria: Society, Culture and Polity*. New York: State University of New York Press, 1991.

Asfour, Edmund Y. *Syria: Development and Monetary Policy*. Cambridge, MA: Harvard University Press, 1959.

El-Attrache, Mohammad. *The Political Philosophy of Michel 'Aflaq and the Ba'th Party in Syria*. Thesis (PhD), Graduate College, University of Oklahoma, 1973.

Baaklini, Abdo Iskandar. *Legislatures, and Political Development: Lebanon 1840–1970*. Thesis (PhD), Graduate School of Public Affairs, Department of Political Science, State University of New York at Albany, 1972.

Badre, Albert Yusuf. *The National Income of Lebanon*. Beirut, 1953.

——————. 'The Economic Development of Lebanon', in Charles Cooper and Sidney Alexander (eds). *Economic Development and Population Growth in the Middle East*. New York: American Elsevier, 1972.

Batatu, Hanna. 'Some Observations on the Social Roots of Syria's Ruling Military Group and the Causes for its Dominance'. *The Middle East Journal* vol. 35 (1981), no. 3.

Barakat, Awad. *Recent Economic Development in Syria*. Middle East Economic Papers. Beirut, 1954.

Barakat, Halim Isber (ed.). *Towards a Viable Lebanon*. London: Croom Helm, 1988.

Beshara, Adel. *Syrian Nationalism: An Inquiry into the Political Philosophy of Antun S'adeh*. Beirut: Bissan, 1995.

Browne, Walter. *Lebanon's Struggle for Independence*. Salisbury, NC: Documentary Publications, 1980.

Buheiry, Marwan Rafat. *Beirut's Role in the Political Economy of the French Mandate, 1919–39*. Oxford: Centre for Lebanese Studies, 1986.

Bustros, Evelyne. *Michel Chiha: Evocations*. Beirut: Cénacle Libanais, 1956.

Carelton, Alford. 'The Syrian Coups d'Etat of 1949'. *Middle East Journal* vol. 4 (1950), no. 1.

Chatti, Bourhan Taher. *The Fiscal System and Economic Development in Syria*. Ann Arbor: University Microfilms, 1957.

Chevalier, Dominique. 'Western Development and Eastern Crisis in the Mid-Nineteenth Century: Syria Confronted with the European Economy', William Polk and Richard Chambers (eds). *Beginning of Modernization in the Middle East*. Chicago: University of Chicago Press, 1968.

——————. *La société du Mont Liban à l'époque de la revolution industrielle en Europe*. Paris: Librairie orientaliste P. Geuthner, 1971.

Choueiri, Youssef. *State and Society in Lebanon and Syria*. New York: St. Martin's Press, 1994.

——————. 'Two Histories of Syria and the Demise of Syrian Patriotism'. *Middle Eastern Studies* vol. 23 (1987), 496–511.

Daher, Masud. *Lubnan, al-istiqlal, al-sigha wa al-mithaq*. Beirut: Ma'had al-inma' al-'arabi, 1997.

Dahir, Masud. *L'histoire socio-politique de la République Libanaise sous mandat Français (1926–1943)*. Thesis (Doctorat d'Etat), Ecole Pratique des Hautes Etudes, Paris, 1980.

Dawn, C. Ernest. 'The Rise of Arabism in Syria'. *The Middle East Journal* vol. 16 (1962), no. 4.

Devlin, John F. *Syria: Modern State in an Ancient Land*. London: Westview Press, 1983.

——————. 'The Syrian Armed Forces in National Politics: The Role of Geographic and Ethnic Periphery', in Roman Kolkowicz and Andrzej Korbonski (eds). *Soldiers, Peasants, and Bureaucrats*. London: Unwin Hyman, 1982.

Douwes, Dick. *The Ottomans in Syria: A History of Justice and Oppression*. London: I.B. Tauris, 2000.

Drewry, James C. *An Analysis of the 1949 Coups d'Etat in Syria in Light of Fertile Crescent Unity*. Thesis (MA), Department of History, American University of Beirut, 1960.

Ducruet, Jean. *Les capitaux européens au Proche-Orient*. Paris: Presses universitaires de France, 1964.

Elias, Joseph. *Al-a'mal al-mukhtara: Najib al-Rayyes*. Beirut: Dar Riad al-Rayyes, 1994.

Fares, Nabih Amin. *Haza al-'alam al-'arabi: dirasa fi al-qawmiyya al-'arabiyya wa fi 'awamel al-taqadum wa al-ta'khur wa al-wihda wa al-tafriq fi al-'alam al-'arabi*. Beirut: Dar al-'ilm li al-malayin, 1953.

Farhani, Muhammad. *Fares al-Khury wa ayam la tunsa*. Beirut: Dar al-Ghad, 1964.

Farshakh, George. *Hamid Franjiyah wa jumhuriat al-istiqlal*. Beirut: al-mu'assassa al-'arabia li al-dirasat wa al-nashir, 1997.

Fawaz, Leila T. *Merchants and Migrants in Nineteenth-Century Beirut*. Cambridge, MA: Harvard University Press, 1983.

Fedden, Robim. *Syria and Lebanon*. London: Murray, 1965.

Firro, Kais K. *Inventing Lebanon: Nationalism and the State under the Mandate*. London: I.B. Tauris, 2003.

Franjiyah, Nabil. *Hamid Franjie, L'autre Liban*. Beirut: Fiches du monde arabe, 1993.

Gates, Carolyn. *The Historical Role of Political Economy in the Development of Modern Lebanon*. Oxford: Center for Lebanese Studies, 1989.

_____. *The Merchant Republic of Lebanon: Rise of an Open Economy*. London: I.B. Tauris, 1998.

_____. 'Laissez-Faire, Outward-Orientation, and Regional Economic Disintegration: A Case Study of the Dissolution of the Syro-Lebanese Customs Union', in Youssef M. Choueiri (ed.). *State and Society in Syria and Lebanon*. Exeter: University of Exeter Press, 1993, 74–83.

Gaunson, A.B. *The Anglo-French Clash in Lebanon and Syria, 1940–45*. New York: Macmillan Press, 1987.

Gehchan, Roger. *Hussein Aoueini: un demi-siècle d'histoire du Liban et du Moyen-Orient (1920–1970)*. Beirut: Fiches du monde arabe, 2000.

Gelvin, James. *Divided Loyalties: Nationalism and Mass Politics in Syria at the Close of Empire*. Berkeley, CA: University of California Press, 1998.

Gendizier, Irene L. *Notes from the Minefield: United States Intervention in Lebanon and the Middle East, 1945–1958*. New York: Columbia University Press, 1997.

Ghaibeh, Haydar. *Syria's Import Capacity and Economic Growth, 1921–1960*. Thesis (PhD), Faculty of Political Science, Columbia University, 1962.

Gomaa, Ahmed M. *The Foundation of the League of Arab States: Wartime Diplomacy and Inter-Arab Politics, 1941 to 1945*. London: Longman Group, 1977.

Haddad, Joseph M. *The Syrian Nationality*. Thesis (MA), American University of Beirut, 1942.

Haffar, Ahmad Rafic. *France in the Establishment of Greater Lebanon: A Study of French Expansionism on the Eve of the First World War*. Thesis (PhD), Princeton University, 1961.

Al-Hajj, Kamal. *Falsafat al-mithaq al-watani*. Beirut, 1961.

El-Helou, Angelina S. *Interrelationships between Agricultural and Industrial Development in Syria*. Thesis (MA), Department of Business Administration, American University of Beirut, 1958.

Heydemann, Steven. *Authoritarianism in Syria: Institutions and Social Conflict, 1946–1970*. Ithaca: Cornell University Press, 1999.

Himadeh, Raja S. *The Fiscal System of Lebanon*. Beirut: Khayat, 1961.

Hitti, Philip Khuri. *Syria: A Short History*. New York: Macmillan, 1959.

Hokayem, Antoine. 'Al-'Alakat al-lubnaniya al-suriya, 1918–1950', in *Al-'Alakat al-lubnaniya al-suriya: muhawala taqwimiya (A'mal al-mu'tamar al-watani fi 14-15 tishrin al-thani*

2000. *Nussus al-itifakiyat wa al-protocolat al-muwaka'a bayn lubnan wa suriya)*. Antelias: al-Haraka al-thaqafiya, 2001.

Hopwood, Derek. *Syria 1945–1986: Politics and Society*. London: Unwin Hyman, 1988.

Hourani, Albert. *Syria and Lebanon: A Political Essay*. London: Oxford University Press, 1946.

Al-Husri, Sati' Abou Khaldun. *Ara' wa ahadith fi al-qawmiyya al-'arabiyya*. Beirut: Markaz dirasat al-wihda al-'arabiyya, 1986.

Johnson, Michael L. *Class and Client in Beirut: The Sunni Muslim Community and the Lebanese State, 1840–1985*. London: Ithaca Press, 1986.

Jurdak, Salwa Mansur. *The Evolution of Lebanese Party Politics: 1919–1947*. Thesis (MA), Department of Political Science, American University of Beirut, 1948.

Khalaf, Samir. *Persistence and Change in 19th Century Lebanon: A Sociological Essay*. Beirut: American University of Beirut, 1979.

Khalil, Muhammad. *The Arab States and the Arab League: A Documentary Record*. Vol. II. London: Archive Editions, 1990.

El-Khazen, Farid. *The Communal Pact of National Identities: The Making and Politics of the 1943 National Pact*. Oxford: Centre for Lebanese Studies, 1991.

Khoury, Philip. *Syria and the French Mandate: The Politics of Arab Nationalism, 1920–1945*. Princeton, NJ: Princeton University Press, 1987.

Lamberkis, George Basil. *Perception and Misperception in Policymaking: The US Relationship with Modern Lebanon, 1943–1967*. Unpublished Doctoral Dissertation, George Washington University, 1989.

Longrigg, Stephen H. *Syria and Lebanon under the French Mandate*. London: Oxford University Press, 1958.

Mardam Bey, Salma. *Syria's Quest for Independence 1939-1945*. Reading UK: Ithaca Press, 1994.

Mallat, Raymond. *Seventy Years of Money Muddling in Lebanon, 1900–1970*. Beirut, 1973.

Ma'oz, Moshe. *Syria and Israel: From War to Peacemaking*. Oxford: Clarendon Press, 1995.

Ma'oz, Moshe, Joseph Ginat and Onn Winckler (eds). *From Ottoman Rule to Pivotal Role in the Middle East*. Brighton: Sussex Academy Press, 1999.

Menassa, Gabriel. *Plan de reconstruction de l'économie libanaise et de réforme de l'état*. Beirut: Société libanaise d'économie politique, 1948.

_____. *For a Lebanese Economic Renovation with the Collaboration of the Lebanon Overseas*. Beirut: Lebanese Political Economy Society, 1959.

Meo, Leila. *The Separation of Lebanon from Greater Syria: A Case Study in Lebanese Politics*. Unpublished Doctoral Dissertation, Indiana University, 1961.

Moubayed, Sami. *The Politics of Damascus, 1920–1946: Urban Notables and the French Mandate*. Damascus: Tlass Publication House, 1999.

Murad, Sa'id. *Al-Haraka al-wihdawiyya fi lubnan bayn al-harbayn al-'alamiyayn*. Beirut: Ma'had al-inma' al-'arabi, 1986.

Nashaba, Adnan. *Al-Mu'ahadat al-duwalia al-suriya al-thuna'iya min al-'am 1923 ila al-'am 1955*. Beirut: Matba'at al-adab, 1955.

Nasr, Asad Yussef. *National Income of Lebanon, Income Arising in the Industrial Sector*. Monograph 3. Beirut: 1953.

Nelson, John. *Political Integration in Lebanon*. Thesis (PhD), Ann Arbor, MI: UMI Dissertation Information Service, 1997.

Odeh, B.J. *Lebanon, Dynamics of Conflict: A Modern Political History*. London: Zed Books, 1985.

Petran, Tabitha. *Syria: A Modern History*. London: Ernest Benn, 1972.

Pipes, Daniel. *Greater Syria: The History of an Ambition*. New York: Oxford University Press, 1990.

Rabbath, Edmond. *La formation historique du Liban politique et constitutionnel: essai de synthèse*. Beirut: Imprimerie Catholique, 1986.

_____. *Unité syrienne et devenir arabe*. Paris: Rivière, 1937.

Rathmell, Andrew. *Secret War in the Middle East: The Covert Struggle for Syria, 1949–1961*. London: Tauris Academic Studies, 1995.

Rosenfeld, Félix. 'Variations des prix de la circulation monétaire en Syrie et au Liban au cours de la deuxième guerre mondiale'. *Journal de la société de statistiques de Paris*. Paris, 1946.

Rustum, Asad. *Lubnan fi 'ahd al-mutasarifiyat*. Beirut: Dar al-nahar, 1973.

Sa'ada, Antun. *Nushu' al-umam*. Beirut: 1938.

_____. *The Principles of the Syrian Nationalist Party*. Beirut: al-hizb al-suri al-qawmi al-ijtima'i, 1949.

Saba, Elias. 'The Syro-Lebanese Customs Union: Causes of Failure and Attempts at Re-Organization'. *Middle East Economic Papers*, 1960.

_____. 'Lebanon's Liberal Foreign Exchange System'. *Middle East Economic Papers*, 1960, 98–112.

_____. *The Foreign Exchange Systems of Lebanon and Syria 1939–1957*. Beirut, 1961.

Salibi, Kamal. *The Modern History of Lebanon*. London: Weidenfeld, 1965.

_____. *A House of Many Mansions: The History of Lebanon Reconsidered*. London: I.B. Tauris, 1988.

Seale, Patrick. *The Struggle for Syria: A Study of Post-War Arab Politics 1945–1958*. London: I.B. Tauris, 1986.

Shambrook, Peter. *French Imperialism in Syria, 1927–1936*. Reading UK: Ithaca Press, 1998.

Shehadi, Nadim. *The Idea of Lebanon: Economy and State in the Cénacle Libanais 1946–54*. Oxford: Center for Lebanese Studies, 1987.

Sokhn, Joseph. *Horizons Libanais*. Beirut: 1983.

El-Solh, Raghid. *Lebanon and Arabism: National Identity and State Formation*. London: I.B. Tauris in association with the Centre for Lebanese Studies, 2004.

Spagnolo, John. *France and Ottoman Lebanon, 1861–1914*. London: Ithaca Press for Middle East Center, St Antony's College, 1977.

Tanenbaum, Jean Karl. *France and the Arab Middle East, 1914–1920*. Philadelphia: The American Philosophical Society, 1978.

Thobie, Jaques. *Interêts et Imperialisme Français dans l'Empire Ottoman: 1895–1914*. Paris: Imprimerie Nationale, 1977.

Tibawi, Abdul Latif. *A Modern History of Syria, Including Lebanon and Palestine*. London: Macmillan, 1969.

Torrey, Gordon H. *Syrian Politics and the Military, 1945–1958*. Columbus: Ohio State University Press, 1964.

_____. *Independent Syria, 1946–54*. Thesis (PhD), Ann Arbor, MI: University Microfilms International, 1961.

Traboulsi, Fawaz. *Silat bila wasl: Michel Chiha wa al-idiolojiya al-lubnaniyya*. Beirut: Riad al-Rayyes, 1999.

Winslow, Charles. *Lebanon: War and Politics in a Fragmented Society*. London: Routledge, 1996.

Zakeh, Samir H. *Lebanon between East and West: Big Power Politics in the Middle East*. Ann Arbor, MI: UMI Dissertation Information Service, 1997.

Zamir, Meir. *Lebanon's Quest: The Road to Statehood 1926–1939*. London: I.B. Tauris, 1997.

_____. *The Formation of Modern Lebanon*. London: Croom Helm, 1985.

_____. 'Faysal and the Lebanese Question, 1918–1920'. *Middle Eastern Studies*, vol. 27 (1991), no. 3, 404–426.

Ziadeh, Nicola A. *Syria and Lebanon*. London: Ernest Benn, 1957.

Zisser, Eyal. *Lebanon: The Challenge of Independence*. London: I.B. Tauris, 2000. *17 Aab 1943–1947, arba' sanawat mina al-hikm al-watani*. Beirut: Dar al 'ahd, 1947 and Damascus: Dar al-yakaza al-'arabiya, 1947.

Zuwiyya Yamak, Labib. *The Syrian Social Nationalist Party: An Ideological Analysis*. Cambridge, MA: Harvard University Press, Center for Middle Eastern Studies, 1966.

INDEX

INDEX